THE COOL KITCHEN COOKBOOK

Taste of Home

RDA ENTHUSIAST BRANDS, LLC • MILWAUKEE, WI

© 2023 RDA Enthusiast Brands, LLC.
1610 N. 2nd St., Suite 102, Milwaukee WI
53212-3906

Visit us at *tasteofhome.com* for other
Taste of Home books and products.

ISBN: 978-1-62145-929-3

INSTANT POT is a trademark of Double Insight Inc.
This publication has not been authorized, sponsored
or otherwise approved by Double Insight, Inc.

Chief Content Officer, Home & Garden:
Jeanne Sidner
Content Director: Mark Hagen
Creative Director: Raeann Thompson
Senior Editor: Christine Rukavena
Editor: Hazel Wheaton
Senior Art Director: Courtney Lovetere
Art Director: Maggie Conners
Designer: Carrie Peterson
Deputy Editor, Copy Desk: Dulcie Shoener
Copy Editor: Elizabeth Pollock Bruch
Contributing Designer: Jennifer Ruetz

Cover Photographer: Dan Roberts
Senior Set Stylist: Melissa Franco
Senior Food Stylist: Shannon Norris

Pictured on front cover:
Summertime Watermelon Punch for a Crowd, p. 18;
Red, White & Blue Summer Salad, p.66;
Banh Mi Skewers, p.40

Pictured on title page:
Crab Lettuce Wraps, p. 43

Pictured on back cover:
Orange Juice Spritzer, p. 23;
Strawberry-Pineapple Coleslaw, p. 83;
Banana Split Icebox Cake, p. 264;
Stuffed Peppers for Four, p. 226;
Hearty Muffuletta, p. 101;
Tzatziki Shrimp Cucumber Rounds, p. 49

Printed in China
1 3 5 7 9 10 8 6 4 2

MORE WAYS TO CONNECT WITH US:

SHOP.TASTEOFHOME.COM

TABLE OF CONTENTS

145

274

SUMMER COOKING THAT WON'T LEAVE YOU OVERHEATED!

In the cooler months, a warm kitchen is cozy and welcome. But in summer, the idea of turning on the oven—and raising the temperature indoors—can be unbearable. It's tempting to resort to takeout or to just hit the deli counter and forget about home cooking until the mercury drops.

Now, even in the worst summer heat, your kitchen can still be a cool place to be, and your family can enjoy scrumptious home-cooked meals. **The Cool Kitchen Cookbook** shows you how, with hundreds of recipes that all come together without once turning on the oven.

Cool, refreshing drinks and crisp salads. Satisfying main courses and inventive side dishes. Quick snacks and crowd-pleasing party food. Desserts and treats to please the most demanding sweet tooth. All with no baking, broiling or roasting required. Even when you do need some heat, recipes are specially chosen to keep things cool, including ultra quick stovetop options and a bonus chapter dedicated to grilling...outdoors!

Every recipe also comes with complete nutritional information, so you can plan meals that make sense for your family. Plus, on the inside back cover, there's a quick guide that will let you convert your favorite oven recipes to cook in a slow cooker, air fryer or Instant Pot, or on the grill.

So dip in and start creating amazing meals that your family will love to eat and you'll love to make—with summertime cooking that won't leave you hot under the collar!

COOL-KITCHEN TIP
Throughout the book, tips from the experts in the *Taste of Home* Test Kitchen guide you to mealtime success!

17

251

295

137

At-a-Glance Icons
Look for these handy icons throughout the book.

- **Fast Fix** dishes are table-ready in 30 minutes or less.

- **Freezer-friendly** recipes include directions for freezing and reheating.

- **Slow Cooker** dishes use one of the most convenient kitchen appliances.

- **Air Fryer** recipes have the flavor and crispness of fried without added fat.

- **Instant Pot** creations are made in the modern electric pressure cooker.

P. 8

REFRESHING SMOOTHIES & OTHER SIPPERS

For a cool drink on a hot day, skip the sugary sodas or canned drinks—these homemade sips are easy and so delicious!

ICED RASPBERRY TEA

Frozen raspberries lend fruity flavor and lovely color to this pretty iced tea. The recipe calls for just a few common ingredients and offers make-ahead convenience.
—*Lois McGrady, Hillsville, VA*

PREP: 10 min. + chilling
MAKES: 16 servings (4 qt.)

- 1½ cups sugar
- 4 qt. water
- 1 pkg. (12 oz.) frozen unsweetened raspberries
- 10 tea bags
- ¼ cup lemon juice
  Ice cubes
  Optional: Fresh raspberries and lemon slices

1. In a Dutch oven over high heat, bring sugar and water to a boil. Remove from heat; stir until sugar is dissolved. Add raspberries, tea bags and lemon juice. Steep, covered, for 3 minutes. Strain; discard berries and tea bags.
2. Transfer tea to a large container or pitcher. Refrigerate until chilled. Serve over ice. If desired, serve with raspberries and lemon slices.
1 cup: 87 cal., 0 fat (0 sat. fat), 0 chol., 8mg sod., 22g carb. (20g sugars, 0 fiber), 0 pro.

Touch-of-Mint Iced Tea: Bring 2 qt. of water to a boil. Steep 5 individual tea bags for 5 minutes and discard; cool for 15 minutes. Add 1⅓ cups packed fresh mint; steep 5 minutes. Strain; stir in 1 cup frozen lemonade concentrate (melted). Refrigerate until chilled. Serve over ice. Yield: about 2 qt.

BLUEBERRY ICED TEA

I enjoy coming up with new ways to use my slow cooker in the kitchen. If it's going to take up space, it needs to earn its keep! Serve this refreshing tea over plenty of ice and garnish with fresh blueberries if desired. For fun, freeze blueberries in your ice cubes.
—Colleen Delawder, Herndon, VA

PREP: 10 min. • **COOK:** 3 hours + cooling
MAKES: 11 servings (2¾ qt.)

- 12 cups water
- 2 cups fresh blueberries
- 1 cup sugar
- ¼ tsp. salt
- 4 family-sized tea bags
   Ice cubes
   Optional: Lemon slices, fresh mint leaves and additional blueberries

1. In a 5-qt. slow cooker, combine water, blueberries, sugar and salt. Cook, covered, on low heat for 3 hours.
2. Turn off slow cooker; add tea bags. Cover and let stand 5 minutes. Discard tea bags; cool 2 hours.
3. Strain and discard blueberries. Pour tea into pitcher; serve over ice cubes. If desired, top each serving with lemon slices, fresh mint leaves and additional fresh blueberries.
1 cup: 73 cal., 0 fat (0 sat. fat), 0 chol., 61mg sod., 19g carb. (18g sugars, 0 fiber), 0 pro.

KALE SMOOTHIES

I enjoy drinking a kale smoothie for breakfast or as an after-school snack. The fruit and agave nectar give this healthy version a pleasant sweetness.
—Kimberly Jackson, Marshfield, MO

TAKES: 15 min. • **MAKES:** 4 servings

- 1 small bunch kale or spinach, chopped
- 1 medium pear, chopped
- 1 cup frozen sweetened mixed berries
- 1 medium banana, halved
- 1 cup unsweetened almond milk
- ½ cup low-fat vanilla almond milk yogurt
- 3 Tbsp. agave nectar

In a large bowl, mix kale and fruits. Pour in almond milk, yogurt and agave nectar; stir to combine. Process in batches in a blender until smooth. Serve immediately or refrigerate.
1 cup: 184 cal., 3g fat (0 sat. fat), 0 chol., 86mg sod., 40g carb. (23g sugars, 6g fiber), 4g pro.

BERRY SLUSH

This make-ahead punch is perfect to serve when hosting a party for a crowd. For a festive touch, garnish with any fresh fruit of your choice.
—*Ruth Seitz, Columbus Junction, IA*

PREP: 10 min. + freezing • **MAKES:** 5 qt.

- 1 pkg. (3 oz.) raspberry or berry blue gelatin
- 2 cups boiling water
- 2 cups sugar
- 1 can (46 oz.) pineapple juice
- 2 liters ginger ale
- 4½ cups cold water
- 1 cup lemon juice
  Red or blue liquid food coloring, optional
  Coarse blue sugar, optional
  Optional: Fresh blueberries, raspberries and watermelon

1. In a large container, dissolve gelatin in boiling water; stir in sugar until dissolved. Add the pineapple juice, ginger ale, water and lemon juice. If desired, add food coloring. Freeze for 8 hours or overnight.
2. Remove from the freezer 20 minutes before serving. Stir until mixture is slushy. Meanwhile, moisten rims of chilled glasses with water. If desired, sprinkle blue sugar on a plate; dip rims in sugar. Spoon slushy mixture into glasses. If desired, top with fruit. Serve immediately.
1 cup: 167 cal., 0 fat (0 sat. fat), 0 chol., 18mg sod., 43g carb. (41g sugars, 0 fiber), 1g pro.

AUNT FRANCES'S LEMONADE

When we were growing up, my sister and I spent a week each summer with our Aunt Frances, who always had this thirst-quenching lemonade in a stoneware crock in her refrigerator.
—*Debbie Reinhart, New Cumberland, PA*

TAKES: 15 min. • **MAKES:** 16 servings (4 qt.)

- 5 lemons
- 5 limes
- 5 oranges
- 3 qt. water
- 1½ to 2 cups sugar
  Ice cubes

1. Squeeze the juice from 4 each of the lemons, limes and oranges; pour into a gallon container.
2. Thinly slice the remaining fruit and set aside for garnish. Add water and sugar to the juice mixture; mix well. Store in the refrigerator. Serve over ice with fruit slices.
1 cup: 92 cal., 0 fat (0 sat. fat), 0 chol., 1mg sod., 24g carb. (21g sugars, 1g fiber), 0 pro.

COOL-KITCHEN TIP
If you don't mind a little bit of stove time, bring the sugar and water to a boil in a saucepan, and stir until the sugar is dissolved. Let the mixture cool before mixing with the juice.

APRICOT ICE CREAM SODA

This ginger ale float recipe came from my husband's aunt, who was born in the early 1900s. It's a delightful drink for hot Texas summers.
—*Joan Hallford, North Richland Hills, TX*

PREP: 20 min. + freezing
MAKES: 4 servings

- 2 **cans (15 oz. each) apricot halves, drained**
- ⅔ **cup sugar**
- 2 **Tbsp. lemon juice**
- 1 **cup heavy whipping cream, whipped**
- 2 **cups chilled ginger ale**

1. Press apricots through a fine-mesh strainer into a bowl; discard skins and pulp. Stir sugar and lemon juice into the apricot puree. Gently fold in whipped cream. Transfer mixture to a 8-in. square dish. Freeze until firm, about 6 hours or overnight.

2. Divide ice cream among 4 glasses; top with ginger ale. Serve immediately.

1 ice cream soda: 554 cal., 22g fat (14g sat. fat), 68mg chol., 34mg sod., 92g carb. (88g sugars, 3g fiber), 3g pro.

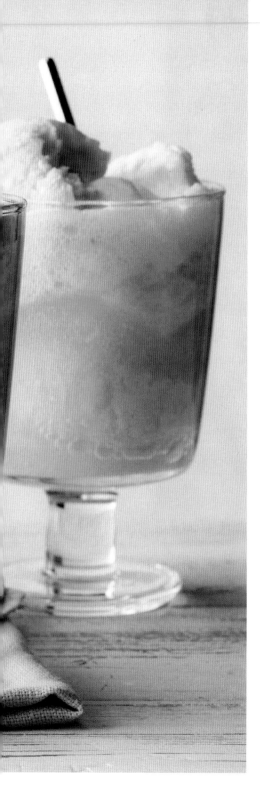

SWEET TEA CONCENTRATE

Sweet iced tea is a southern classic, and this is a fabulous recipes for tea lovers. The concentrate makes 20 servings, so it's great to keep in the fridge for the family, or to make for a party.
—*Natalie Bremson, Plantation, FL*

PREP: 30 min. + cooling
MAKES: 20 servings (5 cups concentrate)

- 2 medium lemons
- 4 cups sugar
- 4 cups water
- 1½ cups English breakfast tea leaves or 20 black tea bags

EACH SERVING
- 1 cup cold water
  Ice cubes

1. Using a vegetable peeler or sharp paring knife, peel the lemon lengthwise into strips, peeling only the zest; reserve. Squeeze fruit, reserving ⅓ cup juice. Save remaining juice for another use.
2. In a large saucepan, combine sugar and water. Bring to a boil over medium heat. Reduce heat; simmer, uncovered, until sugar is dissolved, 3-5 minutes, stirring occasionally. Remove from the heat; add tea leaves and lemon zest strips. Cover and steep for 15 minutes. Strain tea, discarding tea leaves and lemon zest; stir in lemon juice. Cool to room temperature.
3. Transfer to a container with a tight-fitting lid. Store in the refrigerator for up to 2 weeks.
4. To prepare: In a tall glass, combine 1 cup water with ¼ cup concentrate; add ice.
¼ cup concentrate: 165 cal., 0 fat (0 sat. fat), 0 chol., 27mg sod., 43g carb. (40g sugars, 0 fiber), 0 pro.

BLUEBERRY PANCAKE SMOOTHIE

Have your blueberry pancakes and drink them, too! A smoothie loaded with fruit, oatmeal, maple syrup and cinnamon is welcome in the morning or at any time of day. If the berries are fresh instead of frozen, freeze the banana ahead of time.
—*Kailey Thompson, Palm Bay, FL*

TAKES: 5 min. • **MAKES:** 2 servings

- 1 cup unsweetened almond milk
- 1 medium banana
- ½ cup frozen unsweetened blueberries
- ¼ cup instant plain oatmeal
- 1 tsp. maple syrup
- ½ tsp. ground cinnamon
  Dash sea salt

Place the first 6 ingredients in a blender; cover and process until smooth. Pour into 2 chilled glasses; sprinkle with sea salt. Serve immediately.
1 cup: 153 cal., 3g fat (0 sat. fat), 0 chol., 191mg sod., 31g carb. (13g sugars, 5g fiber), 3g pro. **Diabetic exchanges:** 2 starch.

HONEY-CITRUS ICED TEA

Adding a frozen orange or lemon slice helps keep this refreshing punch nice and cold. For an extra-tasty twist, the blend is sweetened with honey.
—*Sheila Bradshaw, Columbus, OH*

PREP: 15 min. + chilling
MAKES: 8 servings (2 qt.)

- 4 tea bags
- 2 cups boiling water
- 3 medium navel oranges
- 2 medium lemons
- 2 cups orange juice
- ¼ cup lemon juice
- 3 Tbsp. honey
- 1 liter ginger ale, chilled
  Ice cubes

1. Place tea bags in a teapot; add boiling water. Cover and steep for 3 minutes; discard tea bags. Pour tea into a pitcher. Peel and section 2 oranges and 1 lemon; add to tea. Stir in the orange juice, lemon juice and honey. Cover and refrigerate for 6 hours or overnight. Cut remaining orange and lemon into slices; freeze.
2. Just before serving, strain and discard fruit from tea. Stir in ginger ale. Serve with frozen fruit slices and ice.
1 cup: 124 cal., 0 fat (0 sat. fat), 0 chol., 11mg sod., 32g carb. (0 sugars, 1g fiber), 1g pro.

STRAWBERRY WATERMELON SLUSH

After a long, hot day, we like to relax on the back porch with glasses of my slush. Strawberries and watermelon blend with lemon juice and sugar for an icy treat that's an instant refresher.
—*Patty Howse, Great Falls, MT*

TAKES: 10 min. • **MAKES:** 4 servings

- ⅓ cup lemon juice
- ⅓ cup sugar
- 2 cups cubed seedless watermelon
- 2 cups fresh strawberries, halved
- 2 cups ice cubes

Place first 4 ingredients in a blender; cover and process until smooth. Add ice; process, covered, until slushy. Serve immediately.
1¼ cups: 112 cal., 0 fat (0 sat. fat), 0 chol., 4mg sod., 30g carb. (27g sugars, 2g fiber), 1g pro.

COCONUT COLD-BREW LATTE

Cold-brew lattes are all the rage at specialty coffee shops, but they're so easy to make at home. This coconut cold-brew latte is ridiculously refreshing—and it's even vegan!
—*Natalie Larsen, Grand Prairie, TX*

PREP: 20 min. + chilling
MAKES: 4 servings

- ½ cup coarsely ground medium-roast coffee
- ½ cup hot water (205°)
- 3½ cups cold water

COCONUT SIMPLE SYRUP
- 1 cup water
- ½ cup sugar
- ½ cup sweetened shredded coconut

EACH SERVING
- Ice cubes
- 2 Tbsp. coconut milk

1. Place ground coffee in a clean glass container. Pour hot water over coffee; let stand 10 minutes. Stir in the cold water. Cover and refrigerate for 12-24 hours. (The longer the coffee sits, the stronger the flavor.)
2. Meanwhile, for coconut simple syrup, in a small saucepan, bring water, sugar and coconut to a boil. Reduce heat; simmer 10 minutes. Strain and discard coconut. Cool completely.
3. Strain coffee through a fine-mesh sieve; discard grounds. Strain coffee again through a coffee filter; discard grounds. Store coffee in the refrigerator for up to 2 weeks.
4. For each serving, fill a large glass with ice. Add 1 cup cold-brewed coffee and 4 Tbsp. coconut syrup; stir. Top with 2 Tbsp. coconut milk.
1 cup: 145 cal., 5g fat (5g sat. fat), 0 chol., 12mg sod., 26g carb. (26g sugars, 0 fiber), 1g pro.

CHERRY LIMEADE

My guests enjoy this refreshing cherry-topped drink. It's just right on a hot southern summer afternoon, and it's pretty too.
—Awynne Thurstenson, Siloam Springs, AR

TAKES: 10 min. • **MAKES:** 8 servings

- ¾ cup lime juice
- 1 cup sugar
- ½ cup maraschino cherry juice
- 2 liters lime carbonated water, chilled
  Ice cubes
- 8 maraschino cherries with stems
- 8 lime slices

In a large pitcher, combine lime juice and sugar. Cover and refrigerate. Just before serving, stir cherry juice, carbonated water and some ice cubes into lime juice mixture. Garnish with maraschino cherries and lime slices.
1 cup: 142 cal., 0 fat (0 sat. fat), 0 chol., 2mg sod., 39g carb. (31g sugars, 2g fiber), 0 pro.

HIBISCUS ICED TEA

This calorie- and caffeine-free tea has a delightful rosy color.
—Taste of Home *Test Kitchen*

TAKES: 10 min. • **MAKES:** 1 serving

- 1 cup water
- 5 dried hibiscus flowers or 1 tsp. crushed dried hibiscus flowers
  Ice cubes

In a saucepan, bring water to a boil. Remove from the heat. Add hibiscus flowers and let stand 5 minutes. Strain tea. Serve in chilled glasses over ice.
Note: Verify that flowers are edible and have not been treated with chemicals.

LUSCIOUS LIME SLUSH

Guests really go for this sweet-tart refresher. If you prefer, swap in lemonade concentrate for the limeade.
—Bonnie Jost, Manitowoc, WI

PREP: 20 min. + freezing
MAKES: 28 servings (5¼ qt.)

- 9 cups water
- 4 green tea bags
- 2 cans (12 oz. each) frozen limeade concentrate, thawed
- 2 cups sugar
- 2 cups lemon rum or rum
- 7 cups lemon-lime soda, chilled
  Lime slices, optional

1. In a Dutch oven, bring water to a boil. Remove from the heat; add tea bags. Cover and steep for 3-5 minutes. Discard tea bags. Stir in the limeade concentrate, sugar and rum.
2. Transfer mixture to a 4-qt. freezer container; cool. Cover and freeze for 6 hours or overnight.
3. Combine the limeade mixture and soda in a 4-qt. pitcher. Or for 1 serving, combine ½ cup limeade mixture and ¼ cup soda in a glass. If desired, garnish with lime slices. Serve immediately.
¾ cup: 177 cal., 0 fat (0 sat. fat), 0 chol., 7mg sod., 36g carb. (35g sugars, 0 fiber), 0 pro.

PEACH-BASIL COOLER

Mix with club soda for a cool and refreshing mocktail, or use champagne, prosecco or another sparkling wine for a sweet summer cocktail!
—*Dana Hinck, Pensacola, FL*

PREP: 25 min. + chilling
MAKES: 12 servings (3 qt.)

- 2 cups sugar
- 4 cups chopped peeled fresh peaches or 1 lb. frozen unsweetened sliced peaches
- 1 pkg. (¾ oz.) fresh basil leaves
- 2 cups cold water
- 1½ cups fresh lemon juice
  Additional cold water
  Ice cubes
  Club soda or champagne
  Additional fresh basil leaves

1. In a large saucepan, combine sugar, peaches, basil and water; bring to a boil. Reduce heat; simmer, uncovered, 5 minutes. Remove from heat; let stand for 30 minutes. Discard basil; stir in lemon juice. Refrigerate until cooled completely.
2. Place peach mixture in a blender; cover and process until blended. Strain into a pitcher; add additional cold water to reach desired consistency. To serve, fill glasses with ice. Pour peach mixture halfway up glass; top with club soda or, if desired, champagne. Garnish with additional basil.
1 cup: 157 cal., 0 fat (0 sat. fat), 0 chol., 1mg sod., 41g carb. (38g sugars, 1g fiber), 1g pro.

SUMMERTIME WATERMELON PUNCH FOR A CROWD

I attended a party years ago where the hostess had made a clever watermelon bowl with a scalloped edge filled with this punch. It was the hit of the party, and she was kind enough to share the recipe.
—*Joan Hallford, North Richland Hills, TX*

PREP: 30 min. + chilling
MAKES: 32 servings

- 30 cups cubed seedless watermelon (about 10 lbs.)
- 1 can (12 oz.) frozen orange juice concentrate, thawed
- ½ cup lemon juice
- 1 bottle (750 milliliters) sweet white wine, chilled
- 3 cups chilled ginger ale
  Ice cubes

1. Process watermelon in batches in a food processor until smooth. Press through a fine-mesh strainer into a bowl; discard pulp. Pour juice into a large pitcher or punch bowl. Stir in juice concentrate and lemon juice. Refrigerate until chilled.
2. Stir in wine and ginger ale before serving. Serve over ice with additional watermelon.
¾ cup: 81 cal., 0 fat (0 sat. fat), 0 chol., 8mg sod., 19g carb. (17g sugars, 1g fiber), 1g pro.

COOL-KITCHEN TIP
We tested this fruity drink with moscato wine. You could also try it with riesling, pinot gris or another sweet wine.

TROPICAL BERRY SMOOTHIES

This fruity, healthy smoothie is a big hit with kids and adults alike because it tastes like a treat while delivering the vitamins. The recipe is easy to increase based on the number of people you'll be serving.
—*Hillary Engler, Cape Girardeau, MO*

TAKES: 10 min. • **MAKES:** 2 servings

- 1 **cup pina colada juice blend**
- 1 **container (6 oz.) vanilla yogurt**
- ⅓ **cup frozen unsweetened strawberries**
- ¼ **cup frozen mango chunks**
- ¼ **cup frozen unsweetened blueberries**

In a blender, combine all ingredients; cover and process for 30 seconds or until smooth. Pour into chilled glasses; serve immediately.

1¼ cups: 172 cal., 2g fat (1g sat. fat), 4mg chol., 62mg sod., 35g carb. (32g sugars, 2g fiber), 5g pro.

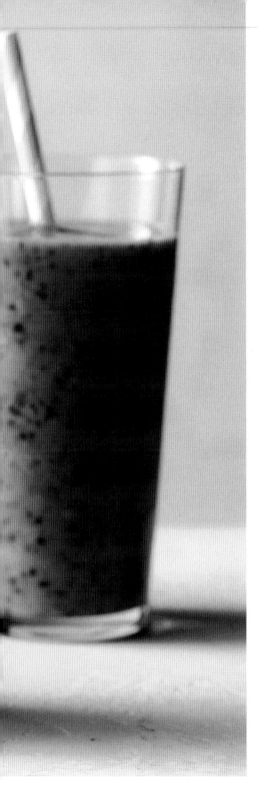

BANANA-ALMOND MILK SHAKES

A few sips of this flavorful shake will curb the hungriest sweet tooth. For a lighter version, substitute a tablespoon of unsweetened cocoa powder for the chocolate chips.
—*Athena Russell, Greenville, SC*

TAKES: 10 min. • **MAKES:** 4 servings

- 1¼ cups unsweetened almond milk
- 6 frozen medium ripe bananas, cut into chunks
- ¼ cup almond butter
- ½ tsp. vanilla extract
- ¼ tsp. almond extract
- ⅓ cup semisweet chocolate chips
  Sweetened whipped cream, optional

1. Place first 5 ingredients in a blender; cover and process until smooth, about 2 minutes. Add chocolate chips; cover and process until blended, about 30 seconds longer.
2. Pour into chilled glasses and garnish with whipped cream if desired. Serve immediately.
1 cup: 342 cal., 14g fat (4g sat. fat), 0 chol., 89mg sod., 55g carb. (33g sugars, 7g fiber), 6g pro.

MANGO LASSI

Learn how to make a mango lassi, the perfect summer drink any mango lover will adore. This sweet and refreshing treat needs only six ingredients!
—*Namrata Telugu, Terre Haute, IN*

TAKES: 10 min. • **MAKES:** 2 servings

- 1 cup fat-free plain yogurt
- 1 medium mango, peeled and cubed
- 2 cups ice cubes
- 3 Tbsp. sugar
- 5 fresh mint leaves
- 2 cardamom pods, crushed, optional

In a blender, combine the yogurt, mango, ice, sugar, mint leaves and cardamom pods if desired. Cover and process for 30-60 seconds or until blended. Pour into 2 chilled glasses; serve immediately.
1½ cups: 226 cal., 1g fat (0 sat. fat), 3mg chol., 73mg sod., 54g carb. (48g sugars, 3g fiber), 6g pro.

COOL-KITCHEN TIP
Make variations on this recipe by using banana, strawberry, peach or cantaloupe instead of mango. To make a vegan lassi, switch the yogurt for a dairy-free option. We recommend a coconut-based yogurt.

ICED HONEYDEW MINT TEA

I grow mint in the garden on my balcony. In this minty tea, I blend two of my favorite beverages—Moroccan mint tea and honeydew *agua fresca*.
—Sarah Batt Throne, El Cerrito, CA

TAKES: 20 min.
MAKES: 10 servings (2½ qt.)

- 4 cups water
- 24 fresh mint leaves
- 8 green tea bags
- ⅔ cup sugar
- 5 cups diced honeydew melon
- 3 cups ice cubes

1. In a large saucepan, bring water to a boil; remove from heat. Add mint leaves and tea bags; steep, covered, 3-5 minutes according to taste, stirring occasionally. Discard mint and tea bags. Stir in sugar.
2. Place 2½ cups honeydew melon, 2 cups tea and 1½ cups ice in a blender; cover and process until blended. Serve over additional ice. Repeat with the remaining ingredients.
1 cup: 83 cal., 0 fat (0 sat. fat), 0 chol., 15mg sod., 21g carb. (20g sugars, 1g fiber), 0 pro.
Diabetic Exchanges: 1 starch, ½ fruit.

PEACHY BUTTERMILK SHAKES

My husband and grandkids sure enjoy the tang of buttermilk blended with sweet peaches in these delightful shakes.
—Anna Mayer, Fort Branch, IN

TAKES: 10 min. • **MAKES:** 3 servings

- 1 cup buttermilk
- 3 cups fresh or frozen unsweetened sliced peaches, thawed
- 1 cup vanilla ice cream, softened
- ¼ cup sugar
- ¾ tsp. ground cinnamon
  Optional: Whipped cream and additional sliced peaches

Place the first 5 ingredients in a blender; cover and process until smooth. Pour into chilled glasses; serve immediately. If desired, top with whipped cream and additional sliced peaches.
1 cup: 250 cal., 6g fat (3g sat. fat), 23mg chol., 191mg sod., 46g carb. (42g sugars, 3g fiber), 6g pro.

ORANGE JUICE SPRITZER

Here's a zippy twist on regular orange juice. It is not too sweet and is refreshing with any breakfast or brunch entree.
—*Michelle Krzmarzick, Torrance, CA*

TAKES: 5 min. • **MAKES:** 8 servings (2 qt.)

- 4 cups orange juice
- 1 liter ginger ale, chilled
- ¼ cup maraschino cherry juice
  Ice cubes
  Optional: Orange wedges and maraschino cherries

In a 2-qt. pitcher, mix orange juice, ginger ale and cherry juice. Serve over ice. If desired, top servings with orange wedges and cherries.

1 cup: 103 cal., 0 fat (0 sat. fat), 0 chol., 9mg sod., 25g carb. (23g sugars, 0 fiber), 1g pro.

A.M. RUSH ESPRESSO SMOOTHIE

Want an early morning pick-me-up that's good for you too? Fruit and flaxseed give this sweet smoothie a nutritious twist.
—*Aimee Wilson, Clovis, CA*

TAKES: 10 min. • **MAKES:** 1 serving

- ½ cup cold fat-free milk
- 1 Tbsp. vanilla flavoring syrup
- 1 cup ice cubes
- ½ medium banana, cut up
- 1 to 2 tsp. instant espresso powder
- 1 tsp. ground flaxseed
- 1 tsp. baking cocoa

In a blender, combine all the ingredients; cover and process 1-2 minutes or until blended. Pour into a chilled glass; serve immediately.

Note: This recipe was tested with Torani brand flavoring syrup.

1½ cups: 148 cal., 2g fat (0 sat. fat), 2mg chol., 54mg sod., 31g carb. (21g sugars, 3g fiber), 6g pro.

STRAWBERRY BANANA YOGURT SMOOTHIES

Frozen strawberries combine with banana to keep these frosty smoothies extra thick. The recipe is a delightful way to get a substantial dose of nutrients early in the day.
—*Christy Adkins, Martinez, GA*

TAKES: 5 min. • **MAKES:** 2 servings

- ½ cup 2% milk
- ⅓ cup strawberry yogurt
- ⅓ cup frozen unsweetened strawberries
- ½ medium firm banana, chopped
- 4 ice cubes
- 8 tsp. sugar

In a blender, combine all of the ingredients; cover and process for 30-45 seconds or until smooth. Stir if necessary. Pour into 2 chilled glasses; serve immediately.
1 cup: 171 cal., 2g fat (1g sat. fat), 7mg chol., 52mg sod., 36g carb. (32g sugars, 1g fiber), 4g pro.

COOL-KITCHEN TIP
Yogurt not only creates a creamy texture but also adds a substantial amount of protein, vitamins and minerals to this smoothie. For a high-protein, low-sugar option, try Greek yogurt. You can replace yogurt with milk in a smoothie in equal amounts. Keep in mind that the smoothie will be thinner, but you can add extra ice cubes to help thicken it up.

BLUEBERRY ORANGE BLAST

I developed this healthful, pretty smoothie after our annual blueberry-picking trip. Using tofu in smoothies adds extra protein, and the frozen banana acts just like ice cream. Blueberries are loaded with antioxidants.
—*Diane Neibling, Overland Park, KS*

TAKES: 5 min. • **MAKES:** 4 servings

- 1 cup orange juice
- 1 cup vanilla yogurt
- 1 medium banana, sliced and frozen
- 1 cup frozen unsweetened blueberries
- ½ cup silken firm tofu

In a blender, combine all ingredients; cover and process until smooth. Pour into chilled glasses; serve immediately.
¾ cup: 140 cal., 2g fat (1g sat. fat), 3mg chol., 49mg sod., 27g carb. (22g sugars, 2g fiber), 5g pro. **Diabetic Exchanges:** 1 starch, 1 fruit.

PINEAPPLE SMOOTHIES

I got this recipe over 30 years ago. I've tried several diabetic recipes, and this is one of the best.
—*Margery Bryan, Moses Lake, WA*

PREP: 5 min. + freezing
MAKES: 5 servings

- 1   can (20 oz.) unsweetened pineapple chunks, undrained
- 1   cup buttermilk
- 2   tsp. vanilla extract
- 2   tsp. sugar or sugar substitute

1. Drain pineapple, reserving ½ cup juice. Freeze pineapple chunks.
2. Place reserved juice, buttermilk, vanilla, sugar and frozen pineapple in a blender; cover and process until smooth. Serve immediately.

¾ cup: 96 cal., 0 fat (0 sat. fat), 2mg chol., 93mg sod., 19g carb. (18g sugars, 1g fiber), 3g pro. **Diabetic Exchanges:** 1 starch.

COOL-KITCHEN TIP
If you're looking to sweeten this recipe without the sugar, try using raw honey or agave nectar instead. Also, pineapple is naturally sweet, so try making this smoothie without the sugar first and see if you like it!

CHERRY FRUIT SMOOTHIES

You need just four ingredients to blend together these super-fast smoothies for breakfast. Try whipping them up on a summer day for a cool treat.
—*Macy Plummer, Avon, IN*

TAKES: 5 min. • **MAKES:** 4 servings

- 1½   cups unsweetened apple juice
- 1   cup frozen unsweetened raspberries
- 1   cup frozen pitted dark sweet cherries
- 1½   cups raspberry sherbet

In a blender, combine the apple juice, raspberries and cherries. Add sherbet; cover and process until well blended. Pour into chilled glasses; serve immediately.
1 cup: 160 cal., 2g fat (1g sat. fat), 3mg chol., 29mg sod., 37g carb. (31g sugars, 2g fiber), 2g pro.

MANGO ORANGE QUENCHER

Serve this beautiful beverage at your next brunch in place of mimosas. Just be sure to chill the base for at least an hour before adding the club soda.
—Taste of Home *Test Kitchen*

PREP: 10 min. + chilling
MAKES: 13 servings (about 2½ qt.)

- 4 **cups mango nectar**
- 2 **cups orange juice**
- 2 **Tbsp. lime juice**
- 1 **bottle (1 liter) club soda, chilled**
  Lime slices, optional

1. In a large pitcher, combine the nectar and juices. Refrigerate for at least 1 hour.
2. Just before serving, stir in club soda. Serve in champagne flutes or wine glasses. Garnish with lime slices if desired.

¾ cup: 58 cal., 0 fat (0 sat. fat), 0 chol., 19mg sod., 14g carb. (12g sugars, 0 fiber), 0 pro. **Diabetic exchanges:** 1 fruit.

NECTARINE SMOOTHIES

This nectarine smoothie recipe tastes great on a warm summer day. Enjoy it on your patio or at a picnic.
—*Joni Rodriguez, Silverton, OR*

PREP: 10 min. + freezing
MAKES: 3 servings

- ¾ **cup lemon Greek yogurt**
- ½ **cup orange juice**
- 2 **Tbsp. lime juice**
- 2 **Tbsp. honey**
- 2 **cups crushed ice**
- 2 **medium nectarines or peaches, peeled, cubed and frozen**

Place all ingredients in a blender; cover and process until blended.

1 cup: 170 cal., 6g fat (4g sat. fat), 15mg chol., 36mg sod., 29g carb. (25g sugars, 2g fiber), 3g pro.

SPARKLING COCONUT GRAPE JUICE

This sparkling drink is a nice change of pace from lemonade and party punch. The lime, coconut and grape combination is so refreshing. Add a splash of gin if you're feeling bold.
—*Shelly Bevington, Hermiston, OR*

TAKES: 5 min. • **MAKES:** 6 servings

- 4 cups white grape juice
- 2 tsp. lime juice
  Ice cubes
- 2 cups coconut-flavored sparkling water, chilled
  Optional: Lime wedges or slices

In a pitcher, combine grape juice and lime juice. Fill 6 tall glasses with ice. Pour juice mixture evenly into glasses; top off with sparkling water. Stir to combine. Garnish with lime wedges if desired.

1 cup: 94 cal., 0 fat (0 sat. fat), 0 chol., 13mg sod., 24g carb. (21g sugars, 0 fiber), 0 pro.

STRAWBERRY SHAKES

Full of summer fruit, these thick berry blends are the perfect way to savor hot days.
—*Ruby Williams, Bogalusa, LA*

TAKES: 5 min. • **MAKES:** 4 servings

- ⅔ cup 2% milk
- 3 cups strawberry ice cream
- 1 cup fresh strawberries
- 2 Tbsp. strawberry syrup
  Optional: Whipped cream and fresh strawberry slices

In a blender, combine all ingredients; cover and process until smooth. Pour into chilled glasses. If desired, top with whipped cream and fresh strawberries. Serve immediately.

1 cup: 253 cal., 10g fat (6g sat. fat), 34mg chol., 81mg sod., 38g carb. (9g sugars, 1g fiber), 5g pro.

PEANUT BUTTER MILK SHAKES

You've already got milk and peanut butter on hand, and probably vanilla ice cream, too! Using just a few ingredients, you can whip up this milkshake in minutes.
—*Joyce Turley, Slaughters, KY*

TAKES: 5 min. • **MAKES:** 3 servings

- 1 cup milk
- 2 cups vanilla ice cream
- ½ cup peanut butter
- 2 Tbsp. sugar

In a blender, combine all ingredients; cover and process for 30 seconds or until smooth. Stir if necessary. Pour into chilled glasses; serve immediately.

1 cup: 519 cal., 34g fat (12g sat. fat), 47mg chol., 287mg sod., 43g carb. (35g sugars, 3g fiber), 15g pro.

GLASS DISMISSED

Want a new way to serve a smoothie?
Skip the glass, and grab a spoon instead!

POWER BERRY SMOOTHIE BOWL

While you can't taste the spinach in these smoothies, you get all its nutrients with big berry flavor.
—*Christine Hair, Odessa, FL*

TAKES: 10 min. • **MAKES:** 3 servings

- ½ cup orange juice
- ½ cup pomegranate juice
- 1 container (6 oz.) mixed berry yogurt
- 1 cup frozen unsweetened strawberries
- 1 cup fresh baby spinach
- ½ medium ripe frozen banana, sliced
- ½ cup frozen unsweetened blueberries
- 2 Tbsp. ground flaxseed
  Optional: Sliced fresh strawberries, fresh blueberries, flaxseed and granola

In a blender, combine first 8 ingredients; cover and process for 30 seconds or until smooth. Pour into chilled bowls; top as desired. Serve immediately.
1 cup: 172 cal., 3g fat (0 sat. fat), 3mg chol., 47mg sod., 35g carb. (28g sugars, 4g fiber), 5g pro.

MEAN GREEN SMOOTHIE BOWLS

This delicious bright green smoothie contains powerful antioxidants. Pour into serving bowls and top with cucumber slices and fresh parsley sprigs for a pretty presentation.
—*Laura Wilhelm, West Hollywood, CA*

TAKES: 20 min. • **MAKES:** 6 servings

- 2 medium green apples, chopped
- 2 celery ribs (with leaves), chopped
- 2 cups fresh baby spinach
- 8 sprigs fresh parsley, stems removed, chopped
- 1 medium cucumber, peeled and chopped
- 1 Tbsp. minced fresh gingerroot
- 1 cup unfiltered or filtered apple juice
- ¼ cup fresh lemon juice
- 2 Tbsp. raw honey
  Optional: Sliced or chopped cucumber, sliced or chopped apples, minced fresh parsley and additional celery leaves

Place first 9 ingredients in a blender; cover and process until blended. Pour into chilled bowls; top as desired. Serve immediately.
¾ cup: 79 cal., 0 fat (0 sat. fat), 0 chol., 22mg sod., 20g carb. (16g sugars, 2g fiber), 1g pro. **Diabetic Exchanges:** 1 starch, 1 vegetable.

LIME COCONUT SMOOTHIE BOWL

This bowl is the most refreshing thing on the planet!
—*Madeline Butler, Denver, CO*

TAKES: 15 min. • **MAKES:** 2 servings

1	medium banana, peeled and frozen
1	cup fresh baby spinach
½	cup ice cubes
½	cup cubed fresh pineapple
½	cup chopped peeled mango or frozen mango chunks
½	cup plain Greek yogurt
¼	cup sweetened shredded coconut
3	Tbsp. honey
2	tsp. grated lime zest
1	tsp. lime juice
½	tsp. vanilla extract
1	Tbsp. spreadable cream cheese, optional

Optional: Lime wedges, sliced banana, sliced almonds, granola, dark chocolate chips and additional shredded coconut

Place the first 11 ingredients in a blender; if desired, add cream cheese. Cover and process until smooth. Pour into chilled bowls. Serve immediately, with optional toppings as desired.

1 cup: 325 cal., 10g fat (7g sat. fat), 15mg chol., 80mg sod., 60g carb. (51g sugars, 4g fiber), 4g pro.

READER RAVE

"Excellent breakfast for a summer morning! Two adults and two kids all loved it!"

—MBDUMEE, TASTEOFHOME.COM

P. 34

LIGHT BITES & SMALL PLATES

The living is easy when you serve these summertime bites, cold canapes, healthy snacks and cool, creamy dips.

WATERMELON TAPAS

I start looking forward to biting into this summery treat when snow is still on the ground here! Whenever I make this for my friends, they swoon. It's also my secret for getting my kids to eat their fruit.
—*Jami Geittmann, Greendale, WI*

TAKES: 25 min. • **MAKES:** 8 servings

- ½ cup plain Greek yogurt
- 1 Tbsp. minced fresh mint
- 1 Tbsp. honey
- 8 wedges seedless watermelon, about 1 in. thick
- 1 medium kiwifruit, peeled and chopped
- 1 tangerine, sliced
- ½ cup sliced ripe mangoes
- ½ cup fresh raspberries
- ¼ cup fresh blueberries
- ¼ cup pomegranate seeds
- 2 Tbsp. pistachios, chopped

In a bowl, combine yogurt, mint and honey. Arrange watermelon wedges on a platter; top each with yogurt mixture, fruit and pistachios. If desired, top with additional honey and mint. Serve immediately.

1 wedge: 103 cal., 2g fat (1g sat. fat), 4mg chol., 18mg sod., 21g carb. (18g sugars, 2g fiber), 2g pro. **Diabetic Exchanges:** 1½ fruit.

PROSCIUTTO SHRIMP WITH TROPICAL MANGO SALSA

Prosciutto and melon are a quintessential pairing. I took things a few steps further by adding an assortment of other fresh ingredients, including mango, pineapple and papaya. Finally, add shrimp and you've got yourself one tasty starter.
—Jane Whittaker, Pensacola, FL

TAKES: 30 min. • **MAKES:** 24 servings

- 24 peeled and deveined cooked shrimp (16-20 per lb.)
- 5 Tbsp. lime juice

MANGO SALSA
- 2 medium ripe mangoes, peeled and chopped
- ¾ cup cubed fresh pineapple
- ¾ cup chopped peeled papaya
- ½ cup finely chopped red onion
- ½ cup finely chopped sweet red pepper
- 2 jalapeno peppers, seeded and minced
- 2 Tbsp. minced fresh cilantro
- 2 Tbsp. lime juice
- 24 thin slices cantaloupe
- 12 thin slices prosciutto, halved lengthwise

1. Place shrimp and lime juice in a large shallow bowl. Refrigerate, covered, while making salsa, turning once. In a large bowl, combine mangoes, pineapple, papaya, red onion, red pepper, jalapenos, cilantro and lime juice. Refrigerate, covered, until serving.
2. Drain shrimp, discarding lime juice. Place 1 cantaloupe slice on each prosciutto slice; top each with 1 shrimp. Fold both sides to close. If desired, secure with toothpicks. Serve with mango salsa.
Note: Wear disposable gloves when cutting hot peppers; the oils can burn skin. Avoid touching your face.
1 wrapped shrimp with 1 Tbsp. salsa: 65 cal., 1g fat (0 sat. fat), 37mg chol., 170mg sod., 7g carb. (6g sugars, 1g fiber), 7g pro.

ZIPPY CURRY DIP

Everyone eats their vegetables when this creamy dip is served alongside them. The curry flavor gets stronger the longer the dip stands, so I like to make it in advance.
—Priscilla Steffke, Wausau, WI

TAKES: 10 min. • **MAKES:** about 1 cup

- ½ cup sour cream
- ½ cup mayonnaise
- 1 Tbsp. sugar
- 1 tsp. prepared horseradish
- 1 tsp. grated onion
- 1 tsp. cider vinegar
- ½ to 1 tsp. curry powder
- ½ tsp. garlic salt
  Assorted fresh vegetables or potato chips

In a small bowl, combine the first 8 ingredients. Refrigerate until serving. Serve with vegetables or chips.
2 Tbsp.: 137 cal., 14g fat (3g sat. fat), 15mg chol., 198mg sod., 2g carb. (2g sugars, 0 fiber), 1g pro.

ANTIPASTO PLATTER

We entertain often, and antipasto is one of our favorite crowd-pleasers. Guests love having their choice of so many delicious nibbles, including pepperoni and cubes of provolone.
—*Teri Lindquist, Gurnee, IL*

PREP: 10 min. + chilling
MAKES: 16 servings (3 qt.)

- 1 jar (24 oz.) pepperoncini, drained
- 1 can (15 oz.) garbanzo beans or chickpeas, rinsed and drained
- 2 cups halved fresh mushrooms
- 2 cups halved cherry tomatoes
- ½ lb. provolone cheese, cubed
- 1 can (6 oz.) pitted ripe olives, drained
- 1 pkg. (3½ oz.) sliced pepperoni
- 1 bottle (8 oz.) Italian vinaigrette dressing
  Lettuce leaves

1. In a large bowl, combine pepperoncini, beans, mushrooms, tomatoes, cheese, olives and pepperoni. Pour vinaigrette over mixture; toss to coat.
2. Refrigerate at least 30 minutes or overnight. Arrange on a lettuce-lined platter. Serve with toothpicks.

¾ cup: 178 cal., 13g fat (4g sat. fat), 15mg chol., 852mg sod., 8g carb. (2g sugars, 2g fiber), 6g pro.

ITALIAN OLIVES

A friend shared this recipe with me more than 25 years ago, and I still get raves when I serve them as part of an antipasto platter.
—*Jean Johnson, Reno, NV*

PREP: 10 min. + chilling • **MAKES:** 4 cups

- 2 cans (6 oz. each) pitted ripe olives, drained
- 1 jar (5¾ oz.) pimiento-stuffed olives, drained
- 2 Tbsp. finely chopped celery
- 2 Tbsp. finely chopped onion
- 2 Tbsp. capers, rinsed and drained
- ¼ cup olive oil
- 2 Tbsp. red wine vinegar
- 2 garlic cloves, minced
- 1 tsp. dried basil
- 1 tsp. dried oregano
- 1 tsp. crushed red pepper flakes
- ¼ tsp. salt

1. In a large bowl, combine the first 5 ingredients. In a small bowl, whisk the oil, vinegar, garlic, basil, oregano, pepper flakes and salt; pour over olive mixture; toss to coat.

2. Cover and refrigerate for at least 3 hours before serving. Store in the refrigerator for up to 3 days.

2 Tbsp.: 36 cal., 4g fat (0 sat. fat), 0 chol., 210mg sod., 1g carb. (0 sugars, 0 fiber), 0 pro.

COOL-KITCHEN TIP
These olives are best enjoyed the week they're made, stored in a well-sealed jar in the refrigerator. They're a great topping for fish fillets or Italian salads. Of course, you can nosh on them with some meat and crackers too.

CUCUMBER PARTY SANDWICHES

This is one of my favorite appetizers. We have lots of pig roasts here in Kentucky, and these little sandwiches are perfect to serve while the pig is cooking.
—*Rebecca Rose, Mount Washington, KY*

PREP: 20 min. + standing
MAKES: 2½ dozen

- 1 pkg. (8 oz.) cream cheese, softened
- 2 Tbsp. mayonnaise
- 2 tsp. Italian salad dressing mix
- 30 slices cocktail rye or pumpernickel bread
- 60 thin cucumber slices
  Optional: Fresh dill sprigs, slivered red pearl onions and cracked black pepper

1. Beat cream cheese, mayonnaise and dressing mix until blended; let stand for 30 minutes.

2. Spread cream cheese mixture on bread. Top each with 2 cucumber slices. If desired, garnish with dill, red onion slivers and cracked black pepper. Refrigerate, covered, until serving.

1 open-faced sandwich: 53 cal., 4g fat (2g sat. fat), 8mg chol., 92mg sod., 4g carb. (1g sugars, 1g fiber), 1g pro.

SPICY PICKLED GRAPES

I love sweet and spicy flavors, so I created these pickled grapes. They are excellent as an appetizer, a sneaky addition to salads or a topper in your favorite Bloody Mary.
—*Carla Hinkle, Memphis, TN*

PREP: 10 min. • **COOK:** 10 min. + chilling
MAKES: 8 cups

- ½ cup sugar
- ½ cup white vinegar
- ½ cup cider vinegar
- 1 banana pepper, sliced
- 2 jalapeno peppers, sliced
- 1 red chili pepper, sliced
- 4 cinnamon sticks (3 in.)
- 2 in. fresh gingerroot, peeled and thinly sliced
- 1 Tbsp. coriander seeds
- 1 tsp. whole allspice
- 4 drops hot pepper sauce
- 1½ lbs. green grapes, halved
- 1½ lbs. seedless red grapes, halved

In a large saucepan, bring the first 11 ingredients to a boil. Reduce heat; simmer 3-5 minutes or until sugar is dissolved. Remove from heat and cool slightly. Place grapes in a large bowl; add pickling liquid. Refrigerate, covered, at least 12 hours before serving.

Note: Wear disposable gloves when cutting hot peppers; the oils can burn skin. Avoid touching your face.

¼ cup: 33 cal., 0 fat (0 sat. fat), 0 chol., 6mg sod., 8g carb. (7g sugars, 0 fiber), 0 pro.

BANG BANG SHRIMP CAKE SLIDERS

My family loves these shrimp sliders. The bang bang slaw dressing and shrimp cake patties can be made ahead. When ready to serve, toss the slaw and sear the cakes.
—*Kim Banick, Turner, OR*

PREP: 30 min. + chilling
COOK: 10 min./batch
MAKES: 12 sliders

- 1 lb. uncooked shrimp (41-50 per lb.), peeled and deveined
- 1 large egg, lightly beaten
- ½ cup finely chopped sweet red pepper
- 6 green onions, chopped and divided
- 1 Tbsp. minced fresh gingerroot
- ¼ tsp. salt
- 1 cup panko bread crumbs
- ¼ cup mayonnaise
- 1 Tbsp. Sriracha chili sauce
- 1 Tbsp. sweet chili sauce
- 5 cups shredded Chinese or napa cabbage
- 12 mini buns or dinner rolls
- 3 Tbsp. canola oil

1. Place shrimp in a food processor; pulse until chopped. In a large bowl, combine the egg, red pepper, 4 green onions, ginger and salt. Add the shrimp and bread crumbs; mix gently. Shape into twelve ½-in.-thick patties. Refrigerate for 20 minutes.

2. Meanwhile, in a large bowl, combine mayonnaise and the chili sauces; stir in cabbage and remaining green onions. In a toaster oven, toast buns, cut sides up, until golden brown, 2-3 minutes.

3. In a large cast-iron or other heavy skillet, heat oil over medium heat. Add shrimp cakes in batches; cook until golden brown on each side, 4-5 minutes. Serve on toasted buns with slaw. Secure with toothpicks if desired. Serve with additional Sriracha chili sauce if desired.

1 slider: 210 cal., 10g fat (1g sat. fat), 63mg chol., 321mg sod., 20g carb. (3g sugars, 1g fiber), 11g pro.

BANH MI SKEWERS

I love banh mi sandwiches, but I wanted to make them easier to serve for a party. These skewers are a fun twist! For easier prep on the day of the party, make the meatballs in advance and freeze them.
—*Elisabeth Larsen, Pleasant Grove, UT*

PREP: 45 min. + chilling
COOK: 10 min./batch • **MAKES:** 12 servings

- 1 cup white vinegar or rice vinegar
- ¼ cup sugar
- ½ tsp. salt
- 1 English cucumber, thinly sliced
- 2 medium carrots, thinly sliced
- 4 radishes, thinly sliced
- 1 cup mayonnaise
- 1 Tbsp. Sriracha chili sauce
- 2 Tbsp. minced fresh cilantro
- 2 green onions, thinly sliced
- 1 Tbsp. soy sauce
- 1 garlic clove, minced
- ¼ tsp. cayenne pepper
- 1½ lbs. ground pork
- 2 Tbsp. canola oil
- 1 French bread baguette (10½ oz.), cut into 24 slices

1. In a large bowl, combine vinegar, sugar and salt; whisk until sugar is dissolved. Add cucumber, carrots and radishes; let stand until serving. Combine mayonnaise and chili sauce; refrigerate until serving.
2. In another large bowl, combine cilantro, green onions, soy sauce, garlic and cayenne. Add pork; mix lightly but thoroughly. Shape into 36 balls.
3. In a large skillet, heat oil over medium heat. Cook meatballs in batches until cooked through, turning occasionally.
4. Drain vegetable mixture. On 12 metal or wooden skewers, alternately thread vegetables and meatballs; start and end each skewer with a baguette slice. Serve with Sriracha mayonnaise.
1 skewer with about 1 Tbsp. sauce:
336 cal., 24g fat (5g sat. fat), 39mg chol., 416mg sod., 16g carb. (2g sugars, 1g fiber), 13g pro.

CREOLE SCALLOP CAKES

Experimenting in the kitchen is a passion of mine ... one I hope to pass along to my daughter. One day I had some scallops and decided to concoct a scallop cake instead of a crab cake. This scrumptious appetizer can be prepared ahead of time; cook the formed, chilled cakes just before serving. Not only does this simplify last-minute prep, it also allows the flavors to infuse into the mixture.

—Iisha Leftridge-Brooks, Sacramento, CA

PREP: 25 min. + chilling
COOK: 5 min./batch
MAKES: 20 scallop cakes (1½ cups aioli)

- 1 large egg, beaten
- ½ cup seasoned bread crumbs
- 2 Tbsp. finely chopped sweet red pepper
- 2 Tbsp. finely chopped leek (white portion only)
- 4 garlic cloves, minced
- 2 Tbsp. honey mustard
- 1 Tbsp. minced fresh thyme
- 1 Tbsp. chopped fennel fronds
- 2 tsp. salt-free lemon-pepper seasoning
- 1½ tsp. Creole seasoning
- 1 lb. sea scallops

COATING
- 1 cup panko bread crumbs
- 4 tsp. dried parsley flakes
- 2 tsp. coarsely ground pepper

SPICY HONEY AIOLI
- 1 cup mayonnaise
- ⅓ cup honey mustard
- 1 Tbsp. lemon juice
- 1 Tbsp. unsweetened apple juice
- 1 tsp. paprika
- 1 tsp. Creole seasoning
- ½ tsp. Cajun seasoning
- ⅓ cup canola oil

1. In a large bowl, combine the first 10 ingredients. Place scallops in a food processor; cover and pulse until just pureed. Fold into egg mixture.

2. In a shallow bowl, combine the bread crumbs, parsley and pepper. Drop 2 Tbsp. scallop mixture into the crumb mixture. Gently coat and shape into a ½-in.-thick patty. Repeat with remaining mixture. Cover patties and refrigerate for at least 30 minutes.

3. Meanwhile, in a small bowl, whisk the mayonnaise, mustard, lemon juice, apple juice and seasonings. Cover; refrigerate until serving.

4. Heat a large cast-iron or other heavy skillet over medium heat. Cook patties in the oil in batches until golden brown, 2-3 minutes on each side. Drain on paper towels. Serve with aioli. If desired, top with additional fennel fronds.

1 scallop cake with 1 Tbsp. aioli: 169 cal., 14g fat (2g sat. fat), 22mg chol., 291mg sod., 7g carb. (2g sugars, 0 fiber), 5g pro.

FRESH SHRIMP & AVOCADO NACHOS

I'm a fan of shrimp, and my family loves nachos. When I combined those favorites and added fresh avocado, the result was a cool yet satisfying snack.
—*Teri Rasey, Cadillac, MI*

PREP: 30 min. + chilling
MAKES: 10 servings

- 4 plum tomatoes, chopped
- 3 tomatillos, husked and chopped
- 4 jalapeno peppers, seeded and finely chopped
- 1 small onion, chopped
- ¼ cup minced fresh cilantro
- 3 Tbsp. olive oil
- 3 Tbsp. lime juice, divided
- 2 Tbsp. seasoned rice vinegar
- 2 garlic cloves, minced
- 1½ tsp. sea salt
- ½ tsp. dried oregano
- 1 lb. peeled and deveined cooked shrimp (31-40 per lb.), coarsely chopped
- 2 medium ripe avocados, peeled and pitted, divided
- ½ cup sour cream
- 8 cups tortilla chips
- 1 cup shredded lettuce

1. Combine tomatoes, tomatillos, peppers, onion, cilantro, oil, 1 Tbsp. lime juice, vinegar, garlic, sea salt and oregano. Cover and refrigerate until chilled, at least 30 minutes. Stir in shrimp.

2. For avocado cream, mash 1 avocado with sour cream and 1 Tbsp. lime juice until smooth. Cube remaining avocado and toss with remaining 1 Tbsp. lime juice.

3. Arrange chips on a platter. Top with shrimp mixture, cubed avocado, lettuce and avocado cream; serve immediately.

Note: Wear disposable gloves when cutting hot peppers; the oils can burn skin. Avoid touching your face.

1 serving: 264 cal., 16g fat (3g sat. fat), 72mg chol., 542mg sod., 20g carb. (3g sugars, 3g fiber), 12g pro.

COCONUT SHRIMP

Jumbo shrimp is the perfect vehicle for crunchy, tropical coconut flakes. The fruity salsa is delightful as a dip for this island-influenced appetizer.
—*Marie Hattrup, Sonoma, CA*

PREP: 20 min. • **COOK:** 5 min./batch
MAKES: 1½ dozen

- 18 uncooked jumbo shrimp (about 1 lb.)
- ⅓ cup cornstarch
- ¾ tsp. salt
- ½ tsp. cayenne pepper
- 3 large egg whites
- 2 cups sweetened shredded coconut
  Oil for deep-fat frying

APRICOT-PINEAPPLE SALSA
- 1 cup diced pineapple
- ½ cup finely chopped red onion
- ½ cup apricot preserves
- ½ cup minced fresh cilantro
- 2 Tbsp. lime juice
- 1 jalapeno pepper, seeded and chopped
  Salt and pepper to taste
  Lime wedges, optional

1. Peel and devein shrimp, leaving tails intact. Make a slit down inner curve of each shrimp, starting with the tail; press lightly to flatten. In a shallow dish, combine the cornstarch, salt and cayenne; set aside. In a bowl, beat egg whites until stiff peaks form. Place the coconut in another shallow dish. Coat shrimp with cornstarch mixture; dip into egg whites, then coat with coconut.
2. In an electric skillet or deep-fat fryer, heat oil to 375°. Fry shrimp, a few at a time, 1-1½ minutes on each side or until golden brown. Drain on paper towels.
3. Combine salsa ingredients. Serve with shrimp and, if desired, lime wedges.
Note: Wear disposable gloves when cutting hot peppers; the oils can burn skin. Avoid touching your face.
1 shrimp with 1 Tbsp. salsa: 505 cal., 12g fat (5g sat. fat), 552mg chol., 677mg sod., 19g carb. (11g sugars, 1g fiber), 75g pro.

CRAB LETTUCE WRAPS

I love dishes you can put together and eat with your hands. These little lettuce wraps are healthy, fast and flavorful.
—*Joyce Huang, New York, NY*

TAKES: 10 min. • **MAKES:** 1 dozen

- 2 cans (6 oz. each) lump crabmeat, drained
- ¼ cup finely chopped celery
- ¼ cup seasoned stuffing cubes, coarsely crushed
- ¼ cup plain Greek yogurt
- ⅛ tsp. salt
- ⅛ tsp. pepper
- 12 Bibb or Boston lettuce leaves
  Finely chopped tomatoes, optional

In a large bowl, mix crab, celery, stuffing cubes, yogurt, salt and pepper. To serve, spoon 2 Tbsp. crab mixture into each lettuce leaf. If desired, sprinkle with tomatoes. Fold lettuce over filling.
1 filled lettuce wrap: 37 cal., 0 fat (0 sat. fat), 25mg chol., 139mg sod., 1g carb. (0 sugars, 0 fiber), 7g pro.

GARLIC BLUE CHEESE DIP

This thick, creamy dip is my mom's recipe, and it's a family favorite for ringing in the season. It also makes a tasty substitute for mayonnaise on chicken and turkey sandwiches.
—*Lillian Nardi, Richmond, CA*

TAKES: 10 min. • **MAKES:** About 1½ cups

- ½ cup milk
- 1 pkg. (8 oz.) cream cheese, cubed
- 1 cup (4 oz.) crumbled blue cheese
- 2 garlic cloves, peeled
  Assorted vegetables or crackers

In a blender, combine the milk, cream cheese, blue cheese and garlic; cover and process until blended. If desired, top with additional crumbled blue cheese just before serving. Serve with vegetables or crackers.
2 Tbsp.: 113 cal., 10g fat (6g sat. fat), 31mg chol., 218mg sod., 1g carb. (1g sugars, 0 fiber), 4g pro.

GREEK OLIVE TAPENADE

Welcome to an olive lover's dream. Mix olives with freshly minced garlic, parsley and a few drizzles of olive oil to have the ultimate in Mediterranean bliss.
—*Lisa Sojka, Rockport, ME*

TAKES: 25 min.
MAKES: 16 servings (about 2 cups)

- 2 cups pitted Greek olives, drained
- 3 garlic cloves, minced
- 3 Tbsp. olive oil
- 1½ tsp. minced fresh parsley
  Toasted baguette slices

In a food processor, pulse olives with garlic until finely chopped. Add oil and parsley; pulse until combined. Serve with toasted baguette slices.
2 Tbsp. tapenade: 71 cal., 7g fat (1g sat. fat), 0 chol., 277mg sod., 2g carb. (0 sugars, 0 fiber), 0 pro.

PERUVIAN FISH CEVICHE

This ceviche is loaded with flavor. Every single bite is uniquely delicious. It is sure to wake up all those taste buds!
—*Melissa Rodriguez, Van Nuys, CA*

PREP: 25 min. + standing
MAKES: 5 servings

- 1½ lbs. halibut, tilapia or mahi mahi fillets, cut into ½-in. pieces
- 1½ tsp. sea salt, divided
- 1 medium red onion, thinly sliced
- 1 celery rib, finely chopped, divided
- 2 Tbsp. minced fresh cilantro, divided
- ¾ tsp. pepper, divided
- 3 garlic cloves, minced
- 1 cup lime juice (10-12 limes)
- 1 minced seeded rocoto pepper
- 2 tsp. minced fresh gingerroot
- 2 Tbsp. evaporated milk
  Optional: Cooked sweet potatoes, lettuce, toasted chulpe corn and corn on the cob

1. In a large bowl, combine uncooked fish, 2 cups cold water and ¼ tsp. salt. Let stand 15 minutes; drain. Meanwhile, place sliced onion in ice water.
2. Stir together drained fish, half the celery, 1 Tbsp. cilantro, ¼ tsp. each salt, pepper and garlic; set aside.
3. In a blender, combine lime juice, 2 Tbsp. fish mixture, the rocoto pepper, ginger, remaining celery and cilantro, and the remaining 1 tsp. salt and ½ tsp. pepper; blend until smooth. Pour mixture over fish; stir to combine. Let stand 10 minutes; stir in evaporated milk. Serve with desired toppings and drained red onions.
Note: Wear disposable gloves when cutting hot peppers; the oils can burn skin. Avoid touching your face.
1 serving: 155 cal., 2g fat (1g sat. fat), 69mg chol., 677mg sod., 7g carb. (2g sugars, 1g fiber), 26g pro.

MARINATED SHRIMP & OLIVES

This is my favorite appetizer to serve party guests. The flavors in this colorful dish blend beautifully, and the shrimp are tender and tasty.
—*Carol A. Gawronski, Lake Wales, FL*

PREP: 15 min. + chilling
MAKES: 20 servings

- 1½ lbs. peeled and deveined cooked shrimp (31-40 per lb.)
- 1 can (6 oz.) pitted ripe olives, drained
- 1 jar (5¾ oz.) pimiento-stuffed olives, drained
- 2 Tbsp. olive oil
- 1½ tsp. curry powder
- ½ tsp. ground ginger
- ¼ tsp. salt
- ¼ tsp. pepper
- 2 Tbsp. lemon juice
- 1 Tbsp. minced fresh parsley or 1 tsp. dried parsley flakes

1. Combine shrimp and olives; set aside.
2. In a small saucepan, heat oil over medium heat. In a small bowl, combine curry powder, ginger, salt and pepper; whisk into hot oil. Cook and stir 1 minute. Remove from heat; stir in lemon juice and parsley. Immediately drizzle over shrimp mixture; toss gently to coat.
3. Refrigerate shrimp, covered, up to 6 hours, stirring occasionally. Serve with toothpicks.

⅓ cup: 71 cal., 4g fat (0 sat. fat), 52mg chol., 292mg sod., 2g carb. (0 sugars, 0 fiber), 7g pro. **Diabetic Exchanges:** 1 lean meat, 1 fat.

SALMON SALAD-STUFFED ENDIVE LEAVES

Salmon creates an elegant appetizer in this vibrant recipe. It's simple to prepare and can even be made ahead of time.
—*Melissa Carafa, Broomall, PA*

TAKES: 15 min. • **MAKES:** 14 pieces

- 1 salmon fillet (6 oz.), cooked and flaked
- ¼ cup tartar sauce
- 2 tsp. capers
- 1 tsp. snipped fresh dill
- ¼ tsp. lemon-pepper seasoning
- 1 head Belgian endive (about 5 oz.), separated into leaves

In a small bowl, combine salmon, tartar sauce, capers, dill and lemon-pepper seasoning. Spoon about 2 teaspoonfuls on each endive leaf. If desired, garnish with additional dill. Refrigerate until serving.
1 piece: 42 cal., 3g fat (1g sat. fat), 9mg chol., 60mg sod., 2g carb. (0 sugars, 1g fiber), 3g pro.

WHIPPED FETA DIP

The basis of this whipped feta dip is a great blank canvas for different flavors. This version is flavored with garlic and lemon, but you might try other flavors like roasted red peppers or Greek olives, or create a spicy version by adding crushed red pepper.
—*Dawn Parker, Surrey, BC*

TAKES: 10 min. • **MAKES:** 1⅓ cups

- 8 oz. feta cheese, crumbled
- ½ cup plain Greek yogurt
- 1 tsp. Greek seasoning
- 1 garlic clove, chopped
- ¾ tsp. grated lemon zest
- 1 Tbsp. extra virgin olive oil
  Fresh mint

Place the first 5 ingredients in a food processor; process until smooth. Spoon into serving dish; drizzle with olive oil and sprinkle with mint.
2 Tbsp.: 85 cal., 7g fat (4g sat. fat), 23mg chol., 311mg sod., 2g carb. (1g sugars, 0 fiber), 4g pro.

COOL-KITCHEN TIP
This recipe was tested with Cavender's Greek seasoning, a blend of salt, oregano, garlic powder, basil, thyme, dill, marjoram and black pepper. If you have za'atar seasoning, you could substitute it.

CRAWFISH BEIGNETS WITH CAJUN DIPPING SAUCE

Get a taste of the Deep South with these slightly spicy beignets. You won't be able to eat just one!
—Donna Lanclos, Lafayette, LA

PREP: 20 min. • **COOK:** 5 min./batch
MAKES: about 2 dozen (¾ cup sauce)

- 1 large egg, beaten
- 1 lb. chopped cooked crawfish tail meat or shrimp
- 4 green onions, chopped
- 1½ tsp. butter, melted
- ½ tsp. salt
- ½ tsp. cayenne pepper
- ⅓ cup bread flour
  Oil for deep-fat frying
- ¾ cup mayonnaise
- ½ cup ketchup
- ¼ tsp. prepared horseradish, optional
- ¼ tsp. hot pepper sauce

1. In a large bowl, combine egg, crawfish, green onions, butter, salt and cayenne. Stir in flour until blended.
2. In an electric skillet or deep fryer, heat 1 in. oil to 375°. Drop batter by tablespoonfuls, a few at a time, into hot oil. Fry until golden brown on both sides. Drain on paper towels.
3. In a small bowl, combine mayonnaise, ketchup, horseradish if desired, and pepper sauce. Serve with the beignets.
1 beignet with 1½ tsp. sauce: 101 cal., 8g fat (1g sat. fat), 35mg chol., 171mg sod., 3g carb. (1g sugars, 0 fiber), 4g pro.

BASIL & PINE NUT GUACAMOLE

Guacamole is typically a Mexican dish, but that doesn't mean you can't try to make it with other global flavors. For a pesto-inspired guac, top it off with toasted pine nuts and fresh basil ribbons. You can also substitute lemon juice for the traditional lime.
—Taste of Home *Test Kitchen*

TAKES: 15 min. • **MAKES:** 6 servings

- 3 medium ripe avocado, peeled and cubed
- 2 to 3 Tbsp. fresh lime juice
- ½ to 1 tsp. kosher salt
- ½ cup fresh basil leaves, thinly sliced
- ¼ cup pine nuts, toasted

In a bowl, mash avocados until almost smooth. Stir in lime juice and ½ tsp. salt. Let stand 10 minutes to allow flavors to blend. Adjust seasoning with additional lime juice and salt if desired. Top with fresh basil and pine nuts.
¼ cup: 153 cal., 14g fat (2g sat. fat), 0 chol., 166mg sod., 7g carb. (0 sugars, 5g fiber), 2g pro. **Diabetic Exchanges:** 3 fat, ½ starch.

TZATZIKI SHRIMP CUCUMBER ROUNDS

I created this recipe with what I had on hand one night, and now it's one of my husband's favorites! The bacon-wrapped shrimp, garlicky sauce and burst of cool cuke flavor make these irresistible.
—*Shannon Trelease, East Hampton, NY*

PREP: 25 min. • **COOK:** 10 min./batch
MAKES: 2 dozen

- ¼ cup reduced-fat plain yogurt
- 2 Tbsp. finely chopped peeled cucumber
- ⅛ tsp. garlic salt
- ⅛ tsp. dill weed
- 6 bacon strips
- 24 uncooked shrimp (31-40 per lb.), peeled and deveined
- 1 to 2 Tbsp. canola oil
- 2 medium cucumbers, cut into ¼-in. slices

1. In a small bowl, combine the yogurt, chopped cucumber, garlic salt and dill; set aside.
2. Cut each bacon strip in half widthwise and then lengthwise. Wrap a piece of bacon around each shrimp. Secure with toothpicks.
3. In a large nonstick skillet, heat oil over medium heat; cook shrimp in batches for 3-4 minutes on each side or until bacon is crisp.
4. Spoon a rounded ½ tsp. yogurt sauce onto each cucumber slice; top with 1 shrimp. If desired, garnish with additional fresh dill.
1 piece: 30 cal., 2g fat (0 sat. fat), 18mg chol., 64mg sod., 1g carb. (0 sugars, 0 fiber), 3g pro.

GREEK PITA SPREAD

I first tried this at a family gathering and was blown away! I have since made it for my co-workers, and they just love it. I've gotten many requests for the recipe.
—*Joyce Benninger, Owen Sound, ON*

TAKES: 30 min. • **MAKES:** 6 cups

- 1 pkg. (8 oz.) cream cheese, softened
- 1 cup sour cream
- ½ cup Greek vinaigrette
- 2 cans (2¼ oz. each) sliced ripe olives, drained
- 2 medium tomatoes, seeded and chopped
- 1 small red onion, chopped
- 1 large green pepper, chopped
- 1 large sweet red pepper, chopped
- 1 large cucumber, seeded and chopped
- 1 cup (4 oz.) crumbled feta cheese
  Pita breads, cut into wedges or baked pita chips

In a small bowl, beat the cream cheese, sour cream and vinaigrette until blended. Spread onto a large serving plate or 2 pie plates. Layer with olives, tomatoes, onion, peppers, cucumber and cheese. Serve with pita breads.

¼ cup: 96 cal., 8g fat (4g sat. fat), 19mg chol., 178mg sod., 3g carb. (2g sugars, 1g fiber), 2g pro.

AUNT KAREN'S SHRIMP SALAD

When unexpected company calls during the holidays, this salad is the perfect fit. It's quick to put together, too, leaving you more time to spend with your guests.
—*Karen Moore, Jacksonville, FL*

PREP: 10 min. • **COOK:** 10 min. + chilling
MAKES: 24 servings

- 2 lbs. uncooked shrimp (26-30 per lb.), peeled, deveined and halved
- 1 Tbsp. white vinegar
- 1 Tbsp. lemon juice
- ⅓ cup plus 1 Tbsp. mayonnaise, divided
- ½ tsp. garlic salt
- 2 celery ribs, chopped
- 5 hard-boiled large eggs, chopped
- ¼ cup chopped sweet red pepper
- 24 Bibb lettuce leaves or Boston lettuce leaves
  Sliced green onions, optional

1. In a Dutch oven or large saucepan, bring 6 cups water to a boil. Add shrimp; cook, uncovered, until shrimp turn pink, 3-5 minutes. Drain. Transfer to a large bowl. Add vinegar, lemon juice, 1 Tbsp. mayonnaise and the garlic salt; toss to coat. Refrigerate, covered, at least 4 hours or overnight.

2. To serve, stir in remaining ⅓ cup mayonnaise, celery, eggs and red pepper. Serve in lettuce leaves. If desired, top with green onions.

¼ cup: 74 cal., 4g fat (1g sat. fat), 85mg chol., 120mg sod., 1g carb. (0 sugars, 0 fiber), 8g pro. **Diabetic Exchanges:** 1 lean meat, 1 fat.

LIME AVOCADO HUMMUS

My mashup of guacamole and hummus is light and bright, but also rich and satisfying. Serve with chips and veggies or as a cool sandwich spread.
—*Andreann Geise, Myrtle Beach, SC*

TAKES: 15 min. • **MAKES:** 2½ cups

- 1 tsp. whole peppercorns
- 1 can (15 oz.) garbanzo beans or chickpeas, rinsed and drained
- 1 ripe avocado, peeled and pitted
- ½ cup fresh parsley sprigs
- ½ cup olive oil
- ¼ cup grated Romano cheese
- ¼ cup fresh cilantro leaves
- ¼ cup lime juice
- 1 garlic clove
- ½ tsp. sugar
- ¼ tsp. salt
  Tortilla chips

Place peppercorns in a food processor; process until ground. Add remaining ingredients; process 2-3 minutes longer or until smooth. Serve with chips.

¼ cup: 174 cal., 15g fat (2g sat. fat), 3mg chol., 168mg sod., 9g carb. (1g sugars, 3g fiber), 3g pro.

READER RAVE

"Comes together super quickly. I doubled the garlic, omitted the cilantro and used more parsley. I served this with bell pepper strips. To add a little crunch, I sprinkled the top with pepitas."

—JMARTINELLI13, TASTEOFHOME.COM

EASY ROAST BEEF ROLL-UPS

For a quick and crowd-pleasing app, you can't beat these flavorful wraps seasoned with salsa. Roll some up for your family and friends!
—*Susan Scott, Asheville, NC*

TAKES: 15 min. • **MAKES:** 10 servings

- ½ cup sour cream
- ¼ cup mayonnaise
- ¼ cup salsa
- 10 flour tortillas (8 in.), room temperature
- 1 lb. thinly sliced cooked roast beef
- 10 large lettuce leaves

Combine the sour cream, mayonnaise and salsa; spread over tortillas. Top with roast beef and lettuce. Roll up each tortilla tightly and secure with toothpicks; cut in half. Serve with additional salsa.

1 wrap: 262 cal., 10g fat (3g sat. fat), 26mg chol., 650mg sod., 28g carb. (1g sugars, 0 fiber), 13g pro.

THYME & FIG GOAT CHEESE SPREAD

When I started growing herbs in my garden it took me a while to find a good way to use thyme, but this easy appetizer spread lets it shine. I usually garnish it with a sprig of thyme, slivered almonds and chopped figs.
—*Laura Cox, Columbia, MO*

TAKES: 15 min. • **MAKES:** 1½ cups

- 1 cup crumbled goat cheese
- ½ cup sour cream
- 1 Tbsp. honey
- ½ tsp. minced fresh thyme
- ½ cup chopped dried figs
- ¼ cup slivered almonds
  Assorted crackers, French bread baguette slices or assorted fresh vegetables

In a small bowl, beat cheese, sour cream, honey and thyme until smooth; stir in figs and almonds. Sprinkle with additional thyme if desired. Refrigerate until serving. Serve with crackers, baguette slices or vegetables.

2 Tbsp.: 81 cal., 6g fat (3g sat. fat), 14mg chol., 49mg sod., 7g carb. (5g sugars, 1g fiber), 3g pro.

COOL-KITCHEN TIP

The ingredients in this recipe are simple and straightforward but, when combined, make an elegant spread. If you don't have fresh thyme on hand, use ¼ tsp. dried thyme.

SIMPLE SALMON DIP

This is my go-to dip recipe for summer barbecues. The secret is the green chiles—they add just enough heat.
—*Susan Jordan, Denver, CO*

PREP: 15 min. + chilling • **MAKES:** 1¼ cups

- 1 pkg. (8 oz.) reduced-fat cream cheese
- 2 Tbsp. canned chopped green chiles
- 1½ tsp. lemon juice
- 2 green onions, chopped, divided
- 2 oz. smoked salmon fillet
  Assorted crackers or toasted French bread baguette slices

1. In a small bowl, mix cream cheese, green chiles, lemon juice and half the green onions. Flake salmon into small pieces; stir into cream cheese mixture. Refrigerate, covered, at least 2 hours before serving.

2. Top dip with remaining green onions. Serve with crackers.

3 Tbsp.: 107 cal., 8g fat (5g sat. fat), 29mg chol., 246mg sod., 2g carb. (1g sugars, 0 fiber), 6g pro.

READER RAVE

"Great dip! We live in an area where steelhead, salmon and kokanee are abundant. This is a saver, and you can use any smoked fish."

—BUTCHER2BOY, TASTEOFHOME.COM

CHEESE-STUFFED CHERRY TOMATOES

We grow plenty of tomatoes, so my husband and I often handpick enough cherry tomatoes for these easy-to-fix appetizers. This is one of our favorite recipes, and it's impossible to eat just one.
—*Mary Lou Robison, Greensboro, NC*

PREP: 15 min. + chilling • **MAKES:** 1 dozen

- 1 pint cherry tomatoes
- 1 pkg. (4 oz.) crumbled feta cheese
- ½ cup finely chopped red onion
- ½ cup olive oil
- ¼ cup red wine vinegar
- 1 Tbsp. dried oregano
  Salt and pepper to taste

1. Cut a thin slice off the top of each tomato. Scoop out and discard pulp. Invert tomatoes onto paper towels to drain. Combine cheese and onion; spoon into tomatoes.

2. In a small bowl, whisk the oil, vinegar, oregano, salt and pepper. Spoon over tomatoes. Cover and refrigerate for 30 minutes or until ready to serve.

1 tomato: 111 cal., 11g fat (2g sat. fat), 5mg chol., 93mg sod., 2g carb. (1g sugars, 1g fiber), 2g pro.

FRIED GREEN TOMATOES

My grandmother came up with her own version of fried green tomatoes years ago. Our family loves them. It's a traditional taste of the South that anyone can enjoy!
—*Melanie Chism, Coker, AL*

PREP: 10 min. + standing • **COOK:** 10 min.
MAKES: 8 servings

- 4   medium green tomatoes
- 1   tsp. salt
- ¼   tsp. lemon-pepper seasoning
- ¾   cup cornmeal
- ½   cup vegetable oil

Slice the tomatoes ¼ in. thick. Sprinkle both sides with salt and lemon-pepper seasoning. Let stand 20-25 minutes. Coat with cornmeal. In a large skillet, heat oil over medium heat. Fry tomatoes until tender and golden brown, 3-4 minutes on each side. Drain on paper towels. Serve immediately.

2 pieces: 166 cal., 11g fat (1g sat. fat), 0 chol., 317mg sod., 16g carb. (4g sugars, 2g fiber), 2g pro.

READER RAVE

"Down in Houston, I use white cornmeal for my tomatoes. I serve them with black-eyed peas and pork chops."

—BENJYY, TASTEOFHOME.COM

SHRIMP & CUCUMBER CANAPES

These cute stacks really stand out in a holiday appetizer buffet. Tasty, cool and crunchy, they come together in a snap.
—*Ashley Nochlin, Port St. Lucie, FL*

TAKES: 25 min. • **MAKES:** 2 dozen

- ½   cup ketchup
- 4   tsp. Creole seasoning, divided
- 1   Tbsp. finely chopped onion
- 1   Tbsp. finely chopped green pepper
- 1   Tbsp. finely chopped celery
- ¼   tsp. hot pepper sauce
- 1   pkg. (8 oz.) cream cheese, softened
- 24   English cucumber slices
- 24   peeled and deveined cooked medium shrimp
- 2   Tbsp. minced fresh parsley

1. For cocktail sauce, in a small bowl, combine the ketchup, 2 tsp. Creole seasoning, onion, green pepper, celery and pepper sauce. In another bowl, combine cream cheese and remaining 2 tsp. Creole seasoning.
2. Spread or pipe the cream cheese mixture onto cucumber slices. Top each with a shrimp and cocktail sauce. Sprinkle with parsley.
Note: If you don't have Creole seasoning, you can make your own using 1 tsp. each salt, garlic powder and paprika, and ¼ tsp. each of dried thyme, ground cumin and cayenne pepper.
1 canape: 50 cal., 3g fat (2g sat. fat), 26mg chol., 218mg sod., 2g carb. (1g sugars, 0 fiber), 3g pro.

DO THE SALSA

Sometimes fruity, frequently spicy, always cool and delicious: Salsa's the ultimate beat-the-heat snack.

CHIPOTLE BERRY FRUIT SALSA

Not too hot, but with a bit of a kick, this salsa is a perfect topping for grilled fish or chicken. It's also a delectable chip dip—just double the recipe and watch it disappear. Cut down on (or increase!) the chipotle peppers to suit your taste.
—*Trisha Kruse, Eagle, ID*

TAKES: 20 min. **MAKES:** 4 cups

- 2 cups chopped fresh strawberries
- 2 cups fresh blackberries, halved
- 2 medium kiwifruit, peeled and chopped
- 2 Tbsp. orange marmalade spreadable fruit
- 2 Tbsp. lime juice
- 1 Tbsp. minced chipotle pepper in adobo sauce
- ⅛ tsp. salt
- ⅛ tsp. cayenne pepper
  Cinnamon sugar pita chips

In a large bowl, combine the first 8 ingredients. Cover and refrigerate until serving. Serve with pita chips.
¼ cup: 26 cal., 0 fat (0 sat. fat), 0 chol., 25mg sod., 6g carb. (4g sugars, 2g fiber), 1g pro.

AVOCADO SALSA

I first made this recipe for a party, and it was an absolute success. People love the garlic, corn and avocado combination.
—*Susan Vandermeer, Ogden, UT*

PREP: 20 min. + chilling
MAKES: about 7 cups

- 1⅔ cups (about 8¼ oz.) frozen corn, thawed
- 2 cans (2¼ oz. each) sliced ripe olives, drained
- 1 medium sweet red pepper, chopped
- 1 small onion, chopped
- 5 garlic cloves, minced
- ⅓ cup olive oil
- ¼ cup lemon juice
- 3 Tbsp. cider vinegar
- 1 tsp. dried oregano
- ½ tsp. salt
- ½ tsp. pepper
- 4 medium ripe avocados, peeled
  Tortilla chips

1. Combine corn, olives, red pepper and onion. In another bowl, mix the next 7 ingredients. Pour over corn mixture; toss to coat. Refrigerate, covered, overnight.
2. Just before serving, chop avocados; stir gently into salsa. Serve with tortilla chips.
¼ cup: 82 cal., 7g fat (1g sat. fat), 0 chol., 85mg sod., 5g carb. (1g sugars, 2g fiber), 1g pro. **Diabetic Exchanges:** 1½ fat.

COOL-KITCHEN TIP
Add a little grated lime zest for a tasty twist on this spicy salsa.

FOUR-TOMATO SALSA

The variety of tomatoes, onions and peppers is what makes this chunky salsa so good. Whenever I try to take a batch to a get-together, it's hard to keep my family from finishing it off first!
—Connie Siese, Wayne, MI

TAKES: 30 min.
MAKES: 14 cups

- 7 plum tomatoes, chopped
- 7 medium red tomatoes, chopped
- 3 medium yellow tomatoes, chopped
- 3 medium orange tomatoes, chopped
- 1 tsp. salt
- 2 Tbsp. lime juice
- 2 Tbsp. olive oil
- 1 medium white onion, chopped
- 1 medium red onion, chopped
- 2 green onions, chopped
- ½ cup each chopped green, sweet red, orange and yellow pepper
- 3 pepperoncini, chopped
- ⅓ cup mild pickled pepper rings, chopped
- ½ cup minced fresh parsley
- 2 Tbsp. minced fresh cilantro
- 1 Tbsp. dried chervil
  Tortilla chips

1. In a colander, combine the tomatoes and salt. Let drain for 10 minutes.
2. Transfer to a large bowl. Stir in lime juice, oil, onions, peppers, pepperoncini, pepper rings, parsley, cilantro and chervil. Serve with tortilla chips. Refrigerate leftovers for up to 1 week.
Note: Look for pepperoncini (pickled peppers) in the pickle and olive section of your grocery store.
¼ cup: 15 cal., 1g fat (0 sat. fat), 0 chol., 62mg sod., 2g carb. (1g sugars, 1g fiber), 0 pro. **Diabetic Exchanges:** 1 free food.

PEPPY PEACH SALSA

Garden-fresh salsas are one of my favorite condiments. So when I saw a recipe for fruity peach salsa in the newspaper, I couldn't think of anything that sounded better.
—Jennifer Abbott, Moraga, CA

TAKES: 20 min. • **MAKES:** 1¼ cups

- 2 Tbsp. lime juice
- 1 Tbsp. honey
- ½ tsp. minced garlic
- ⅛ tsp. ground ginger
- 2 fresh peaches, peeled and diced
- ½ green serrano chile pepper, seeded and minced
- ½ red serrano chile pepper, seeded and minced
- ½ small yellow chile pepper, seeded and minced
- 2 tsp. minced fresh cilantro
  Tortilla chips

In a small bowl, combine the lime juice, honey, garlic and ginger; let stand for 5 minutes. Stir in the peaches, peppers and cilantro. Serve with chips. Refrigerate the leftovers.
Note: Wear disposable gloves when cutting hot peppers; the oils can burn skin. Avoid touching your face.
¼ cup: 30 cal., 0 fat (0 sat. fat), 0 chol., 1mg sod., 8g carb. (6g sugars, 1g fiber), 0 pro.

P. 62

SUMMER SALADS

Summertime is when salads are best, with fresh fruits
and vegetables from the store, farmers markets
and your own garden.

ISRAELI PEPPER TOMATO SALAD

This Israeli salad, which is traditionally eaten at breakfast, lends itself to endless variety. You can add other items like olives, beets or potatoes.
—*Sandy Long, Lees Summit, MO*

PREP: 25 min. + chilling
MAKES: 9 servings

- 6 medium tomatoes, seeded and chopped
- 1 each medium green, sweet red and yellow peppers, chopped
- 1 medium cucumber, seeded and chopped
- 1 medium carrot, chopped
- 3 green onions, thinly sliced
- 1 jalapeno pepper, seeded and chopped
- 2 Tbsp. each minced fresh cilantro, parsley, dill and mint
- ¼ cup lemon juice
- 2 Tbsp. olive oil
- 3 garlic cloves, minced
- ½ tsp. salt
- ¼ tsp. pepper

In a large bowl, combine tomatoes, peppers, cucumber, carrot, green onions, jalapeno and herbs. In a small bowl, whisk together the remaining ingredients. Pour over tomato mixture; toss to coat evenly. Cover and refrigerate for at least 1 hour. Serve with a slotted spoon.
Note: Wear disposable gloves when cutting hot peppers; the oils can burn skin. Avoid touching your face.
1 cup: 64 cal., 3g fat (0 sat. fat), 0 chol., 143mg sod., 8g carb. (5g sugars, 3g fiber), 2g pro. **Diabetic Exchanges:** 1 vegetable, ½ fat.

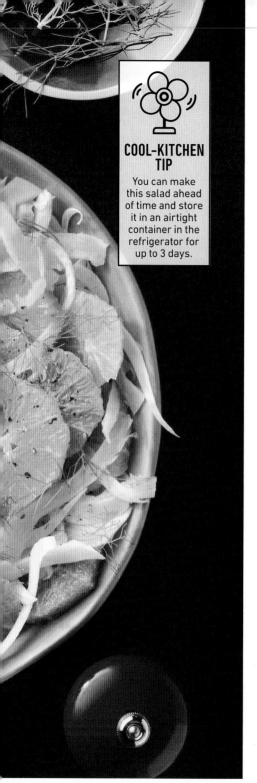

COOL-KITCHEN TIP

You can make this salad ahead of time and store it in an airtight container in the refrigerator for up to 3 days.

FENNEL ORANGE SALAD

You'll need just a few ingredients to fix this fresh-tasting salad. The combination of crisp fennel and juicy oranges is delightful. To reduce last-minute prep, make it the day before you plan to serve it.
—*Nina Hall, Spokane, WA*

TAKES: 30 min. • **MAKES:** 4 servings

- 1   fennel bulb with fronds (about ¾ lb.)
- 4   medium oranges, peeled and sliced
- ⅓   cup orange juice
- 4   tsp. olive oil
- 1   Tbsp. grated orange zest
- ¼   tsp. salt
- ⅛   tsp. pepper
       Pomegranate seeds, optional

1. Finely chop enough fennel fronds to measure ¼ cup; set aside. Cut fennel bulb in half lengthwise; remove and discard the tough outer layer, fennel core and any green stalks. Cut widthwise into thin slices and measure 3 cups; reserve remaining fennel for another use. Place fennel slices in a large bowl. Add orange slices.
2. In a jar with a tight-fitting lid, combine orange juice, oil, orange zest, salt and pepper; shake well. Pour over fennel and oranges; toss gently. Sprinkle with the reserved fronds and, if desired, pomegranate seeds.
1 cup: 143 cal., 5g fat (1g sat. fat), 0 chol., 193mg sod., 25g carb. (0 sugars, 6g fiber), 3g pro. **Diabetic Exchanges:** 1 fruit, 1 vegetable, 1 fat.

SUMMER AVOCADO SALAD

Garden-fresh veggies, creamy avocado and a sprinkling of feta cheese make this chunky salad a healthy summer standout!
—*Deborah Williams, Peoria, AZ*

TAKES: 30 min. • **MAKES:** 2 servings

- ½   cup chopped seeded peeled cucumber
- ⅓   cup chopped sweet yellow pepper
- 6   cherry tomatoes, seeded and quartered
- 2   Tbsp. finely chopped sweet onion
- 1   Tbsp. minced fresh basil or 1 tsp. dried basil
- 1½   tsp. lemon juice
- 1½   tsp. olive oil
       Dash garlic powder
- 1   medium ripe avocado, peeled and chopped
- 2   Tbsp. crumbled feta cheese

In a bowl, combine the first 8 ingredients; cover and refrigerate 15-20 minutes. Add avocado; toss gently. Sprinkle with feta. Serve immediately.
1 cup: 186 cal., 15g fat (3g sat. fat), 4mg chol., 77mg sod., 12g carb. (4g sugars, 6g fiber), 4g pro. **Diabetic Exchanges:** 3 fat, 1 vegetable.

SESAME ALMOND SLAW

Crunchy veggies and noodles are coated in a tangy dressing in this pleasant slaw.
—Taste of Home *Test Kitchen*

TAKES: 20 min. • **MAKES:** 2 servings

1	pkg. (3 oz.) ramen noodles
¾	cup shredded cabbage
¾	cup shredded romaine
2	Tbsp. sliced green onion
2	tsp. slivered almonds, toasted
2	tsp. sesame seeds, toasted
1	Tbsp. rice vinegar
1½	tsp. sugar
1½	tsp. canola oil
1	tsp. water
½	tsp. sesame oil
¼	tsp. reduced-sodium soy sauce
	Dash salt
	Dash pepper

1. Split ramen noodles in half and save the seasoning and half of the noodles for another use. Break apart remaining noodles; place in a bowl. Add cabbage, romaine, green onion, almonds and sesame seeds.

2. For dressing, in a jar with a tight-fitting lid, combine the vinegar, sugar, canola oil, water, sesame oil, soy sauce, salt and pepper; shake well. Add dressing to salad and toss to coat. Serve immediately.

1 cup: 187 cal., 10g fat (3g sat. fat), 0 chol., 193mg sod., 20g carb. (4g sugars, 2g fiber), 4g pro. **Diabetic Exchanges:** 1½ fat, 1 starch, 1 vegetable.

SUMMER SQUASH SALAD

Packing a perfect crunch, this salad is a tasty alternative to coleslaw. Like most gardeners, we usually have an abundance of squash and zucchini in summer, so this dish is an amazing way to use our fresh produce.
—*Diane Hixon, Niceville, FL*

PREP: 15 min. + chilling
MAKES: 12 servings

- 4 cups julienned zucchini
- 4 cups julienned yellow squash
- 2 cups sliced radishes
- 1 cup canola oil
- ⅓ cup cider vinegar
- 2 Tbsp. Dijon mustard
- 2 Tbsp. snipped fresh parsley
- 1½ tsp. salt
- 1 tsp. dill weed
- ½ tsp. pepper

In a large bowl, toss the zucchini, squash and radishes. In a small bowl, whisk the remaining ingredients. Pour over the vegetables. Cover and refrigerate for at least 2 hours. If desired, top with additional snipped fresh parsley.
¾ cup: 188 cal., 19g fat (1g sat. fat), 0 chol., 368mg sod., 4g carb. (3g sugars, 1g fiber), 1g pro.

YUMMY CORN CHIP SALAD

Corn chips give a special crunch and an unexpected flavor to this potluck favorite. Bacon adds a hint of smokiness, while the cranberries bring a touch of sweetness. It's the perfect picnic companion!
—*Nora Friesen, Aberdeen, MS*

TAKES: 25 min. • **MAKES:** 12 servings

- ¾ cup canola oil
- ¼ cup cider vinegar
- ¼ cup mayonnaise
- 2 Tbsp. yellow mustard
- ½ tsp. salt
- ¾ cup sugar
- ½ small onion
- ¾ tsp. poppy seeds

SALAD
- 2 bunches leaf lettuce, chopped (about 20 cups)
- 1 pkg. (9¼ oz.) corn chips
- 8 bacon strips, cooked and crumbled
- 1 cup shredded part-skim mozzarella cheese
- 1 cup dried cranberries

1. For dressing, place first 7 ingredients in a blender. Cover; process until smooth. Stir in poppy seeds.
2. Place salad ingredients in a large bowl; toss with dressing. Serve immediately.
1⅓ cups: 436 cal., 30g fat (4g sat. fat), 12mg chol., 456mg sod., 38g carb. (24g sugars, 2g fiber), 7g pro.

RED, WHITE & BLUE SUMMER SALAD

In this dish, I combine traditional Caprese salad flavors with peaches and blueberries I also add prosciutto for saltiness, creating a balanced, flavor-packed summer side dish.
—*Emily Falke, Santa Barbara, CA*

TAKES: 25 min. • **MAKES:** 12 servings

- ⅔ cup extra virgin olive oil
- ½ cup julienned fresh basil
- ⅓ cup white balsamic vinegar
- ¼ cup julienned fresh mint leaves
- 2 garlic cloves, minced
- 2 tsp. Dijon mustard
- 1 tsp. sea salt
- 1 tsp. sugar
- 1 tsp. pepper
- 2 cups cherry tomatoes
- 8 cups fresh arugula
- 1 carton (8 oz.) fresh mozzarella cheese pearls, drained
- 2 medium peaches, sliced
- 2 cups fresh blueberries
- 6 oz. thinly sliced prosciutto, julienned
  Additional mint leaves

1. Whisk the first 9 ingredients. Add the tomatoes; let stand while preparing salad.
2. In a large bowl, combine the arugula, mozzarella, peach slices, blueberries and prosciutto. Pour tomato mixture over top; toss to coat. Garnish with additional mint leaves. Serve immediately.

1 cup: 233 cal., 18g fat (5g sat. fat), 27mg chol., 486mg sod., 10g carb. (8g sugars, 2g fiber), 8g pro.

VEGAN QUINOA SALAD

Toasting the quinoa before it simmers isn't essential, but it does add a nice nuttiness to the flavor of this dish. You can mix and match whatever fresh herbs and veggies you have on hand.
—Taste of Home *Test Kitchen*

TAKES: 30 min. • **MAKES:** 6 cups

- 1½ cups quinoa, rinsed and well drained
- 3 cups water
- ¼ cup plus 2 Tbsp. olive oil
- 1 Tbsp. grated lemon zest
- ¼ cup lemon juice
- 4 garlic cloves, minced
- 6 Tbsp. minced fresh parsley
- 6 Tbsp. minced fresh mint
- 1½ tsp. salt
- 1 cup cherry tomatoes, halved
- 2 mini cucumbers, sliced
- 1 medium sweet red pepper, chopped
- ½ cup chopped red onion

1. In a large saucepan, cook and stir quinoa over medium-high until toasted, 3-5 minutes. Add the water; bring to a boil. Reduce heat; simmer, covered, until liquid is absorbed, 12-15 minutes. Transfer to a large bowl. Cool slightly.
2. In a small bowl, whisk oil, lemon zest, lemon juice, garlic, parsley, mint and salt. Add vegetables to quinoa; drizzle with dressing and toss to combine. Cover and refrigerate until ready to serve.

¾ cup: 227 cal., 12g fat (2g sat. fat), 0 chol., 449mg sod., 25g carb. (3g sugars, 3g fiber), 5g pro. **Diabetic Exchanges:** 2 fat, 1½ starch.

COOL-KITCHEN TIP
White balsamic vinegar keeps the colors bright in this sweet-salty salad.

RAMEN NOODLE CRANBERRY COLESLAW

Adults and children love this colorful dish featuring cabbage and dried cranberries, and I'm often asked to bring it to potlucks and other big dinners. Refrigerate any leftovers—it'll still taste great for a day or two, if you can keep people out of it that long!
—*Cornelia Cree, Waynesville, NC*

PREP: 25 min. + chilling
MAKES: 24 servings

- 1   cup peanut or canola oil
- ¾   cup sugar
- ¼   cup cider vinegar
- 1   head Chinese or napa cabbage, thinly sliced
- 1   small head red cabbage, shredded
- 1   small red onion, halved and sliced
- ¾   cup dried cranberries
- 1   pkg. (3 oz.) ramen noodles
- 1   cup salted peanuts or sunflower kernels

1. Whisk together oil, sugar and vinegar until smooth. In a large bowl, combine the cabbages, red onion and cranberries. Pour 1 cup dressing over coleslaw; toss to coat. Refrigerate, covered, several hours or overnight. Cover and refrigerate the remaining dressing.

2. Drain coleslaw. Discard the seasoning packet from noodles or save for another use. Break noodles into small pieces; add to coleslaw. Stir in peanuts and remaining dressing; toss to coat.

¾ cup: 154 cal., 11g fat (2g sat. fat), 0 chol., 39mg sod., 14g carb. (10g sugars, 1g fiber), 2g pro.

MARINATED CUCUMBERS

These cucumber slices make a cool side dish dressed in a light, tangy vinegar-and-oil mixture seasoned with herbs. The refreshing salad is perfect alongside sandwiches and a variety of grilled meats.
—*Mary Helen Hinson, Lamberton, NC*

PREP: 10 min. + marinating
MAKES: 12 servings

- 6   medium cucumbers, thinly sliced
- 1   medium onion, sliced
- 1   cup white vinegar
- ¼   to ⅓ cup sugar
- ¼   cup olive oil
- 1   tsp. salt
- 1   tsp. dried oregano
- ½   tsp. garlic powder
- ½   tsp. dried marjoram
- ½   tsp. lemon-pepper seasoning
- ½   tsp. ground mustard

In a large bowl, combine the cucumbers and onion. In a jar with a tight-fitting lid, combine remaining ingredients; cover and shake well. Pour over cucumber mixture; toss to coat. Cover and refrigerate for at least 4 hours. Serve with a slotted spoon.

¾ cup: 48 cal., 2g fat (0 sat. fat), 0 chol., 106mg sod., 6g carb. (4g sugars, 2g fiber), 2g pro.

PEACH CAPRESE SALAD

During summer, I like to showcase the fresh ingredients I receive weekly from my local food share, and that's how this salad was created. I use large balls of mozzarella torn into pieces, but you could use smaller mozzarella pearls.
—*MOUNIR ECHARITI, MENDHAM, NJ*

TAKES: 15 min. • **MAKES:** 2 servings

- 4 oz. fresh buffalo mozzarella cheese
- 2 cups torn leaf lettuce
- 1 medium peach, cut into wedges
- 1 large heirloom tomato, cut into wedges
- ½ cup loosely packed basil leaves
- 2 Tbsp. extra virgin olive oil
- 1 Tbsp. balsamic vinegar
- ¼ tsp. flaky sea salt
- ⅛ tsp. coarsely ground pepper

Tear the mozzarella into large pieces. On 2 large plates, arrange the lettuce, peach wedges, tomato wedges, mozzarella and basil. Drizzle with oil and vinegar; sprinkle with salt and pepper.

1 salad: 343 cal., 26g fat (10g sat. fat), 45mg chol., 336mg sod., 15g carb. (12g sugars, 3g fiber), 12g pro.

COOL-KITCHEN TIP
When buying peaches, look for ones that are plump and free from bruises. Ripe peaches will give slightly when pressed. Avoid those that are rock hard.

JUICY WATERMELON SALAD

This fruit salad has such a surprising yet fabulous mix of flavors that friends often ask for the recipe. Combine seedless watermelon varieties in yellow, red and pink for a colorful twist.
—*Heidi Haight, Macomb, MI*

PREP: 20 min. + chilling
MAKES: 10 servings

- 8 cups cubed seedless watermelon (about 1 medium)
- 1 small red onion, cut into rings
- 1 cup coarsely chopped macadamia nuts or sliced almonds, toasted
- 1 cup fresh arugula or baby spinach
- ⅓ cup balsamic vinaigrette
- 3 Tbsp. canola oil
  Watermelon slices, optional
- 1 cup (4 oz.) crumbled blue cheese

In a large bowl, combine watermelon and onion; cover and refrigerate until cold, about 30 minutes. Just before serving, add macadamia nuts and arugula to the watermelon mixture. In a small bowl, whisk vinaigrette and oil; drizzle over salad and toss to coat. Serve over sliced watermelon, if desired. Sprinkle with cheese.

Note: To toast nuts, bake in a shallow pan in a 350° oven for 5-10 minutes or cook in a skillet over low heat until lightly browned, stirring occasionally.

1 cup: 232 cal., 20g fat (5g sat. fat), 10mg chol., 295mg sod., 15g carb. (12g sugars, 2g fiber), 4g pro.

BERRY NECTARINE SALAD

In my circle, no summer celebration is complete without this most-requested vibrant fruit medley. The creamy topping is the perfect accent, so don't skimp!
—*Mindee Myers, Lincoln, NE*

PREP: 15 min. + chilling
MAKES: 8 servings

- 4 medium nectarines, sliced
- ¼ cup sugar
- 1 tsp. lemon juice
- ½ tsp. ground ginger
- 3 oz. reduced-fat cream cheese
- 2 cups fresh raspberries
- 1 cup fresh blueberries

1. In a large bowl, toss nectarines with sugar, lemon juice and ginger. Refrigerate, covered, 1 hour, stirring once.
2. Drain the nectarines, reserving juices. Gradually beat reserved juices into cream cheese. Gently combine nectarines and berries; serve with cream cheese mixture.
1 serving: 109 cal., 3g fat (2g sat. fat), 8mg chol., 46mg sod., 21g carb. (15g sugars, 4g fiber), 2g pro. **Diabetic Exchanges:** 1 fruit, ½ starch, ½ fat.

QUICK CORN SALAD

This sensational salad is a delight to serve because you can make it ahead, and it's an easy way to put garden bounty to good use. With colorful ingredients like corn, tomato and green pepper, it's also pretty in the bowl and on your plate.
—*Rita Reifenstein, Evans City, PA*

TAKES: 10 min. • **MAKES:** 4 servings

- 2 cups fresh or frozen sweet corn
- ¾ cup chopped tomato
- ½ cup chopped green pepper
- ½ cup chopped celery
- ¼ cup chopped onion
- ¼ cup ranch salad dressing

In a large bowl, combine the vegetables; stir in the dressing. Cover and refrigerate until serving.

¾ cup: 138 cal., 7g fat (1g sat. fat), 2mg chol., 169mg sod., 18g carb. (7g sugars, 3g fiber), 3g pro. **Diabetic Exchanges:** 1½ fat, 1 starch.

COOL-KITCHEN TIP
Jazz up this salad by tossing in toasted nuts, adding extra veggies, sprinkling with feta cheese or blending in fresh minced parsley, cilantro or basil.

CRUNCHY ASIAN COLESLAW

This flavor-packed twist on traditional creamy coleslaw is a perfect complement to Asian-themed meals. The light, tangy vinaigrette enhances the fresh veggies.
—*Erin Chilcoat, Central Islip, NY*

PREP: 15 min. + chilling
MAKES: 2 servings

- 1 cup shredded Chinese or napa cabbage
- ½ cup sliced water chestnuts, chopped
- ½ small zucchini, julienned
- 2 Tbsp. chopped green pepper
- 4½ tsp. rice vinegar
- 1 tsp. sugar
- 1 tsp. sesame seeds, toasted
- 1 tsp. reduced-sodium soy sauce
- ½ tsp. sesame oil
  Dash crushed red pepper flakes

In a small bowl, combine the cabbage, water chestnuts, zucchini and green pepper. In another small bowl, whisk the remaining ingredients. Drizzle over salad; toss to coat. Refrigerate for at least 1 hour.
1 cup: 65 cal., 2g fat (0 sat. fat), 0 chol., 120mg sod., 11g carb. (5g sugars, 2g fiber), 2g pro. **Diabetic Exchanges:** 2 vegetable.

GREEN BEAN, CORN & BUTTERMILK SALAD

I love the crunch of green beans and fresh corn, so I combined them with a buttermilk Caesar dressing. This salad is good served immediately, but it's even better after chilling for a few hours.
—*Arlene Erlbach, Morton Grove, IL*

PREP: 25 min. • **COOK:** 15 min. + chilling
MAKES: 6 servings

- ½ cup reduced-fat mayonnaise
- ½ cup buttermilk
- ½ cup shredded Parmesan cheese, plus more for topping
- 1 Tbsp. lemon juice
- 1 tsp. Worcestershire sauce
- ½ tsp. garlic powder
- ½ tsp. salt
- ½ tsp. pepper
- ¾ lb. fresh green beans, trimmed and cut into 1-in. pieces
- 4 medium ears sweet corn
- 1 Tbsp. olive oil

1. In a small bowl, whisk mayonnaise, buttermilk, ½ cup Parmesan, lemon juice, Worcestershire sauce, garlic powder, salt and pepper. Refrigerate, covered, until serving.
2. Meanwhile, in a Dutch oven, bring 8 cups water to a boil. Add beans; cook, uncovered, just until crisp-tender, 2-3 minutes. Drain and immediately drop into ice water. Drain and pat dry; transfer to a serving bowl.
3. Cut corn from cobs. In a large heavy skillet, heat 1 Tbsp. oil over medium-high heat. Add corn; cook and stir until tender, 6-8 minutes. Remove from heat and add to beans; refrigerate, covered, until chilled.
4. Stir the mayonnaise mixture into the vegetables; toss to coat. Sprinkle with additional Parmesan.
1 cup: 201 cal., 12g fat (3g sat. fat), 13mg chol., 498mg sod., 20g carb. (8g sugars, 3g fiber), 7g pro.

COUSCOUS TABBOULEH WITH FRESH MINT & FETA

Using couscous instead of bulgur really speeds up the process of making this colorful salad. You can easily double the recipe if feeding more people.
—Elodie Rosinovsky, Brighton, MA

TAKES: 20 min. • **MAKES:** 3 servings

- ¾ cup water
- ½ cup uncooked couscous
- 1 can (15 oz.) garbanzo beans or chickpeas, rinsed and drained
- 1 large tomato, chopped
- ½ English cucumber, halved and thinly sliced
- 3 Tbsp. lemon juice
- 2 tsp. grated lemon zest
- 2 tsp. olive oil
- 2 tsp. minced fresh mint
- 2 tsp. minced fresh parsley
- ¼ tsp. salt
- ⅛ tsp. pepper
- ¾ cup crumbled feta cheese
  Lemon wedges, optional

1. In a small saucepan, bring water to a boil. Stir in couscous. Remove from heat; cover and let stand for 5-8 minutes or until water is absorbed. Fluff with a fork.
2. In a large bowl, combine the beans, tomato and cucumber. In a small bowl, whisk lemon juice, lemon zest, oil, herbs and seasonings. Drizzle over bean mixture. Add couscous; toss to combine. Serve immediately or refrigerate until chilled. Sprinkle with cheese. If desired, serve with lemon wedges.
Note: Make this refreshing main dish salad gluten-free by replacing the couscous with about 1½ cups cooked quinoa.
1⅔ cups: 362 cal., 11g fat (3g sat. fat), 15mg chol., 657mg sod., 52g carb. (7g sugars, 9g fiber), 15g pro.

CAPRESE SALAD

My husband and I love Caprese salad, but not the high prices we pay for it in restaurants. Here, we created our own version which tastes incredibly close, if not better, than any restaurant version we've tried.
—Melissa Pearson, Sandy, UT

TAKES: 15 min. • **MAKES:** 4 servings

- 4 medium tomatoes, sliced
- ½ lb. fresh mozzarella cheese, sliced
- ¼ cup fresh basil leaves
  BALSAMIC VINAIGRETTE
- 2 Tbsp. olive oil
- 2 Tbsp. balsamic vinegar
- 1 tsp. ground mustard
- ⅛ tsp. salt
- ⅛ tsp. pepper

Arrange the tomatoes, cheese and basil on a serving platter. Whisk the vinaigrette ingredients; drizzle over salad. If desired, sprinkle with additional salt and pepper.
1 serving: 256 cal., 19g fat (9g sat. fat), 45mg chol., 161mg sod., 8g carb. (6g sugars, 2g fiber), 11g pro.

GREEK ORZO SALAD

Tart and refreshing, this side salad is a big hit at my home. With all the tasty toppings—including red onion, tomatoes, olives, feta cheese and a zesty dressing—you'd never know it has under 8 grams of fat.

—Judy Roberts, Las Vegas, NV

PREP: 15 min. + chilling
MAKES: 8 servings

- 1 cup uncooked orzo pasta
- 6 tsp. olive oil, divided
- 1 medium red onion, finely chopped
- ½ cup minced fresh parsley
- ⅓ cup red wine vinegar
- 1½ tsp. dried oregano
- 1 tsp. salt
- ½ tsp. sugar
- ⅛ tsp. pepper
- 2 large tomatoes, seeded and chopped
- 1 medium cucumber, peeled, seeded and chopped
- 12 pitted ripe or Greek olives, halved
- ½ cup crumbled feta cheese

1. Cook the orzo according to package directions; drain. In a large serving bowl, toss orzo with 2 tsp. oil.
2. In another bowl, combine onion, parsley, vinegar, oregano, salt, sugar, pepper and remaining 4 tsp. oil; pour over orzo and toss to coat. Cover and refrigerate until chilled. Just before serving, gently stir in tomatoes, cucumber, olives and cheese.
¾ cup: 167 cal., 6g fat (1g sat. fat), 4mg chol., 427mg sod., 24g carb. (3g sugars, 2g fiber), 6g pro. **Diabetic Exchanges:** 1½ starch, 1 fat.

MANGO SALAD WITH MINT YOGURT DRESSING

An abundant planter full of mint inspired me to create this summery salad. The flavors pair together so well and really let the freshness of the mint shine.
—*Natalie Klein, Albuquerque, NM*

PREP: 25 min. + chilling
MAKES: 8 servings

- 3 medium mangoes, peeled and cut into ¼-in. slices
- 3 medium Gala apples, cut into ¼-in. slices
- 2 Tbsp. lime juice, divided
- ½ cup plain yogurt
- 2 Tbsp. honey
- 1 tsp. minced fresh gingerroot
- ¼ tsp. salt
- ¼ cup fresh mint leaves, thinly sliced

1. In a large bowl, combine the mangoes and apples. Drizzle with 1 Tbsp. lime juice; toss to coat.

2. In a small bowl, combine yogurt, honey, ginger, salt and remaining 1 Tbsp. lime juice. Stir into mango mixture. Sprinkle with mint and toss to coat. Refrigerate for at least 15 minutes before serving.

1 cup: 105 cal., 1g fat (0 sat. fat), 2mg chol., 84mg sod., 26g carb. (22g sugars, 3g fiber), 1g pro. **Diabetic Exchanges:** 2 fruit.

COOL BEANS SALAD

This protein-filled dish could be served as a colorful side dish or a meatless main entree. The basmati rice adds texture and flavor, and the dressing gives every bite a bit of a tang.
—*Janelle Lee, Appleton, WI*

TAKES: 20 min. • **MAKES:** 6 servings

- ½ cup olive oil
- ¼ cup red wine vinegar
- 1 Tbsp. sugar
- 1 garlic clove, minced
- 1 tsp. salt
- 1 tsp. ground cumin
- 1 tsp. chili powder
- ¼ tsp. pepper
- 3 cups cooked basmati rice
- 1 can (16 oz.) kidney beans, rinsed and drained
- 1 can (15 oz.) black beans, rinsed and drained
- 1½ cups frozen corn, thawed
- 4 green onions, sliced
- 1 small sweet red pepper, chopped
- ¼ cup minced fresh cilantro

In a large bowl, whisk first 8 ingredients. Add the remaining ingredients; toss to coat. Chill until serving.

1⅓ cups: 440 cal., 19g fat (3g sat. fat), 0 chol., 659mg sod., 58g carb. (5g sugars, 8g fiber), 12g pro.

COOL-KITCHEN TIP

Making this salad for a party? Simply double the recipe and serve portions in 2-oz. plastic cups for easy serving and cleanup.

CUCUMBER CRUNCH COLESLAW

This recipe came about as a way to use a julienne peeler that I received as a gift. Leftover sparkling wine was my other inspiration, and I combined it with cucumbers to make a refreshing slaw. It's a nice way to round out a picnic.
—*Merry Graham, Newhall, CA*

TAKES: 30 min. • **MAKES:** 8 servings

- ⅓ cup olive oil
- ¼ cup sparkling or dry white wine
- 1 Tbsp. minced fresh basil
- 1 Tbsp. Key lime juice
- 1 serrano pepper, seeded and minced
- 1½ tsp. minced fresh mint
- 1½ tsp. molasses
- 1 tsp. sugar
- 1 garlic clove, minced
- ¾ tsp. salt
- ¾ tsp. grated lime zest
- ½ tsp. pepper

COLESLAW
- 3 English cucumbers, julienned
- 2 cups fresh arugula or baby spinach, coarsely chopped
- 1 cup fresh snow peas, cut into ½-in. pieces
- ½ cup sliced almonds, toasted
- 1 cup dried cranberries

1. In a small bowl, combine the first 12 ingredients. In a large bowl, combine the cucumbers, arugula, peas, almonds and cranberries.

2. Just before serving, pour dressing over salad; toss to coat.

Note: Wear disposable gloves when cutting hot peppers; the oils can burn skin. Avoid touching your face.

¾ cup: 178 cal., 12g fat (2g sat. fat), 0 chol., 227mg sod., 16g carb. (11g sugars, 2g fiber), 2g pro. **Diabetic Exchanges:** 2 fat, 1 vegetable, ½ starch.

SANTA FE SALAD

My family loves this colorful salad. People always ask for the recipe when I bring it to potlucks. The zippy dressing and mix of crunchy veggies with beans is a winning combination.
—*Gail Park, Newport News, VA*

TAKES: 30 min. • **MAKES:** 10 servings

- 2½ cups cut fresh green beans
- 1 cup minced fresh cilantro
- ¼ cup fat-free sour cream
- 2 Tbsp. lime juice
- 2 Tbsp. balsamic vinegar
- 2 garlic cloves, minced
- 1½ tsp. ground cumin
- ¼ tsp. salt
  Dash cayenne pepper
- 2 cups frozen corn, thawed
- 1 can (15 oz.) pinto beans, rinsed and drained
- 1 can (15 oz.) black beans, rinsed and drained
- 1 small sweet red pepper, finely chopped
- 1 small red onion, chopped
- 1 can (4 oz.) chopped green chiles
- 1 can (2¼ oz.) sliced ripe olives, drained
- ½ cup shredded reduced-fat cheddar cheese

1. Place green beans in a small saucepan and cover with water. Bring to a boil; cover and cook for 3-5 minutes or until crisp-tender. Drain and immediately place beans in ice water. Drain and pat dry.
2. For dressing, in a small bowl, combine cilantro, sour cream, lime juice, vinegar, garlic, cumin, salt and cayenne.
3. In a large bowl, combine green beans, corn, pinto beans, black beans, red pepper, onion, chiles and olives. Sprinkle with cheese. Pour the dressing over salad; toss gently to coat. Cover and refrigerate until serving.

¾ cup: 151 cal., 2g fat (1g sat. fat), 5mg chol., 374mg sod., 26g carb. (4g sugars, 6g fiber), 8g pro. **Diabetic Exchanges:** 1½ starch, ½ fat.

COOL-KITCHEN TIP

You can add other types of beans to this salad, such as cannellini, kidney or wax beans. For extra nutrition, toss in other fresh veggies like celery, cucumber and green pepper. Or to make this salad even more hearty, stir in cubed cooked chicken.

TABBOULEH

Tabbouleh is a classic Middle Eastern salad. The fresh veggies and mint leaves make it light and refreshing on a hot day.
—*Michael & Mathil Chebat, Lake Ridge, VA*

TAKES: 30 min. • **MAKES:** 8 servings

- ¼ cup bulgur
- 3 bunches fresh parsley, minced (about 2 cups)
- 3 large tomatoes, finely chopped
- 1 small onion, finely chopped
- ¼ cup lemon juice
- ¼ cup olive oil
- 5 fresh mint leaves, minced
- ½ tsp. salt
- ½ tsp. pepper
- ¼ tsp. cayenne pepper

Prepare bulgur according to package directions; cool. Transfer to a large bowl. Stir in remaining ingredients. If desired, chill before serving.

⅔ cup: 100 cal., 7g fat (1g sat. fat), 0 chol., 164mg sod., 9g carb. (3g sugars, 2g fiber), 2g pro. **Diabetic Exchanges:** 1½ fat, ½ starch.

 COOL-KITCHEN TIP
To store fresh parsley, add about an inch of water to a sturdy tumbler. Place parsley in the water; tie a produce bag around the top. Refrigerate. hange the water each time you use the parsley.

FOUR-BERRY SPINACH SALAD

Enjoy some of nature's candy in this berry-filled salad. The slightly tart dressing contrasts deliciously with the sweet, in-season fruit.
—*Betty Lise Anderson, Gahanna, OH*

TAKES: 15 min. • **MAKES:** 4 servings

- 1 Tbsp. canola oil
- 1 Tbsp. orange juice
- 1 Tbsp. red wine vinegar
- 1 Tbsp. balsamic vinegar
- 1 Tbsp. water
- 2 tsp. lemon juice
- ½ tsp. sugar
- ½ tsp. poppy seeds
- ⅛ tsp. ground allspice
  Dash ground cinnamon
- 4 cups fresh baby spinach
- ½ cup each fresh raspberries, blueberries, blackberries and sliced strawberries
- 2 tsp. chopped walnuts, toasted

In a small bowl, whisk first 10 ingredients until blended. In a medium bowl, combine spinach and berries. Drizzle with dressing and sprinkle with walnuts; toss to coat.

1¼ cups: 89 cal., 5g fat (0 sat. fat), 0 chol., 25mg sod., 12g carb. (6g sugars, 4g fiber), 2g pro. **Diabetic Exchanges:** 1 vegetable, 1 fat, ½ fruit.

TANGERINE TOSSED SALAD

My mother taught me how to cook when I was a young girl. The sweet tangerines and crunchy caramelized almonds make this one of my favorite recipes.
—Helen Musenbrock, O'Fallon, MO

PREP: 40 min. • **MAKES:** 6 servings

- ½ cup sliced almonds
- 3 Tbsp. sugar, divided
- 2 medium tangerines or 1 navel orange
- 6 cups torn lettuce
- 3 green onions, chopped
- 2 Tbsp. cider vinegar
- 2 Tbsp. olive oil
- ¼ tsp. salt
- ¼ tsp. pepper

1. In a small skillet, cook and stir almonds and 2 Tbsp. sugar over medium-low heat for 25-30 minutes or until the sugar is melted and the almonds are toasted. Remove from the heat. Peel and section the tangerines, reserving 1 Tbsp. juice.
2. In a large bowl, combine the lettuce, green onions, tangerines and almonds. In a small bowl, whisk the vinegar, oil, salt, pepper, reserved juice and remaining 1 Tbsp. sugar. Pour over salad; toss to coat.
1 cup: 138 cal., 9g fat (1g sat. fat), 0 chol., 105mg sod., 14g carb. (11g sugars, 3g fiber), 3g pro. **Diabetic Exchanges:** 2 fat, 1 vegetable, ½ starch.

READER RAVE

"An excellent salad! The dressing was wonderful, and something I'll make to put on other salads too."

—JULIE, TASTEOFHOME.COM

STRAWBERRY-PINEAPPLE COLESLAW

Sweet fruit, tangy coleslaw dressing and colorful, crisp cabbage make a wonderful combination to share with others. I like to include the nuts because they add a healthy crunch.
—*Victoria Pederson, Ham Lake, MN*

PREP: 15 min. + chilling
MAKES: about 14 servings

- 2 pkg. (14 oz. each) coleslaw mix
- 1 jar (13 oz.) coleslaw salad dressing
- 1 cup salted cashews or macadamia nuts
- 1 cup dried cranberries
- 1 cup chopped fresh or canned pineapple
- 1 cup chopped fresh sugar snap peas
- 1 cup chopped fresh strawberries
- ½ cup sweetened shredded coconut
- ½ cup chopped green onions

Combine all ingredients in a large bowl; toss to coat. Cover and refrigerate until serving. Stir before serving.

¾ cup: 244 cal., 15g fat (3g sat. fat), 3mg chol., 272mg sod., 26g carb. (19g sugars, 3g fiber), 3g pro.

RICE NOODLE SALAD

This salad is easy, sweet, spicy, nutty and light. Many friends request this for get-togethers, and our family enjoys it at least once a month for dinner. To make it a main dish, I add marinated and grilled teriyaki chicken.
—*Krista Frank, Rhododendron, OR*

TAKES: 25 min. • **MAKES:** 10 servings

- 1 pkg. (8.8 oz.) thin rice noodles
- 2 cups fresh spinach, cut into strips
- 1 large carrot, shredded
- ½ cup pineapple tidbits
- ¼ cup minced fresh cilantro
- 1 green onion, chopped

SESAME PEANUT DRESSING

- ¼ cup unsalted peanuts
- ¼ cup water
- ¼ cup lime juice
- 2 Tbsp. soy sauce
- 1 Tbsp. brown sugar
- 1 Tbsp. canola oil
- 1 tsp. sesame oil
- ½ tsp. ground ginger
- ¼ tsp. crushed red pepper flakes
  Optional: Salted peanuts and additional lime juice

1. Cook noodles according to package directions. Meanwhile, in a large salad bowl, combine spinach, carrot, pineapple, cilantro and green onion.
2. In a blender, combine the 9 dressing ingredients; cover and process until blended. Drain noodles and rinse in cold water; drain well. Add to spinach mixture. Drizzle with dressing and toss to coat. If desired, sprinkle with salted peanuts and additional lime juice.

¾ cup: 149 cal., 4g fat (1g sat. fat), 0 chol., 238mg sod., 26g carb. (4g sugars, 1g fiber), 2g pro. **Diabetic Exchanges:** 1½ starch, 1 fat.

COOL-KITCHEN TIP

Green onions should be stored in your refrigerator's crisper bin. They usually only last about a week before they start getting slimy.

ACINI DI PEPE SALAD

Looking for a quick lunch idea or fun new side dish? Try this blend of veggies, tiny pasta and juicy pineapple bits for a change-of-pace salad jam-packed with flavor.
—*June Herke, Watertown, SD*

PREP: 20 min. + chilling
MAKES: 2 servings

- ¼ cup uncooked acini di pepe pasta
- ¼ cup mayonnaise
- ¼ cup whipped topping
- 1 Tbsp. finely chopped onion
  Dash celery seed
- ¾ cup chopped fresh cauliflower
- 1 snack-size cup (4 oz.) pineapple tidbits, drained
- ⅓ cup frozen peas, partially thawed
- 1 Tbsp. raisins
  Optional: Lettuce leaves and minced fresh parsley

Cook the pasta according to package directions; drain and rinse in cold water. In a small bowl, combine mayonnaise, whipped topping, onion and celery seed. Add the cauliflower, pineapple, peas, raisins and pasta; toss to coat. Cover and refrigerate for 1 hour. If desired, serve on a lettuce-lined plate and sprinkle with minced parsley.

¾ cup: 295 cal., 11g fat (3g sat. fat), 11mg chol., 284mg sod., 42g carb. (14g sugars, 4g fiber), 7g pro.

COOL-KITCHEN TIP
Orzo and ditalini are two other pasta shapes you could use for this recipe if you don't have acini di pepe on hand.

RAVISHING RADISH SALAD

Showcase radishes in all their glory with a fresh, crunchy salad. Herbs and fennel take it up another notch.
—*Maggie Ruddy, Altoona, IA*

PREP: 30 min. + chilling
MAKES: 6 servings

- 24 radishes, quartered
- 1 tsp. salt
- 1 tsp. pepper
- 6 green onions, chopped
- ½ cup thinly sliced fennel bulb
- 6 fresh basil leaves, thinly sliced
- ¼ cup snipped fresh dill
- ¼ cup olive oil
- 2 Tbsp. champagne vinegar
- 2 Tbsp. honey
- 2 garlic cloves, minced
- ½ cup chopped walnuts, toasted

1. Place radishes in a large bowl. Sprinkle with salt and pepper; toss to coat. Add the green onions, fennel, basil and dill. In a small bowl, whisk the oil, vinegar, honey and garlic. Pour over salad; toss to coat.
2. Cover and refrigerate for at least 1 hour. Sprinkle with walnuts just before serving.
⅔ cup: 177 cal., 15g fat (2g sat. fat), 0 chol., 408mg sod., 10g carb. (7g sugars, 2g fiber), 2g pro. **Diabetic Exchanges:** 3 fat, 1 vegetable.

HONEY-MUSTARD BRUSSELS SPROUTS SALAD

Even if you dislike Brussels sprouts, you will love this dish. The dressing is truly tasty, and it pairs so nicely with the apples, grapes and walnuts. You can add whatever cheese, nuts or fruit you prefer.
—*Sheila Sturrock, Coldwater, ON*

TAKES: 25 min. • **MAKES:** 10 servings

- 1 lb. fresh Brussels sprouts, trimmed and shredded
- 2 medium tart apples, chopped
- 1 medium red onion, chopped
- 1 small sweet orange pepper, chopped
- ½ cup chopped walnuts
- ½ cup green grapes, sliced
- ½ cup shredded cheddar cheese
- 3 bacon strips, cooked and crumbled
- ¼ cup olive oil
- 2 Tbsp. red wine vinegar
- 2 Tbsp. honey mustard
- 1 garlic clove, minced
- ¼ tsp. salt
- ¼ tsp. pepper

In a large bowl, combine the first 8 ingredients. In a small bowl, whisk remaining ingredients; pour over salad. Toss to coat.
1 cup: 170 cal., 12g fat (3g sat. fat), 8mg chol., 177mg sod., 13g carb. (7g sugars, 3g fiber), 5g pro. **Diabetic exchanges:** 2 fat, 1 starch.

HONEY POPPY SEED FRUIT SALAD

The subtle honey sauce in this salad steals the show. The colorful dish pairs well with any morning entree and takes just 10 minutes to assemble.
—*Dorothy Dinnean, Harrison, AR*

TAKES: 10 min. • **MAKES:** 8 servings

- 2 medium firm bananas, chopped
- 2 cups fresh blueberries
- 2 cups fresh raspberries
- 2 cups sliced fresh strawberries
- 5 Tbsp. honey
- 1 tsp. lemon juice
- ¾ tsp. poppy seeds

In a large bowl, combine the bananas and berries. In a small bowl, combine honey, lemon juice and poppy seeds. Pour over fruit and toss to coat. Serve immediately.
¾ cup: 117 cal., 1g fat (0 sat. fat), 0 chol., 2mg sod., 30g carb. (23g sugars, 5g fiber), 1g pro.

COOL-KITCHEN TIP
Fruit will naturally oxidize and release more juice over time, which can make fruit salad soggy. But the good news is that the lemon juice in this recipe will help slow that process down. If you're making this fruit salad ahead of time, wait to add the bananas until right before you serve it.

THAI SALAD WITH PEANUT DRESSING

This salad is very fresh and flavorful. The peanut garnish adds a satisfying crunch.
—*James Schend, Pleasant Prairie, WI*

TAKES: 25 min. • **MAKES:** 8 servings

- 2 cups spring mix salad greens
- ½ cup fresh cilantro leaves
- 1 small napa cabbage, shredded
- 1 small cucumber, sliced
- 1 small red onion, julienned
- 2 small carrots, shredded
- 2 green onions, sliced

PEANUT DRESSING
- ¼ cup creamy peanut butter
- 3 Tbsp. hot water
- 1 Tbsp. lime juice
- 1 Tbsp. sesame oil
- 1 Tbsp. fish sauce
- 1 Tbsp. rice vinegar
- ½ tsp. crushed red pepper flakes
- 1 small garlic clove, minced
- ¼ cup dry roasted peanuts
  Jalapeno pepper slices, optional

1. In a large bowl, toss salad greens and next 6 ingredients.
2. For the dressing, in a small bowl, whisk the next 8 ingredients. Add to the salad mixture and toss to coat. Divide mixture between 4 plates; top with peanuts and, if desired, jalapenos.
1 cup: 111 cal., 8g fat (1g sat. fat), 0 chol., 286mg sod., 7g carb. (3g sugars, 2g fiber), 4g pro. **Diabetic Exchanges:** 1½ fat, 1 vegetable.

YOU SAY POTATO ...

Potato salads are not all the same! Try some new flavors and methods to see just how deliciously different one vegetable can be.

SPICY CAJUN POTATO SALAD

Here in the South, we have a lot of get-togethers. If you want your dish to be chosen over all of the rest, it has to have a kick! This does the trick.
—*Amanda West, Shelbyville, TN*

PREP: 20 min. • **COOK:** 10 min. + chilling
MAKES: 20 servings

- 5 lbs. medium Yukon Gold potatoes, peeled and cut into ¾-in. cubes
- 1 large yellow onion
- ½ medium lemon
- ½ tsp. salt
- 8 hard-boiled large eggs, chopped
- 1½ cups mayonnaise with olive oil and coarsely ground pepper
- 1 cup dill pickle relish
- ¼ cup yellow mustard
- 1 to 2 Tbsp. Cajun seasoning
- ¼ cup minced fresh parsley
  Paprika

1. Place potatoes in a Dutch oven; add water to cover. Cut onion in half crosswise; add 1 half to saucepan. Bring to a boil. Add lemon and salt to cooking water. Reduce heat; cook, uncovered, until the potatoes tender, 5-6 minutes.

2. Meanwhile, chop remaining half onion. Combine with eggs, mayonnaise, pickle relish, mustard and Cajun seasoning.

3. Drain potatoes; rinse under cold water. Discard onion and lemon. Add potatoes to egg mixture; gently toss until well mixed (do not overmix, or potatoes will break down). Refrigerate, covered, 1-2 hours. Just before serving, sprinkle with parsley and paprika.

¾ cup: 229 cal., 10g fat (2g sat. fat), 81mg chol., 400mg sod., 31g carb. (3g sugars, 2g fiber), 5g pro.

COOL-KITCHEN TIP

Adding lemon to the water when boiling potatoes will help keep the taters on the firm side, which is a great tactic for potato salads!

MOM'S SWEET POTATO SALAD

My mother used to make this potato salad. We all liked it back then— and now my family likes it, too!
—*Willard Wilson, Woodsfield, OH*

PREP: 10 min. + chilling
MAKES: 12 servings

- 3 lbs. sweet potatoes, cooked, peeled and cubed
- ½ cup chopped onion
- 1 cup chopped sweet red pepper
- 1¼ cups mayonnaise
- 1½ tsp. salt
- ½ tsp. pepper
- ¼ tsp. hot pepper sauce
  Sliced green onions, optional

In a large bowl, combine sweet potatoes, onion and red pepper. In a small bowl, combine remaining ingredients; add to potato mixture and toss to coat. Cover and refrigerate until serving. If desired, garnish with green onions.

¾ cup: 292 cal., 19g fat (3g sat. fat), 8mg chol., 436mg sod., 29g carb. (7g sugars, 4g fiber), 2g pro.

PRESSURE-COOKER POTATO SALAD

It's not a summer party without a tasty potato salad, but I rarely make it because it can be time consuming. However, now that I know I can quickly cook the potatoes in the pressure cooker, I'll be making this much more! We prefer this salad with unpeeled red potatoes, but you can use another potato—with or without the skin.
—*Courtney Stultz, Weir, KS*

PREP: 15 min. + chilling
COOK: 5 min. + cooling
MAKES: 10 servings

- 2½ lbs. red potatoes, cubed (about 8 cups)
- 1 cup mayonnaise
- ⅓ cup sour cream
- ¼ cup finely chopped onion
- ¼ cup finely chopped celery
- 2 Tbsp. prepared mustard
- 1 Tbsp. dill weed
- 1 Tbsp. cider vinegar
- 1 tsp. garlic salt
- ½ tsp. salt
- ½ tsp. pepper

1. Place the potatoes and 1½ cups water in a 6-qt. electric pressure cooker. Lock the lid; close pressure-release valve. Adjust to pressure-cook on high for 3 minutes. Quick-release pressure. Drain; cool completely.
2. In a large bowl, combine remaining ingredients. Add the potatoes; toss to coat. Refrigerate, covered, at least 1 hour.
¾ cup: 247 cal., 18g fat (3g sat. fat), 3mg chol., 471mg sod., 19g carb. (2g sugars, 2g fiber), 3g pro.

COOL-KITCHEN TIP

To bring a little bold, salty flavor to this salad, stir in some finely chopped capers to the dressing. Or use whole capers as a garnish.

FRENCH POTATO SALAD

French potato salad is vinegar-based instead of creamy, made with Dijon mustard, olive oil, scallions or shallots, and fresh herbs.
—*Denise Cassady, Phoenix, MD*

TAKES: 25 min.
MAKES: 6 cups

- 1 lb. baby red potatoes
- 1 lb. baby yellow potatoes
- 1 garlic clove
- ¼ cup olive oil
- 2 Tbsp. champagne vinegar or white wine vinegar
- 2 tsp. Dijon mustard
- ½ tsp. salt
- ½ tsp. pepper
- 1 shallot, finely chopped
- 1 Tbsp. each minced fresh chervil, parsley and chives
- 1 tsp. minced fresh tarragon

1. Place potatoes in a large saucepan; add water to cover. Bring to a boil. Reduce the heat; cook, uncovered, 10-15 minutes or until tender. With a slotted spoon, remove potatoes to a colander; cool slightly. Return water to a boil. Add the garlic; cook, uncovered, 1 minute. Remove garlic and immediately drop into ice water. Drain and pat dry; mince. Reserve ¼ cup cooking liquid.
2. Cut cooled potatoes into ¼-in. slices. Transfer potatoes to a large bowl. In a small bowl, whisk reserved cooking liquid, oil, vinegar, mustard, minced garlic, salt and pepper until blended. Pour over potato mixture; toss gently to coat. Gently stir in remaining ingredients. Serve warm or at room temperature.
1 cup: 201 cal., 9g fat (1g sat. fat), 0 chol., 239mg sod., 29g carb. (1g sugars, 2g fiber), 3g pro. **Diabetic Exchanges:** 2 starch, 2 fat.

SANDWICHES, WRAPS & MORE

For lunches, picnics or a light dinner, sandwiches are a perfect choice. And even hot sandwiches can be made with minimal kitchen time!

GUACAMOLE CHICKEN SALAD SANDWICHES

This chicken salad recipe is inspired by a local restaurant's inventive guacamole, which was served studded with pomegranate seeds. I serve this salad on homemade tomato bread—it's a great contrast in flavor and color. It can also be served on lettuce leaves instead of bread.
—*Debra Keil, Owasso, OK*

TAKES: 20 min. • **MAKES:** 10 servings

- 1 rotisserie chicken, skin removed, cubed
- 2 medium ripe avocados, peeled and mashed
- ¾ cup pomegranate seeds
- 6 green onions, chopped
- 8 cherry tomatoes, halved
- 1 jalapeno pepper, seeded and minced
- ¼ cup fresh cilantro leaves, chopped
- 3 Tbsp. mayonnaise
- 2 Tbsp. lime juice
- 1 garlic clove, minced
- ½ tsp. salt
- ½ tsp. ground cumin
- ¼ tsp. pepper
- 20 slices multigrain bread, toasted

In a large bowl, combine all the ingredients but the bread. Spread chicken salad over 10 bread slices; top with remaining bread.

Note: Wear disposable gloves when cutting hot peppers; the oils can burn skin. Avoid touching your face.

1 sandwich: 295 cal., 12g fat (2g sat. fat), 35mg chol., 370mg sod., 28g carb. (6g sugars, 6g fiber), 19g pro.

Diabetic Exchanges: 2 starch, 2 lean meat, 2 fat.

COOL-KITCHEN TIP
For variety, try adding bacon bits, chopped pickled jalapenos or garlic powder. You could also swap out the cheddar cheese for a smoky Gouda, or serve with chipotle mayo instead of sour cream.

MAYAN POTATO QUESADILLAS

I make potato-filled rolled tacos all the time and wanted to switch it up, so I made quesadillas from my original recipe. I serve the creamy, crispy quesadillas with salsa and sour cream. As an extra, serve homemade guacamole too!
—*Marina Castle-Kelley, Canyon Country, CA*

PREP: 20 min. • **COOK:** 15 min.
MAKES: 4 servings

- 1 cup mashed potatoes (without added milk and butter)
- 1 cup tomatillo salsa, divided
- ¼ cup thinly sliced green onions
- 2 flour tortillas (10 in.)
- 1 cup shredded cheddar cheese
- 2 Tbsp. butter, softened
- ½ cup sour cream

1. In a large bowl, combine mashed potatoes, ½ cup tomatillo salsa and the green onions. Top half of each tortilla with half the potato mixture; sprinkle with ½ cup cheese. Fold tortilla to close. Lightly butter top and bottom of quesadillas.
2. In a large cast-iron skillet or griddle, in batches, cook quesadillas over medium heat until golden brown and heated through, 2-3 minutes on each side. Cut each quesadilla into 4 wedges. Serve with sour cream and the remaining ½ cup tomatillo salsa. If desired, sprinkle with additional green onions.
2 wedges: 394 cal., 24g fat (14g sat. fat), 64mg chol., 877mg sod., 32g carb. (5g sugars, 5g fiber), 11g pro.

READER RAVE

"Delicious! Now I have another option for leftover mashed potatoes!"

—JELLYBUG, TASTEOFHOME.COM

LOADED AVOCADO BLT

My husband invented this twist on a bacon, lettuce and tomato sandwich. I like to make it with double the bacon, and I sometimes add the Gorgonzola cheese to the avocado spread.
—*Lori Grant, Kingsport, TN*

TAKES: 15 min. • **MAKES:** 2 servings

- ½ small ripe avocado, peeled
- 2 Tbsp. mayonnaise
- ½ tsp. lemon juice
- 2 Tbsp. crumbled Gorgonzola cheese
- 4 slices Italian bread, toasted
- 1½ cups fresh baby spinach
- 4 tomato slices
- 4 thick-sliced applewood smoked bacon strips, cooked

1. Mash avocado with a fork; stir in the mayonnaise and lemon juice. Gently stir in cheese. Spread over all toast slices.
2. Top 2 slices of toast with spinach, tomato, bacon and the remaining toast.
1 sandwich: 420 cal., 29g fat (7g sat. fat), 27mg chol., 921mg sod., 27g carb. (3g sugars, 5g fiber), 15g pro.

HEARTY MEATBALL SUB SANDWICHES

Making the saucy meatballs in advance and reheating them saves me precious time when expecting company. These satisfying sandwiches are excellent for casual parties.
—*Deena Hubler, Jasper, IN*

TAKES: 30 min. • **MAKES:** 12 servings

- 2 large eggs, lightly beaten
- 1 cup dry bread crumbs
- 2 Tbsp. grated Parmesan cheese
- 2 Tbsp. finely chopped onion
- 1 tsp. salt
- ½ tsp. pepper
- ½ tsp. garlic powder
- ¼ tsp. Italian seasoning
- 2 lbs. ground beef
- 1 jar (28 oz.) spaghetti sauce
- 12 sandwich rolls, split
  Optional: Sliced onion and sliced green pepper

1. In a large bowl, combine the first 8 ingredients. Crumble beef over mixture and mix lightly but thoroughly. Shape into 1-in. balls. Place in a single layer in a 3-qt. microwave-safe dish.

2. Microwave, covered, on high for 3-4 minutes. Turn meatballs; cook until no longer pink, 3-4 minutes longer. Drain.

3. Add spaghetti sauce. Microwave, covered, on high until heated through, 2-4 minutes. Serve on rolls. If desired, top with slices of onion and green pepper, and additional grated Parmesan.

1 sandwich: 464 cal., 18g fat (7g sat. fat), 88mg chol., 1013mg sod., 49g carb. (10g sugars, 3g fiber), 26g pro.

SLOW-COOKED CHICKEN CAESAR WRAPS

I first created this recipe for our daughter who loves Caesar salads, then later for our extended family on vacation. It's such an easy meal—perfect for vacations when you'd rather be outside than inside cooking all day.
—*Christine Hadden, Whitman, MA*

PREP: 10 min. • **COOK:** 3 hours
MAKES: 6 servings

- 1½ lbs. boneless skinless chicken breast halves
- 2 cups chicken broth
- ¾ cup creamy Caesar salad dressing
- ½ cup shredded Parmesan cheese
- ¼ cup minced fresh parsley
- ½ tsp. pepper
- 6 flour tortillas (8 in.)
- 2 cups shredded lettuce
  Optional: Salad croutons and crumbled cooked bacon

1. Place chicken and broth in a 1½- or 3-qt. slow cooker. Cook, covered, on low 3-4 hours or until a thermometer inserted in chicken reads 165°. Remove chicken and discard cooking juices. Shred chicken with 2 forks; return to slow cooker.

2. Stir in dressing, Parmesan, parsley and pepper; heat through. Serve in tortillas with lettuce and, if desired, salad croutons, crumbled bacon and additional shredded Parmesan cheese.

1 wrap: 472 cal., 25g fat (5g sat. fat), 79mg chol., 795mg sod., 29g carb. (1g sugars, 2g fiber), 31g pro.

BASIL CHICKEN SANDWICHES

I got the inspiration for this recipe when family members with food allergies were coming to see our new home. I created this chicken sandwich with fresh basil for our lunch.
—*Kerry Durgin Krebs, New Market, MD*

TAKES: 15 min. • **MAKES:** 6 sandwiches

- ½ tsp. pepper
- ¼ tsp. salt
  Dash paprika
- 1 lb. boneless skinless chicken breasts, cut into ½-in. slices
- 6 Tbsp. prepared olive oil vinaigrette salad dressing, divided
- 6 ciabatta rolls, split
- 18 basil leaves
- 1 jar (7 oz.) roasted sweet red peppers, drained
- ¼ cup shredded Romano cheese

1. Combine the pepper, salt and paprika; sprinkle over chicken slices. In a nonstick skillet over medium-high heat, cook chicken in 2 Tbsp. salad dressing for 4-5 minutes on each side or until chicken is no longer pink.

2. Brush remaining 4 Tbsp. salad dressing on rolls. Place basil leaves on rolls; top with chicken and red peppers. Sprinkle with Romano cheese.

1 sandwich: 308 cal., 8g fat (2g sat. fat), 45mg chol., 824mg sod., 33g carb. (3g sugars, 2g fiber), 22g pro. **Diabetic Exchanges:** 2 starch, 2 lean meat, 1 fat.

1. Place sour cream, chiles, cilantro and lime juice in a food processor; cover and process until blended. Set aside.

2. Cut each tilapia fillet lengthwise into 2 portions. Place flour, egg white and bread crumbs in separate shallow bowls. Dip the tilapia in flour, then egg white, then crumbs.

3. Preheat air fryer to 400°. In batches, arrange fillets in a single layer on greased tray in air-fryer basket; spritz with cooking spray. Cook until fish flakes easily with a fork, 10-12 minutes, turning once.

4. Combine seasonings; sprinkle over fish. Place a portion of fish on each tortilla; top with about 2 Tbsp. of the sour cream mixture. Sprinkle with tomato. If desired, top with additional cilantro.

Note: In our testing, we find cook times vary dramatically among brands of air fryers. As a result, we give wider than normal ranges on suggested cook times. Begin checking at the first time listed and adjust as needed.

1 taco: 178 cal., 3g fat (1g sat. fat), 30mg chol., 269mg sod., 22g carb. (2g sugars, 2g fiber), 16g pro. **Diabetic Exchanges:** 2 lean meat, 1½ starch, ½ fat.

COOL-KITCHEN TIP
A mild whitefish like the tilapia in this recipe works best for fish tacos. Good alternatives include snapper, mahi mahi, grouper, flounder, halibut or cod. If you have a local fresh fish you want to use, that's great too!

AIR-FRYER FISH TACOS

These crispy tacos are good enough to challenge the best food truck. I love that the fish is deliciously guilt-free because it's air-fried instead of deep-fried.
—Lena Lim, Seattle, WA

PREP: 30 min. • **COOK:** 10 min./batch
MAKES: 8 servings

¾ cup reduced-fat sour cream
1   can (4 oz.) chopped green chiles
1   Tbsp. fresh cilantro leaves
1   Tbsp. lime juice
4   tilapia fillets (4 oz. each)
½ cup all-purpose flour
1   large egg white, beaten
½ cup panko bread crumbs
     Cooking spray
½ tsp. salt
½ tsp. each white pepper, cayenne pepper and paprika
8   corn tortillas (6 in.), warmed
1   large tomato, finely chopped

2. Preheat air fryer to 375°. In a shallow bowl, mix flour, herbes de Provence, sea salt, garlic powder, pepper and cayenne. In a separate shallow bowl, whisk egg, milk and hot pepper sauce. Place coconut in a third shallow bowl. Dip shrimp in the flour to coat both sides; shake off excess. Dip in egg mixture, then in coconut, patting to help adhere.

3. In batches, arrange shrimp in a single layer on greased tray in air-fryer basket; spritz with cooking spray. Cook until coconut is lightly browned and shrimp turn pink, 3-4 minutes on each side.

4. Spread cut side of buns with remoulade. Top with shrimp, lettuce and tomato.

1 sandwich: 716 cal., 40g fat (16g sat. fat), 173mg chol., 944mg sod., 60g carb. (23g sugars, 4g fiber), 31g pro.

COBB SALAD WRAP SANDWICHES

These wraps are easy for a summer night—and, even better, I don't have to turn on my oven. There are smiles all around when I make them for dinner.
—Bonnie Hawkins, Elkhorn, WI

TAKES: 15 min. • **MAKES:** 2 servings

- ¼ cup blue cheese salad dressing
- 2 spinach or whole wheat tortillas (8 in.)
- 1 cup shredded cooked chicken
- 1 cup spring mix salad greens
- 1 medium tomato, halved and sliced
- 4 cooked bacon strips
- ½ medium ripe avocado, peeled and sliced
- 1 Tbsp. sliced ripe olives
- 1 Tbsp. crumbled blue cheese

Spread dressing over tortillas to within ½ in. of edges. Layer with the remaining ingredients. Roll up tortillas.

1 wrap: 610 cal., 37g fat (8g sat. fat), 91mg chol., 880mg sod., 36g carb. (3g sugars, 5g fiber), 33g pro.

AIR-FRYER SHRIMP PO'BOYS

My husband loves crispy coconut shrimp and po'boys, so I combined them with a spicy remoulade and *voila*! This air-fryer shrimp is a big hit with family and friends and is frequently requested. For catfish po'boys, substitute cornmeal for the coconut and add a few minutes to the cooking time.
—Marla Clark, Albuquerque, NM

PREP: 35 min. • **COOK:** 10 min./batch
MAKES: 4 servings

- ½ cup mayonnaise
- 1 Tbsp. Creole mustard
- 1 Tbsp. chopped cornichons or dill pickles
- 1 Tbsp. minced shallot
- 1½ tsp. lemon juice
- ⅛ tsp. cayenne pepper

COCONUT SHRIMP
- 1 cup all-purpose flour
- 1 tsp. herbes de Provence
- ½ tsp. sea salt
- ½ tsp. garlic powder
- ½ tsp. pepper
- ¼ tsp. cayenne pepper
- 1 large egg
- ½ cup 2% milk
- 1 tsp. hot pepper sauce
- 2 cups sweetened shredded coconut
- 1 lb. uncooked shrimp (26-30 per lb.), peeled and deveined
  Cooking spray
- 4 hoagie buns, split
- 2 cups shredded lettuce
- 1 medium tomato, thinly sliced

1. For remoulade, combine the first 6 ingredients. Refrigerate, covered, until serving.

COOL-KITCHEN TIP

If the tortillas are brittle, wrap them in a damp paper towel and warm them in the microwave for a few seconds before assembling to make them more pliable.

BISTRO APPLE PANINI

The bacon, apple and tarragon in this recipe go together so well. If you don't have a panini maker or an indoor grill, you can easily pan-fry these excellent sandwiches.
—Noelle Myers, Grand Forks, ND

PREP: 20 min. • **COOK:** 5 min./ batch
MAKES: 6 servings

- 12 thick-sliced bacon strips, cut in half
- 1 medium apple, thinly sliced
- 1 Tbsp. ginger ale
- 1 tsp. lemon juice
- ¼ cup apple jelly
- 4 tsp. minced fresh tarragon
- 12 slices sourdough bread
- 6 slices Havarti cheese
- 2 Tbsp. Dijon mustard
- 3 Tbsp. butter, softened

1. In a large skillet, cook bacon over medium heat until crisp. Remove to paper towels to drain. In a small bowl, toss apple with ginger ale and lemon juice; set aside.
2. Place jelly in a small microwave-safe bowl; microwave on high until softened, 20-30 seconds. Stir in tarragon.
3. Spread jelly mixture over 6 bread slices. Top with cheese, apple and bacon. Spread mustard over the remaining 6 bread slices; place over bacon. Spread outsides of sandwiches with butter.
4. Cook on a panini maker or indoor grill for 3-4 minutes or until bread is browned and cheese is melted.
1 sandwich: 512 cal., 25g fat (12g sat. fat), 62mg chol., 1235mg sod., 50g carb. (13g sugars, 2g fiber), 22g pro.

COOL-KITCHEN TIP
Fry bacon in bulk in cool weather, then drain the slices well and freeze them. The slices don't stick together, so it's easy to remove a few as needed for a sandwich or to crumble for a recipe.

HEARTY MUFFULETTA

Famous in Louisiana, a muffuletta is a combo of cold cuts, cheese and olive salad layered into an Italian bread shell. I was happy when a friend and co-worker gave me this recipe so I could make it myself. More than a meal, it's a dining experience!
—*Ruth Hayward, Lake Charles, LA*

PREP: 55 min. + chilling
MAKES: 10 servings

- ½ cup finely chopped celery
- ½ cup sliced pimiento-stuffed olives, drained
- ½ cup sliced ripe olives, drained
- ½ cup giardiniera
- ⅓ cup finely chopped onion
- ⅓ cup olive oil
- ¼ cup finely chopped green onions
- ¼ cup minced fresh parsley
- 3 Tbsp. lemon juice
- 1 tsp. dried oregano
- 1 garlic clove, minced
- ⅛ tsp. pepper
- 1 round loaf (24 oz.) unsliced Italian bread
- ¼ lb. thinly sliced hard salami
- ¼ lb. provolone cheese
- ¼ lb. thinly sliced deli ham

1. Combine the first 12 ingredients. Refrigerate, covered, at least 8 hours. Drain, reserving 2 Tbsp. liquid.
2. Cut loaf of bread in half horizontally; hollow out top and bottom, leaving a 1-in. shell (discard removed bread or save for another use). Brush cut sides of bread with reserved liquid. Layer bottom of bread shell with salami, half the olive mixture, cheese, remaining olive mixture and ham. Replace bread top. Cut into wedges to serve.
Note: Giardiniera is a vegetable mixture available in mild and hot varieties. Look for it in the Italian or pickle section of your local grocery store.
1 serving: 378 cal., 19g fat (5g sat. fat), 25mg chol., 1103mg sod., 38g carb. (2g sugars, 3g fiber), 14g pro.

SPICY BUFFALO CHICKEN WRAPS

This recipe has a real kick, and it's one of my husband's favorites. It's ready in a flash, easily doubled, and the closest thing to restaurant Buffalo wings I've ever tasted in a light version.
—*Jennifer Beck, Meridian, ID*

TAKES: 25 min. • **MAKES:** 2 servings

- ½ lb. boneless skinless chicken breast, cubed
- ½ tsp. canola oil
- 2 Tbsp. Louisiana-style hot sauce
- 1 cup shredded lettuce
- 2 flour tortillas (6 in.), warmed
- 2 tsp. reduced-fat ranch salad dressing
- 2 Tbsp. crumbled blue cheese

1. In a large nonstick skillet, cook chicken in oil over medium heat for 6 minutes; drain. Stir in hot sauce. Bring to a boil. Reduce heat; simmer, uncovered, until sauce is thickened and chicken is no longer pink, 3-5 minutes.
2. Place lettuce on tortillas; drizzle with ranch dressing. Top with chicken mixture and blue cheese; roll up.
1 wrap: 273 cal., 11g fat (3g sat. fat), 70mg chol., 453mg sod., 15g carb. (1g sugars, 1g fiber), 28g pro. **Diabetic Exchanges:** 3 lean meat, 1½ fat, 1 starch.

CLUB ROLL-UPS

Packed with meat, cheese and olives, these roll-ups are always a hit at parties. Experiment with different lunch meats and salad dressing flavors.
—*Linda Searl, Pampa, TX*

TAKES: 25 min. • **MAKES:** 8 servings

- 3 oz. cream cheese, softened
- ½ cup ranch salad dressing
- 2 Tbsp. ranch salad dressing mix
- 8 bacon strips, cooked and crumbled
- ½ cup finely chopped onion
- 1 can (2¼ oz.) sliced ripe olives, drained
- 1 jar (2 oz.) diced pimientos, drained
- ¼ cup diced canned jalapeno peppers
- 8 flour tortillas (10 in.), room temperature
- 8 thin slices deli ham
- 8 thin slices deli turkey
- 8 thin slices deli roast beef
- 2 cups shredded cheddar cheese

1. In a small bowl, beat the cream cheese, ranch dressing and dressing mix until well blended. In another bowl, combine the bacon, onion, olives, pimientos and jalapenos.

2. Spread cream cheese mixture over tortillas; layer with ham, turkey and roast beef. Sprinkle with bacon mixture and cheddar cheese; roll up.

1 roll-up: 554 cal., 29g fat (12g sat. fat), 80mg chol., 1802mg sod., 39g carb. (2g sugars, 7g fiber), 27g pro.

READER RAVE
"Delicious, easy and they looked professional."

—DEANNER, TASTEOFHOME.COM

SLOW-COOKER ITALIAN SLOPPY JOES

These tasty sloppy joes are perfect for a gathering. If you're taking them to an event, simplify things by cooking the beef mixture and stirring in other ingredients the night before. Cool the meat sauce in shallow bowls in the fridge, then cover and refrigerate them overnight. The next day, transfer the mixture to the slow cooker to keep it warm for the party.
—Hope Wasylenki, Gahanna, OH

PREP: 30 min. • **COOK:** 4 hours
MAKES: 36 servings

- 2 lbs. lean ground beef (90% lean)
- 2 lbs. bulk Italian sausage
- 2 medium green peppers, chopped
- 1 large onion, chopped
- 4 cups spaghetti sauce
- 1 can (28 oz.) diced tomatoes, undrained
- ½ lb. sliced fresh mushrooms
- 1 can (6 oz.) tomato paste
- 2 garlic cloves, minced
- 2 bay leaves
- 36 hamburger buns, split

1. Cook the beef, sausage, peppers and onion in a Dutch oven over medium heat until meat is no longer pink, breaking it into crumbles; drain. Transfer to a 6-qt. slow cooker. Stir in the spaghetti sauce, tomatoes, mushrooms, tomato paste, garlic and bay leaves.
2. Cover and cook on high until flavors are blended, 4-5 hours. Discard bay leaves. Serve on buns, ½ cup on each.
Freeze option: Freeze cooled meat mixture in freezer containers. To use, partially thaw in refrigerator overnight. Heat through in a saucepan, stirring occasionally; add a little broth or water if necessary.
1 sandwich: 246 cal., 9g fat (3g sat. fat), 29mg chol., 522mg sod., 27g carb. (6g sugars, 2g fiber), 13g pro. **Diabetic Exchanges:** 2 starch, 2 lean meat.

SALMON SALAD SANDWICHES

These are perfect to pack in lunchboxes when your kids can't face another boring sandwich. We love this salmon, cream cheese and dill tucked inside a crusty roll. The carrots and celery add a nice crunch.
—Yvonne Shust, Shoal Lake, MB

TAKES: 10 min. • **MAKES:** 2 servings

- 3 oz. cream cheese, softened
- 1 Tbsp. mayonnaise
- 1 Tbsp. lemon juice
- 1 tsp. dill weed
- ¼ to ½ tsp. salt
- ⅛ tsp. pepper
- 1 can (6 oz.) pink salmon, drained, bones and skin removed
- ½ cup shredded carrot
- ½ cup chopped celery
  Lettuce leaves
- 2 whole wheat buns, split
  Sliced tomatoes

In a large bowl, beat the cream cheese, mayonnaise, lemon juice, dill, salt and pepper until smooth. Add salmon, carrot and celery; mix well. Place a lettuce leaf and about ½ cup salmon salad on each bun; top with tomato.
1 sandwich: 463 cal., 29g fat (12g sat. fat), 87mg chol., 1158mg sod., 28g carb. (5g sugars, 5g fiber), 25g pro.

PRESSURE-COOKER SHREDDED CHICKEN GYROS

Our family has no links of any kind to Greece, but we always have such a marvelous time at the annual Salt Lake City Greek Festival. One of my favorite parts is all the awesome food. This meal is a good way to mix up our menu at home, and my kids are big fans.
—Camille Beckstrand, Layton, UT

TAKES: 30 minutes • **MAKES:** 8 servings

- 2 medium onions, chopped
- 6 garlic cloves, minced
- 1 tsp. lemon-pepper seasoning
- 1 tsp. dried oregano
- ½ tsp. ground allspice
- ½ cup lemon juice
- ¼ cup red wine vinegar
- 2 Tbsp. olive oil
- 2 lbs. boneless skinless chicken breasts
- 8 whole pita breads
  Toppings: Tzatziki sauce, torn romaine and sliced tomato, cucumber and onion

1. In a 6-qt. electric pressure cooker, combine the first 8 ingredients; add chicken. Lock lid; close pressure-release valve. Adjust to pressure-cook on high for 6 minutes. Quick-release pressure. A thermometer inserted in chicken should read at least 165°.
2. Remove chicken; shred with 2 forks. Return to pressure cooker. Using tongs, place chicken mixture on pita breads. Serve with toppings.
Freeze option: Freeze cooled chicken mixture and juices in freezer containers. To use, partially thaw in refrigerator overnight. Heat through in a saucepan, stirring occasionally and adding a little water if necessary.
1 gyro: 335 cal., 7g fat (1g sat. fat), 63mg chol., 418mg sod., 38g carb. (2g sugars, 2g fiber), 29g pro. **Diabetic Exchanges:** 3 lean meat, 2½ starch, ½ fat.

CORNED BEEF SANDWICHES

My daughter shared this recipe with me. It has become a favorite of our entire family.
—Kathryn Binder, Pickett, WI

TAKES: 20 min. • **MAKES:** 10 servings

- ¾ cup mayonnaise
- 3 Tbsp. chili sauce
- 1 can (14 oz.) sauerkraut, rinsed and well drained
- 2 cups shredded Swiss cheese
- 12 oz. sliced deli corned beef
- 20 slices rye bread
- ½ cup butter, softened
  Thousand Island salad dressing, optional

1. In a large bowl, combine mayonnaise, chili sauce, sauerkraut and Swiss cheese; spread over all 20 slices of bread, about ¼ cup on each. Top half the bread slices with corned beef; top with remaining bread slices, spread side down, to form sandwiches. Lightly butter the outside of each sandwich.
2. Toast sandwiches on a hot griddle for 4-5 minutes on each side or until golden brown. Serve with Thousand Island dressing if desired.
1 sandwich: 486 cal., 32g fat (13g sat. fat), 69mg chol., 1308mg sod., 34g carb. (4g sugars, 5g fiber), 17g pro.

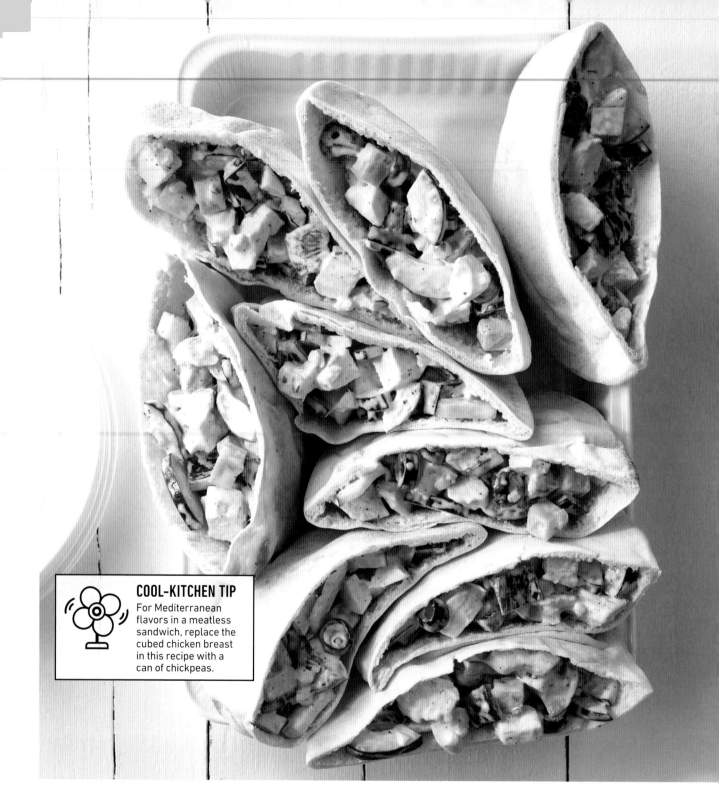

COOL-KITCHEN TIP
For Mediterranean flavors in a meatless sandwich, replace the cubed chicken breast in this recipe with a can of chickpeas.

CHICKEN CUCUMBER PITAS

I wanted a good recipe for pitas. Seeing the large stack of garden-fresh cucumbers on my counter, I decided to improvise and create my own filling. It was a huge hit.
—Sheena Wellard, Nampa, ID

TAKES: 25 min. • **MAKES:** 6 servings

- 2 cups cubed cooked chicken breast
- 1 large cucumber, quartered, seeded and sliced
- 1 can (2¼ oz.) sliced ripe olives, drained
- 1 medium tomato, seeded and chopped
- 1 small sweet red pepper, chopped
- ½ cup cubed cheddar cheese
- ¼ cup chopped red onion

DRESSING

- ½ cup ranch salad dressing
- ¼ cup mayonnaise
- 1 Tbsp. Italian salad dressing
- ¼ tsp. garlic powder
- ¼ tsp. pepper
- 12 pita pocket halves

In a large bowl, combine the first 7 ingredients. In a small bowl, combine the ranch dressing, mayonnaise, Italian dressing, garlic powder and pepper; pour over the chicken mixture and toss to coat. Fill each pita half with a scant ½ cup chicken mixture.

NOTE: A simple swap to reduced-fat mayo and dressings would save 60 calories and 8 grams of fat per serving.

2 filled pita halves: 445 cal., 22g fat (5g sat. fat), 49mg chol., 747mg sod., 37g carb. (4g sugars, 2g fiber), 22g pro.

SMOKED SALMON EGG SALAD

Smoked salmon and croissants elevate egg salad sandwiches to a delicious and decidedly grown-up level.
—Cathy Tang, Redmond, WA

TAKES: 10 min. • **MAKES:** 6 servings

- ¾ cup mayonnaise
- 1 tsp. dill weed
- ½ tsp. lemon juice
- ¼ tsp. salt
- ⅛ tsp. pepper
- 6 hard-boiled large eggs, chopped
- 4 oz. smoked salmon, chopped
- 6 croissants, split
- 1½ cups fresh baby spinach

In a large bowl, combine the first 5 ingredients. Stir in eggs and salmon. Place ⅓ cup mixture on the bottom of each croissant; top with spinach leaves and replace the croissant tops.

1 sandwich: 533 cal., 40g fat (11g sat. fat), 265mg chol., 889mg sod., 27g carb. (7g sugars, 2g fiber), 15g pro.

MOROCCAN LAMB LETTUCE WRAPS

I am a huge fan of both lamb and lettuce wraps. This combination—with creamy dressing and crunchy cucumber—makes a tasty slow-cooked dish. Wine and chili powder add even more flavor elements.
—*Arlene Erlbach, Morton Grove, IL*

PREP: 25 min. • **COOK:** 5 hours
MAKES: 8 servings

- 2 lbs. lamb stew meat
- 1 cup chunky salsa
- ⅓ cup apricot preserves
- 6 Tbsp. dry red wine, divided
- 1 to 2 Tbsp. Moroccan seasoning (ras el hanout)
- 2 tsp. chili powder
- ½ tsp. garlic powder
- 1 English cucumber, very thinly sliced
- 2 Tbsp. prepared ranch salad dressing
- 16 Bibb or Boston lettuce leaves

1. Combine lamb, salsa, preserves, 4 Tbsp. wine, Moroccan seasoning, chili powder and garlic powder. Transfer to a 3-qt. slow cooker. Cook, covered, on low 5-6 hours, or until lamb is tender.

2. Remove lamb; shred with 2 forks. Strain cooking juices; skim fat. Return lamb and cooking juices to the slow cooker; heat through. Stir in remaining 2 Tbsp. wine; heat through.

3. Combine cucumber and ranch dressing; toss to coat. Serve lamb mixture in lettuce leaves; top with cucumber mixture.

2 filled lettuce wraps: 221 cal., 8g fat (2g sat. fat), 74mg chol., 257mg sod., 13g carb. (8g sugars, 1g fiber), 24g pro. **Diabetic Exchanges:** 3 lean meat, 1 starch.

CRANBERRY-WALNUT CHICKEN SALAD SANDWICHES

I made these simple, yet special, sandwiches for a birthday party. Tangy cranberries and crunchy celery pep up the chicken. Leftover turkey works well, too.
—Shannon Tucker, Land O Lakes, FL

TAKES: 15 min. • **MAKES:** 8 servings

- ½ cup mayonnaise
- 2 Tbsp. honey Dijon mustard
- ¼ tsp. pepper
- 2 cups cubed rotisserie chicken
- 1 cup shredded Swiss cheese
- ½ cup chopped celery
- ½ cup dried cranberries
- ¼ cup chopped walnuts
- ½ tsp. dried parsley flakes
- 8 lettuce leaves
- 16 slices pumpernickel bread

1. In a large bowl, combine mayonnaise, mustard and pepper. Stir in the chicken, cheese, celery, cranberries, walnuts and parsley.

2. Place lettuce on 8 slices of bread; top each with ½ cup chicken salad. Top with the remaining bread slices.

1 sandwich: 411 cal., 22g fat (5g sat. fat), 49mg chol., 469mg sod., 35g carb. (7g sugars, 5g fiber), 20g pro.

COOL-KITCHEN TIP

We all get a little limp in the summer heat, but you can give limp celery a second chance! Cut the ends from the celery stalks and place the stalks in a glass of cold water in the refrigerator for several hours or overnight. You'll be surprised how refreshed the celery will be.

CAPRESE SANDWICH

This is a staple sandwich in my family that we make at least several times a month when things are hectic and we need a fast, fresh and healthy dinner. The sandwiches are excellent for a picnic lunch or for a warm-weather dinner when you don't want to turn on your oven. Pair with a crisp, fruity white wine and a pasta salad or fancy potato chips.
—Stacey Johnson, Tacoma, WA

TAKES: 15 min. • **MAKES:** 4 servings

- 6 Tbsp. wasabi mayonnaise or plain mayonnaise
- 8 slices sourdough bread (½ in. thick), toasted
- 2 large heirloom tomatoes, sliced
- ½ tsp. sea salt
- ½ tsp. coarsely ground pepper
- ½ large sweet onion, thinly sliced
- 8 oz. fresh mozzarella cheese, sliced
- ½ cup fresh basil leaves

Spread mayonnaise on 1 side of each slice of toast. Top half the toast slices with tomatoes, salt and pepper. Add onion, mozzarella and basil; top with remaining bread slices.

1 sandwich: 463 cal., 29g fat (11g sat. fat), 52mg chol., 753mg sod., 34g carb. (6g sugars, 2g fiber), 17g pro.

PRESSURE-COOKER TANDOORI CHICKEN PANINI

The tandoori-style spices in this chicken give it a bold flavor that's hard to resist. It tastes incredible tucked between pieces of naan, then grilled for Indian-inspired panini sandwiches.

—*Yasmin Arif, Manassas, VA*

PREP: 25 min. • **COOK:** 10 min.
MAKES: 6 servings

- 1½ lbs. boneless skinless chicken breasts
- ½ cup reduced-sodium chicken broth
- 2 garlic cloves, minced
- 2 tsp. minced fresh gingerroot
- 1 tsp. paprika
- ¼ tsp. salt
- ¼ to ½ tsp. cayenne pepper
- ¼ tsp. ground turmeric
- 6 green onions, chopped
- 6 Tbsp. chutney
- 6 naan flatbreads

1. Place the first 8 ingredients in a 6-qt. electric pressure cooker. Lock lid; close pressure-release valve. Adjust to pressure-cook on high for 6 minutes. Quick-release pressure. A thermometer inserted in the chicken should read at least 165°.

2. Remove chicken; shred with 2 forks. Return to pressure cooker. Stir in green onions; heat through.

3. Spread chutney over 1 side of each naan. Using a slotted spoon, top chutney side of 3 naan with chicken mixture; top with the remaining naan, chutney side down.

4. Cook sandwiches on a panini maker or indoor grill until golden brown, 6-8 minutes. To serve, cut each sandwich in half.

Freeze option: Freeze cooled meat mixture and juices in freezer containers. To use, partially thaw in refrigerator overnight. Heat through in a saucepan, stirring occasionally and adding a little broth if necessary.

½ sandwich: 351 cal., 6g fat (2g sat. fat), 68mg chol., 853mg sod., 44g carb. (13g sugars, 2g fiber), 28g pro.

LOBSTER ROLLS

Mayonnaise infused with dill and lemon lends refreshing flavor to these super sandwiches. Try pan-toasting the buns in butter for something special.

—Taste of Home *Test Kitchen*

TAKES: 30 min. • **MAKES:** 8 sandwiches

- 1 cup chopped celery
- ⅓ cup mayonnaise
- 2 Tbsp. lemon juice
- ½ tsp. dill weed
- 5 cups cubed cooked lobster meat (about 4 small lobsters)
- 8 hoagie rolls, split and toasted

In a large bowl, combine the celery, mayonnaise, lemon juice and dill weed. Gently stir in lobster. Serve on rolls.

1 sandwich: 354 cal., 12g fat (2g sat. fat), 133mg chol., 887mg sod., 36g carb. (5g sugars, 1g fiber), 25g pro.

MEDITERRANEAN TURKEY PANINI

The word *panini* refers to sandwiches that are pressed and toasted. I love making panini for my fellow teachers and friends. For potlucks, make several and cut them into fourths. The sandwiches work well as an appetizer for any occasion. If you don't have a panini press, you can make this sandwich on the grill or in a skillet.
—*Martha Muellenberg, Vermillion, SD*

TAKES: 25 min. • **MAKES:** 4 servings

- 4 ciabatta rolls, split
- 1 jar (24 oz.) marinara or spaghetti sauce, divided
- 1 container (4 oz.) crumbled feta cheese
- 1 jar (7½ oz.) marinated quartered artichoke hearts, drained and chopped
- 2 plum tomatoes, sliced
- 1 lb. sliced deli turkey

1. Spread each ciabatta bottom with 2 Tbsp. marinara sauce. Top with half the cheese; add the artichokes, tomato, turkey and remaining cheese. Spread each ciabatta top with 2 Tbsp. marinara; place over turkey.
2. Cook on a panini maker or indoor grill until cheese is melted, 4-5 minutes. Place remaining marinara sauce in a small microwave-safe bowl; cover and microwave on high until heated through. Serve with sandwiches.
1 sandwich with ⅓ cup sauce: 701 cal., 18g fat (5g sat. fat), 55mg chol., 2314mg sod., 98g carb. (18g sugars, 8g fiber), 40g pro.

VEGGIE BROWN RICE WRAPS

Salsa gives a bit of zip to the savory veggie, brown rice and bean filling in these meatless tortilla wraps.
—Lisa Sullivan, St. Marys, OH

TAKES: 20 min. • **MAKES:** 6 servings

- 1 medium sweet red or green pepper, diced
- 1 cup sliced fresh mushrooms
- 1 Tbsp. olive oil
- 2 garlic cloves, minced
- 2 cups cooked brown rice
- 1 can (16 oz.) kidney beans, rinsed and drained
- 1 cup frozen corn, thawed
- ¼ cup chopped green onions
- ½ tsp. ground cumin
- ½ tsp. pepper
- ¼ tsp. salt
- 6 flour tortillas (8 in.), room temperature
- ½ cup shredded reduced-fat cheddar cheese
- ¾ cup salsa

1. In a large cast-iron or other heavy skillet, saute red pepper and mushrooms in oil until tender. Add garlic; cook 1 minute. Add the rice, beans, corn, green onions, cumin, pepper and salt. Cook and stir until heated through, 4-6 minutes.
2. Spoon ¾ cup onto each tortilla. Sprinkle with cheese; drizzle with salsa. Fold sides of tortilla over filling; roll up. Serve immediately.
1 wrap: 377 cal., 8g fat (2g sat. fat), 7mg chol., 675mg sod., 62g carb. (4g sugars, 7g fiber), 15g pro.

TANDOORI MASALA CHICKEN SANDWICHES

This recipe combines spices from my Indian roots with a modern twist. If you want to add some extra heat to your sandwiches, add half a serrano pepper to the slaw.
—Mary Lou Timpson, Centennial Park, AZ

PREP: 30 min. + marinating
COOK: 10 min. • **MAKES:** 4 servings

- 2 Tbsp. plain Greek yogurt
- 2 Tbsp. tandoori masala seasoning
- 4 boneless skinless chicken thighs (about 1 lb.)

SLAW
- 1 cup shredded daikon radish
- 2 Tbsp. grated onion
- 2 Tbsp. lime juice
- 2 Tbsp. minced fresh cilantro
- ¼ tsp. salt

SAUCE
- ½ cup plain Greek yogurt
- 2 Tbsp. minced fresh mint
- 1 Tbsp. lime juice
- ½ tsp. minced garlic
- ⅛ tsp. salt
- ⅛ tsp. pepper
- 1 Tbsp. canola oil
- 4 brioche hamburger buns, split and toasted
- 4 lettuce leaves

1. In a large bowl, whisk yogurt and tandoori seasoning until blended. Add chicken and turn to coat. Cover and refrigerate at least 30 minutes or overnight, turning occasionally.
2. Meanwhile, in a small bowl, combine slaw ingredients. Refrigerate, covered, until serving. For sauce, combine yogurt, mint, lime juice, garlic, salt and pepper. Refrigerate, covered, until serving.
3. Drain chicken, discarding marinade. In a large cast-iron or other heavy skillet, heat oil over medium heat. Add chicken; cook until a thermometer reads 170°, 5-6 minutes on each side. Spread sauce over toasted bun tops. On each bun bottom, layer lettuce, chicken and slaw. Replace tops.
1 sandwich: 415 cal., 19g fat (6g sat. fat), 114mg chol., 559mg sod., 32g carb. (9g sugars, 4g fiber), 28g pro. 0

COOL-KITCHEN TIP
For a lower carb version of this sweet-savory sandwich, serve the chicken mixture in lettuce cups.

MOROCCAN CHICKEN TAGINE POCKETS

I enjoy shredded chicken dishes, Moroccan seasonings and pita sandwiches. The addition of carrot salad laced with dates and pomegranate seeds lends an extra punch and crunch. Mini flour tortillas can be substituted for the pitas. One pocket makes an appetizer; two makes lunch!
—Arlene Erlbach, Morton Grove, IL

PREP: 20 min. • **COOK:** 5 hours
MAKES: 14 sandwiches

- 1½ lbs. boneless skinless chicken thighs
- 1 cup chunky salsa
- ½ cup pomegranate juice, divided
- ½ cup pitted dates, chopped and divided
- 2 Tbsp. honey
- 1 Tbsp. Moroccan seasoning (ras el hanout)
- 1½ tsp. garlic powder
- 1¼ cups shredded carrots
- 3 Tbsp. mayonnaise
- 2 Tbsp. pomegranate seeds
- 7 miniature pita pockets, halved
  Minced fresh cilantro, optional

1. Place chicken in a greased 3- or 4-qt. slow cooker. Combine the salsa, 6 Tbsp. pomegranate juice, ⅓ cup dates, the honey, Moroccan seasoning and garlic powder; pour over chicken. Cook, covered, on low, until chicken is tender, 5-6 hours.
2. Meanwhile, combine the carrots, mayonnaise, pomegranate seeds and remaining dates. Refrigerate, covered, until serving.
3. Remove chicken from slow cooker; cool slightly. Skim fat from cooking juices. Shred chicken with 2 forks. Return chicken and juices to slow cooker. Stir in remaining 2 Tbsp. pomegranate juice; heat through. Serve in pitas with carrot slaw and, if desired, cilantro.
Note: Using skinless chicken thighs instead of breast meat keeps the chicken tender, juicy and flavorful, and only adds about 20 calories per serving.
1 sandwich: 164 cal., 6g fat (1g sat. fat), 33mg chol., 194mg sod., 17g carb. (7g sugars, 1g fiber), 11g pro.

TUNA PATTY

Salmon can also be used for this burger. My husband likes his topped with melted Swiss cheese and Dijon mustard.
—Joann Brasington, Sumter, SC

TAKES: 20 min. • **MAKES:** 4 servings

- 1 can (6 oz.) tuna, drained and flaked
- 1 large egg
- ½ cup Italian-seasoned bread crumbs
- ⅓ cup finely chopped onion
- ¼ cup chopped celery
- ¼ cup chopped sweet red pepper
- ¼ cup mayonnaise
- 2 Tbsp. chili sauce
- ½ tsp. dill weed
- ¼ tsp. salt
- ⅛ tsp. pepper
  Dash hot pepper sauce
  Dash Worcestershire sauce
- 1 tsp. olive oil
- 4 hamburger buns, split
  Tomato slices and lettuce leaves, optional

1. Combine tuna and next 12 ingredients; mix well. Shape into 4 patties (mixture will be soft).
2. In a nonstick skillet, cook patties in oil over medium-high heat until golden brown and cooked through, 3-4 minutes per side. Serve on buns. If desired, add tomato and lettuce.
1 sandwich: 363 cal., 16g fat (3g sat. fat), 71mg chol., 962mg sod., 36g carb. (6g sugars, 2g fiber), 18g pro.

READER RAVE

"Great alternative to hamburgers. A delicious, healthy and low-cost meal."

—JBDUPUIS, TASTEOFHOME.COM

COOL-KITCHEN TIP

To keep your patties from crumbling, use a firm touch when shaping, especially at the edges. Placing the patties on a sheet pan and chilling them for 15-20 minutes should also help. When frying, avoid moving them too much—brown well on one side before flipping.

SAY (GRILLED) CHEESE!

Just a few minutes in a skillet delivers a gooey, flavorful sandwich filled with surprising extras!

BLACKBERRY GRILLED CHEESE SANDWICH

If you're looking for a fabulous gourmet grilled cheese recipe, your search is over. With five kinds of cheese and fresh blackberries, this sandwich is impressive enough to serve to guests.
—*Josh Rink, Milwaukee, WI*

PREP: 30 min. • **COOK:** 10 min.
MAKES: 4 servings

- 6 Tbsp. softened butter, divided
- 8 slices sourdough bread
- ½ cup shredded sharp white cheddar cheese
- ½ cup shredded Monterey Jack cheese
- ½ cup shredded Gruyere cheese
- 3 Tbsp. finely shredded Manchego or Parmesan cheese
- 3 Tbsp. mayonnaise
- ⅛ tsp. onion powder
- 4 oz. Brie cheese, sliced, rind removed
- 1 cup fresh blackberries

1. Spread half the butter over 1 side of bread slices. In a large skillet, toast bread, buttered side down, over medium-low heat until golden brown, 2-3 minutes.
2. In a small bowl, combine cheddar, Monterey Jack and Gruyere cheeses. In another bowl, combine Manchego cheese, mayonnaise, remaining 3 Tbsp. butter and the onion powder.
3. With toasted side up, layer 4 slices of bread with Brie cheese, cheddar cheese mixture and blackberries. Top with the remaining slices, toasted side down. Spread outsides of sandwiches with mayonnaise mixture. Toast sandwiches over medium heat until golden brown and the cheese is melted, 5-6 minutes on each side. Serve immediately.
1 sandwich: 674 cal., 50g fat (27g sat. fat), 122mg chol., 1018mg sod., 34g carb. (5g sugars, 3g fiber), 25g pro.

ITALIAN GRILLED CHEESE SANDWICHES

I made up this recipe for the students in my class. The kids like it so much, they often go home and fix it for their families.
—*Beth Hiott, York, SC*

TAKES: 25 min. • **MAKES:** 4 servings

- 8 slices Italian bread
- 4 Tbsp. prepared pesto
- 4 slices provolone cheese
- 4 slices part-skim mozzarella cheese
- 5 tsp. olive oil
  Marinara sauce, warmed, optional

1. Spread 4 bread slices with pesto. Layer with cheeses; top with remaining bread. Brush outsides of sandwiches with oil.
2. Using a large cast-iron skillet or electric griddle, toast sandwiches over medium heat until cheese is melted, 3-4 minutes on each side. If desired, serve with warm marinara.
1 sandwich: 445 cal., 27g fat (10g sat. fat), 35mg chol., 759mg sod., 32g carb. (1g sugars, 2g fiber), 20g pro.

SUN-DRIED TOMATO GRILLED CHEESE SANDWICH

I love experimenting with grilled cheese combinations. This is one of my favorites.
—*Jess Apfe, Berkeley, CA*

TAKES: 30 min. • **MAKES:** 4 servings

- ½ cup oil-packed sun-dried tomatoes
- ¼ cup grated Parmesan cheese
- ¼ cup chopped fresh basil
- 2 Tbsp. olive oil
- 1 tsp. balsamic vinegar
- 1 garlic clove, crushed
- ⅛ tsp. salt
- ⅛ tsp. pepper
- 8 slices sourdough bread
- 1¼ cups shredded part-skim mozzarella cheese
- ½ cup crumbled goat cheese
- ¼ cup fresh arugula
- 2 Tbsp. chopped roasted sweet red pepper
- 3 Tbsp. butter, melted

1. Place the first 8 ingredients in a food processor; process until blended.
2. Spread over each of 4 bread slices; top with cheeses, arugula, red pepper and the remaining bread. Brush outsides of sandwiches with butter.
3. On a griddle, toast sandwiches over medium heat until golden brown and cheese is melted, 3-4 minutes per side.
1 sandwich: 491 cal., 31g fat (14g sat. fat), 67mg chol., 942mg sod., 37g carb. (4g sugars, 3g fiber), 19g pro.

COOL-KITCHEN TIP
Make these sandwiches on the grill for a hint of smoky flavor. If you don't love the mild tang of sourdough, use a loaf of Italian bread instead.

GRILLED PIMIENTO CHEESE SANDWICHES

Rich and creamy pimiento cheese is a southern favorite. It makes a tasty grilled cheese sandwich, especially with sweet hot pepper jelly.
—*Amy Freeze, Avon Park, FL*

TAKES: 20 min. • **MAKES:** 2 servings

- 4 slices sourdough bread
- ¼ cup butter, melted
- ½ cup refrigerated pimiento cheese
- 2 Tbsp. pepper jelly
- 6 cooked thick-sliced bacon strips

1. Brush 1 side of each bread slice with melted butter. In a large skillet, toast bread, buttered side down, over medium heat until golden brown, 3-4 minutes.
2. Remove from heat; place toasted side up. Spread cheese over toasted bread slices. Top 2 slices with jelly, then with bacon. Top with remaining bread slices, cheese facing inward. Brush outside of each sandwich with remaining melted butter. Cook until bread is golden brown and cheese is melted, 3-4 minutes on each side. If desired, serve with additional jelly.
1 sandwich: 869 cal., 52g fat (28g sat. fat), 105mg chol., 1856mg sod., 70g carb. (19g sugars, 2g fiber), 27g pro.

P. 120

MARVELOUS MAINS

Main courses can be a cool-kitchen challenge.
Here are your solutions—ultra quick stovetop dinners,
main-dish salads and more to the rescue!

PISTACHIO-CRUSTED FRIED FISH

This nut-crusted fish is so novel compared to standard breaded fillets. Plus, the pistachios give it a lovely color.
—Taste of Home *Test Kitchen*

TAKES: 30 min. • **MAKES:** 6 servings

- ½ cup dry bread crumbs
- ½ cup chopped pistachios
- ½ tsp. seafood seasoning
- ¼ tsp. salt
- ¼ tsp. garlic powder
- ¼ tsp. pepper
- ½ cup all-purpose flour
- ½ cup 2% milk
- 1½ lbs. whitefish or cod fillets
- 3 Tbsp. canola oil

1. In a shallow bowl, combine the first 6 ingredients. Place flour and milk in separate shallow bowls. Dip fillets in the flour, then in milk; coat with the pistachio mixture.
2. In a large nonstick skillet, heat oil over medium heat; add fish. Cook until fish just begins to flake easily with a fork, 4-5 minutes on each side.
3 oz. cooked fish: 325 cal., 18g fat (2g sat. fat), 71mg chol., 260mg sod., 14g carb. (2g sugars, 1g fiber), 26g pro. **Diabetic Exchanges:** 3 lean meat, 3 fat, 1 starch.

NICOISE SALAD

This garden-fresh salad is a feast for the eyes as well as the palate. Add some crusty bread and you have a mouthwatering meal.
—*Marla Fogderud, Mason, MI*

PREP: 40 min.
MAKES: 2 servings

- ⅓ cup olive oil
- 3 Tbsp. white wine vinegar
- 1½ tsp. Dijon mustard
- ⅛ tsp. each salt, onion powder and pepper

SALAD
- 2 small red potatoes
- ½ cup cut fresh green beans
- 3½ cups torn Bibb lettuce
- ½ cup cherry tomatoes, halved
- 10 Greek olives, pitted and halved
- 2 hard-boiled large eggs, quartered
- 1 can (5 oz.) albacore white tuna in water, drained and flaked

1. In a small bowl, whisk the oil, vinegar, mustard, salt, onion powder and pepper; set aside.
2. Place potatoes in a small saucepan and cover with water. Bring to a boil. Reduce heat; cover and simmer until tender, 15-20 minutes. Drain and cool; cut into quarters.
3. Place beans in another saucepan and cover with water. Bring to a boil. Cover and cook until crisp-tender, 3-5 minutes; drain and rinse in cold water.
4. Divide lettuce between 2 salad plates; top with potatoes, beans, tomatoes, olives, eggs and tuna. Drizzle with the dressing.
1 salad: 613 cal., 49g fat (8g sat. fat), 242mg chol., 886mg sod., 18g carb. (3g sugars, 3g fiber), 26g pro.

PROSCIUTTO PASTA TOSS

I love quick, simple pasta dishes, and this is one of my favorites. I prepare a tossed green salad while the pasta cooks and serve up a lovely light supper in minutes!
—*Laura Murphy-Ogden, Charlotte, NC*

TAKES: 20 min. • **MAKES:** 6 servings

- 1 pkg. (16 oz.) linguine
- ½ cup fresh or frozen peas, thawed
- 2 Tbsp. minced garlic
- 1 Tbsp. Italian seasoning
- 1 tsp. pepper
- ¼ cup olive oil
- ½ lb. thinly sliced prosciutto or deli ham, chopped
- ¼ cup shredded Parmesan cheese

1. Cook linguine according to package directions, adding peas during the last 3 minutes. Meanwhile, in a large cast-iron or other heavy skillet, saute garlic, Italian seasoning and pepper in oil until garlic is tender, about 1 minute. Stir in prosciutto.
2. Drain linguine and peas; add to skillet and toss to coat. Sprinkle with cheese.
1⅓ cups: 461 cal., 16g fat (4g sat. fat), 36mg chol., 802mg sod., 58g carb. (3g sugars, 3g fiber), 22g pro.

SAUSAGE & SQUASH PENNE

I love using frozen cooked winter squash because the hard work—all the peeling, chopping and cooking—is already done for me.
—*Jennifer Roberts, South Burlington, VT*

TAKES: 30 min. • **MAKES:** 4 servings

- 2   cups uncooked penne pasta
- 1   pkg. (12 oz.) frozen cooked winter squash
- 2   Tbsp. olive oil
- 3   cooked Italian sausage links (4 oz. each), sliced
- 1   medium onion, chopped
- ¼   cup grated Parmesan cheese
- ¼   tsp. salt
- ¼   tsp. dried parsley flakes
- ¼   tsp. pepper
   Optional: Minced fresh parsley and additional grated Parmesan cheese

1. Cook pasta and squash according to package directions. Meanwhile, in a large skillet, heat oil over medium heat. Add sausage and onion; cook and stir until the sausage is browned and the onion is tender; keep warm.

2. In a small bowl, mix the squash, cheese, salt, parsley and pepper until blended. Drain pasta; transfer to a serving plate. Spoon squash mixture over pasta; top with sausage mixture. If desired, sprinkle with parsley and additional cheese.

¾ cup pasta with ½ cup sausage and ¼ cup squash: 468 cal., 26g fat (8g sat. fat), 40mg chol., 705mg sod., 41g carb. (4g sugars, 4g fiber), 19g pro.

STEAK WITH CREAMY PEPPERCORN SAUCE

My wife, Mailynn, and I both love spicy foods. This is one of her favorite dishes. I've been cooking it as a treat on her birthday for years.
—*David Collin, Martinez, CA*

PREP: 5 min. + chilling • **COOK:** 15 min.
MAKES: 4 servings

- 2   to 3 Tbsp. whole black peppercorns, crushed
- 1½   tsp. white pepper
- 4   boneless beef top loin steaks (12 oz. each)
- 1   tsp. salt
- ¼   cup butter, melted
- ¼   cup Worcestershire sauce
- 1   tsp. hot pepper sauce
- ¼   cup half-and-half cream

1. Combine peppercorns and pepper; rub over both sides of steaks. Chill for 1 hour.

2. Sprinkle salt in a large skillet; heat on high until salt begins to brown. Add steaks and brown on both sides. Add butter; reduce heat to medium-high; cook steaks 1-2 minutes on each side.

3. Add Worcestershire and hot pepper sauce; cook until meat reaches desired doneness (for medium-rare, a thermometer should read 135°; medium, 140°; medium-well, 145°), 2-3 minutes longer. Remove steaks and keep warm. Add cream to the skillet; cook and stir until smooth. Serve with steaks.

Note: Top loin steak may be labeled as strip steak, Kansas City steak, New York strip steak, ambassador steak or boneless club steak in your region.

1 steak with 2 Tbsp. sauce: 487 cal., 17g fat (7g sat. fat), 157mg chol., 919mg sod., 5g carb. (2g sugars, 0 fiber), 73g pro.

SWEET & TANGY SHRIMP

With its delightfully sweet-tangy flavor, this easy entree is destined to become a hit with your gang! My husband and I adapted the recipe from one in a magazine, and we just love it.
—Kathleen Davis, North Bend, WA

TAKES: 30 min. • **MAKES:** 4 servings

- ½ cup ketchup
- 2 Tbsp. sugar
- 2 Tbsp. cider vinegar
- 2 Tbsp. reduced-sodium soy sauce
- 1 tsp. sesame oil
- ¼ tsp. crushed red pepper flakes
- 1½ lbs. uncooked medium shrimp, peeled and deveined
- 1 Tbsp. minced fresh gingerroot
- 1 Tbsp. canola oil
- 3 garlic cloves, minced
- 2 green onions, sliced
- 1 tsp. sesame seeds, toasted
  Hot cooked rice, optional

1. In a small bowl, combine the first 6 ingredients; set aside. In a large nonstick skillet or wok, stir-fry shrimp and ginger in oil until the shrimp turn pink. Add garlic; cook 1 minute longer.

2. Add the ketchup mixture; cook and stir until heated through, 2-3 minutes. Sprinkle with green onions and sesame seeds. If desired, serve with rice.

¾ cup: 241 cal., 7g fat (1g sat. fat), 252mg chol., 954mg sod., 17g carb. (10g sugars, 1g fiber), 28g pro.

COOL-KITCHEN TIP
To speed things up, use precooked shrimp; just add them at the same time as the ketchup mixture.

SHRIMP & NOODLE BOWLS

It'll look as if you got takeout, but this dish comes from your kitchen. Convenience items reduce the prep time.
—*Mary Bergfeld, Eugene, OR*

TAKES: 25 min. • **MAKES:** 6 servings

- 8 oz. uncooked angel hair pasta
- 1 lb. cooked small shrimp
- 2 cups broccoli coleslaw mix
- 6 green onions, thinly sliced
- ½ cup minced fresh cilantro
- ⅔ cup reduced-fat sesame ginger salad dressing

Cook pasta according to package directions; drain and rinse in cold water. Transfer to a large bowl. Add the shrimp, coleslaw mix, green onions and cilantro. Drizzle with dressing; toss to coat. Cover and refrigerate until serving.
Note: Swap in whole wheat pasta and you'll boost the fiber to 5g per serving.
1⅓ cups: 260 cal., 3g fat (0 sat. fat), 147mg chol., 523mg sod., 36g carb. (6g sugars, 2g fiber), 22g pro. **Diabetic exchanges:** 2 starch, 2 lean meat, 1 vegetable.

STEAK STIR-FRY

No one would guess this elegant entree is a snap to prepare at the last minute. To save even more prep time, use frozen mixed veggies instead of fresh. I will sometimes substitute chicken, chicken bouillon and curry for the beef, beef bouillon and ginger.
—*Janis Plourde, Smooth Rock Falls, ON*

TAKES: 25 min. • **MAKES:** 4 servings

- 1 tsp. beef bouillon granules
- 1 cup boiling water
- 2 Tbsp. cornstarch
- ⅓ cup soy sauce
- 1 lb. beef top sirloin steak, cut into thin strips
- 1 garlic clove, minced
- 1 tsp. ground ginger
- ¼ tsp. pepper
- 2 Tbsp. canola oil, divided
- 1 large green pepper, julienned
- 1 cup julienned carrots or sliced celery
- 5 green onions, cut into 1-in. pieces Hot cooked rice

1. Dissolve bouillon in the boiling water. Combine the cornstarch and soy sauce until smooth; add to bouillon. Set aside. Toss beef with garlic, ginger and pepper. In a large skillet or wok over medium-high heat, stir-fry beef in 1 Tbsp. oil until meat is no longer pink; remove and keep warm.
2. In the same pan, heat remaining 1 Tbsp. oil; stir-fry vegetables until crisp-tender. Stir soy sauce mixture and add to the pan; bring to a boil. Cook and stir for 2 minutes. Return meat to pan and heat through. Serve with rice.
1 cup: 266 cal., 13g fat (3g sat. fat), 63mg chol., 1484mg sod., 12g carb. (4g sugars, 2g fiber), 25g pro.

SAKE-STEAMED SOLE WITH SPICY SLAW

This healthy fish and zippy slaw can be prepared easily on a weeknight or for a special occasion. I like to serve this dish with rice.
—*Donna Noel, Gray, ME*

PREP: 25 min. • **COOK:** 10 min.
MAKES: 4 servings

- ¾ cup chicken broth
- ½ cup sake
- ½ cup mirin (sweet rice wine)
- ¼ cup reduced-sodium soy sauce
- 2 Tbsp. sugar
- ⅛ tsp. salt
- ⅛ tsp. pepper
- 4 sole or whitefish fillets (4 oz. each)

SLAW
- 1½ cups shredded Chinese or napa cabbage
- ⅓ cup each julienned cucumber, radishes, carrot and sweet red pepper
- 2 jalapeno peppers, seeded and julienned
- 2 Tbsp. minced fresh cilantro
- 2 Tbsp. minced fresh mint
- 2 Tbsp. plus 2 tsp. rice vinegar
- 4½ tsp. reduced-sodium soy sauce
- ⅛ tsp. salt
- ⅛ tsp. pepper

1. In a large skillet, combine the first 7 ingredients. Bring to a boil; add fish. Reduce heat; cover and simmer until fish just begins to flake easily with a fork, 8-10 minutes.
2. Combine cabbage, cucumber, radishes, carrot, red pepper, jalapenos, cilantro and mint. In a second bowl, combine vinegar, soy sauce, salt and pepper; pour over vegetables and toss to coat. Serve with fish.
Note: Wear disposable gloves when cutting hot peppers; the oils can burn skin. Avoid touching your face.
1 fillet with ⅔ cup slaw: 271 cal., 7g fat (1g sat. fat), 71mg chol., 1357mg sod., 19g carb. (15g sugars, 1g fiber), 25g pro.

PORK FRIED RICE

My husband anxiously awaits the nights we have pork because he knows I'll use the leftovers in this recipe. Add a few fortune cookies to make the meal special.
—*Norma Reynolds, Overland Park, KS*

TAKES: 20 min. • **MAKES:** 4 servings

- 2 Tbsp. canola oil, divided
- ½ cup diced carrots
- ½ cup diced celery
- ½ cup diced sweet red pepper
- ½ cup sliced green onions
- 3 large eggs, lightly beaten
- 2 cups cubed cooked pork (about 1 lb.)
- 2 cups cold cooked rice
- 4 to 5 tsp. soy sauce
  Salt and pepper to taste

1. In a large skillet, heat 1 Tbsp. oil over medium heat. Add vegetables; cook and stir until crisp-tender. Remove from pan and keep warm.
2. Heat the remaining 1 Tbsp. oil over medium heat. Add eggs; cook and stir until completely set. Break up eggs. Add the pork, rice, soy sauce, salt, pepper and vegetables; cook, stirring, until heated through.
1¼ cups: 382 cal., 17g fat (4g sat. fat), 203mg chol., 428mg sod., 26g carb. (2g sugars, 2g fiber), 28g pro.

NECTARINE CHICKEN SALAD

When guests are coming for lunch or dinner in the warm summer months, I like to serve this attractive, colorful salad. The dressing is refreshingly tart. A neighbor shared the recipe years ago and I've passed it on many times.
—*Cathy Ross, Van Nuys, CA*

TAKES: 15 min. • **MAKES:** 4 servings

- ¼ cup lime juice
- 1 Tbsp. sugar
- 1 Tbsp. minced fresh thyme or 1 tsp. dried thyme
- 1 Tbsp. olive oil
- 1 garlic clove, minced
- 6 cups torn mixed salad greens
- 1 lb. boneless skinless chicken breasts, cooked and sliced
- 5 medium ripe nectarines, thinly sliced

1. In a jar with a tight-fitting lid, combine the lime juice, sugar, thyme, oil and garlic; shake well.

2. On a serving platter, arrange salad greens, chicken and nectarines. Drizzle with dressing. Serve immediately.

1½ cups: 266 cal., 7g fat (1g sat. fat), 63mg chol., 76mg sod., 27g carb. (21g sugars, 5g fiber), 26g pro. **Diabetic Exchanges:** 3 lean meat, 1½ starch, 1 vegetable, 1 fat.

READER RAVE

"Wonderfully light and refreshing. The dressing is delicious. I added a touch of crumbled blue cheese, scallions and celery."

—ANNRMS, TASTEOFHOME.COM

CUMIN QUINOA PATTIES

These easy-to-make veggie burgers pack an amazing taste, and the crunch from the quinoa makes the texture to die for. Pan-frying them brings the crunch to the next level. The mixture can be made ahead of time and it freezes very well. Enjoy!
—*Beth Klein, Arlington, VA*

TAKES: 30 min. • **MAKES:** 4 servings

- 1 cup water
- ½ cup quinoa, rinsed
- 1 medium carrot, cut into 1-in. pieces
- 1 cup canned cannellini beans, rinsed and drained
- ¼ cup panko bread crumbs
- 3 green onions, chopped
- 1 large egg, lightly beaten
- 3 tsp. ground cumin
- ¼ tsp. salt
- ⅛ tsp. pepper
- 2 Tbsp. olive oil
  Optional: Sour cream, salsa and minced fresh cilantro

1. In a small saucepan, bring the water to a boil. Add quinoa. Reduce heat; simmer, covered, until the liquid is absorbed, 12-15 minutes. Remove from heat; fluff with a fork.
2. Meanwhile, place carrot in a food processor; pulse until coarsely chopped. Add beans; process until chopped. Transfer mixture to a large bowl. Mix in cooked quinoa, bread crumbs, green onions, egg and seasonings. Shape mixture into 8 patties.
3. In a large skillet, heat oil over medium heat. Add patties; cook until a thermometer reads 160°, 3-4 minutes on each side, turning carefully. If desired, serve with sour cream, salsa and minced fresh cilantro.
Freeze option: Freeze cooled patties in freezer containers, separating layers with waxed paper. Reheat patties on a baking sheet in a 325° oven until heated through.
2 patties: 235 cal., 10g fat (1g sat. fat), 47mg chol., 273mg sod., 28g carb. (2g sugars, 5g fiber), 8g pro. **Diabetic Exchanges:** 2 starch, 1½ fat, 1 lean meat.

PESTO SHRIMP PASTA

A dash of red pepper puts zip in this lively main dish.
—*Gloria Jones Grenga, Newnan, GA*

TAKES: 30 min. • **MAKES:** 4 servings

- 8 oz. uncooked spaghetti
- 3 Tbsp. olive oil, divided
- 1 cup loosely packed fresh basil leaves
- ¼ cup lemon juice
- 2 garlic cloves, peeled
- ½ tsp. salt
- 1 lb. fresh asparagus, trimmed and cut into 2-in. pieces
- ¾ lb. uncooked medium shrimp, peeled and deveined
- ⅛ tsp. crushed red pepper flakes

1. Cook spaghetti according to package directions. Meanwhile, in a blender, combine 1 Tbsp. oil, the basil, lemon juice, garlic and salt; cover and process until smooth.
2. In a large skillet, saute asparagus in remaining 2 Tbsp. oil until crisp-tender. Add shrimp and pepper flakes. Cook and stir until shrimp turn pink.
3. Drain spaghetti; place in a large bowl. Add basil mixture; toss to coat. Add shrimp mixture and mix well.
1 cup: 393 cal., 12g fat (2g sat. fat), 103mg chol., 406mg sod., 47g carb. (3g sugars, 3g fiber), 23g pro.

MUGHALI CHICKEN

I enjoy cooking for my family, and I try to incorporate healthy new foods into our menus. This authentic Indian dish is a favorite.
—Aruna Kancharla, Bentonville, AR

TAKES: 30 min. • **MAKES:** 6 servings

- 4 cardamom pods
- 10 garlic cloves, peeled
- 6 whole cloves
- 4½ tsp. chopped fresh gingerroot
- 1 Tbsp. unblanched almonds
- 1 Tbsp. salted cashews
- 1 tsp. ground cinnamon
- 6 small red onions, halved and sliced
- 4 jalapeno peppers, seeded and finely chopped
- ¼ cup canola oil
- 3 Tbsp. water
- 1½ lbs. boneless skinless chicken breasts, cut into ½-in. cubes
- 1 cup coconut milk
- 1 cup plain yogurt
- 1 tsp. ground turmeric
  Fresh cilantro leaves
  Optional: Naan flatbreads or hot cooked basmati rice

1. Remove seeds from cardamom pods; place in a food processor. Add the garlic, cloves, ginger, almonds, cashews and cinnamon; cover and process until blended. Set aside.

2. In a large skillet, saute onions and jalapenos in oil until tender. Stir in water and the garlic mixture. Add the chicken, coconut milk, yogurt and turmeric. Bring to a boil. Reduce heat; simmer, uncovered, until chicken juices run clear, 8-10 minutes. Sprinkle with cilantro. Serve with naan or rice if desired.

Note: Wear disposable gloves when cutting hot peppers; the oils can burn skin. Avoid touching your face.

1 cup: 367 cal., 23g fat (10g sat. fat), 68mg chol., 93mg sod., 14g carb. (5g sugars, 3g fiber), 27g pro.

BEST VEAL SCALLOPINI

I found the original version of this dish in a magazine and adjusted it to suit my family's tastes. Delicate, fine-textured veal needs only a short cooking time, which makes this simple entree even more attractive.
—*Ruth Lee, Troy, ON*

TAKES: 25 min. • **MAKES:** 2 servings

2	veal cutlets (about 4 oz. each)
2	Tbsp. all-purpose flour
½	tsp. salt
¼	tsp. pepper
3	Tbsp. butter, divided
1	Tbsp. olive oil
¼	lb. fresh mushrooms, thinly sliced
⅓	cup chicken broth
2	tsp. minced fresh parsley

1. Flatten veal cutlets to ⅛-in. thickness. In a shallow dish, combine flour, salt and pepper. Add the cutlets; turn to coat. In a skillet, heat 2 Tbsp. butter and the oil over medium heat. Add veal; cook until juices run clear, about 1 minute on each side. Remove and keep warm.
2. Add mushrooms to skillet; cook and stir until tender, 2-3 minutes. Spoon over veal. Stir broth into the skillet, stirring to loosen any browned bits. Add parsley and the remaining 1 Tbsp. butter; cook and stir until slightly thickened, 1-2 minutes longer. Pour over veal and mushrooms.
1 serving: 435 cal., 35g fat (16g sat. fat), 120mg chol., 941mg sod., 8g carb. (0 sugars, 0 fiber), 21g pro.
Wiener Schnitzel: Omit the oil, mushrooms, chicken broth and parsley. Coat cutlets with flour mixture, then dip in 1 beaten egg and coat with ⅓ cup dry bread crumbs. Cook veal in the entire amount of butter. Serve with lemon slices.

TILAPIA WITH CUCUMBER RELISH

My husband isn't big on fish, but he enjoys this mild-tasting tilapia. The relish adds garden-fresh flavor and pretty color to the lightly browned fillets.
—*Mary VanHollebeke, Wyandotte, MI*

TAKES: 15 min. • **MAKES:** 4 servings

⅔	cup chopped seeded cucumber
½	cup chopped radishes
1	Tbsp. tarragon vinegar
1	tsp. olive oil
½	tsp. salt, divided
¼	tsp. pepper, divided
⅛	tsp. sugar
⅛	tsp. paprika
4	tilapia fillets (6 oz. each)
1	Tbsp. butter

1. In a small bowl, combine cucumber and radishes. In another small bowl, whisk the vinegar, oil, ¼ tsp. salt, ⅛ tsp. pepper and the sugar. Pour over cucumber mixture; toss to coat evenly. Combine paprika and remaining ¼ tsp. salt and ⅛ tsp. pepper; sprinkle over fillets.
2. In a large nonstick skillet coated with cooking spray, melt butter. Add fish; cook for 3-4 minutes on each side or until fish flakes easily with a fork. Serve with cucumber relish.
1 fillet with ¼ cup relish: 181 cal., 6g fat (3g sat. fat), 90mg chol., 384mg sod., 1g carb. (1g sugars, 0 fiber), 32g pro. **Diabetic Exchanges:** 4 lean meat, 1 fat.

CHICKEN STREET TACOS WITH CORN-JICAMA SALSA

Here's a light, speedy meal you can enjoy anytime. These tacos are quite tasty, and the jicama in the salsa boosts the nutritional value. Win-win!
—*Priscilla Gilbert, Indian Harbour Beach, FL*

PREP: 30 min. • **COOK:** 15 min.
MAKES: 4 servings

- 1 cup Mexicorn, drained
- ½ cup canned black beans, rinsed and drained
- ½ cup finely chopped peeled jicama
- 2 Tbsp. minced fresh cilantro
- 1 Tbsp. lime juice
- ¼ tsp. ground cumin
- ¼ tsp. salt

GUACAMOLE
- 1 medium ripe avocado, peeled and pitted
- 1 small tomato, seeded and chopped
- 4½ tsp. lime juice
- ¼ tsp. salt

TACOS
- 2 tsp. chili powder
- 1 tsp. ground cumin
- 1 tsp. dried oregano
- ¼ tsp. salt
- 1 lb. boneless skinless chicken breasts, cut into thin strips
- 8 flour tortillas (6 in.), warmed

1. In a small bowl, combine corn, beans, jicama, cilantro, lime juice, cumin and salt. Cover and refrigerate until serving.
2. In another small bowl, mash avocado. Stir in the tomato, lime juice and salt. Cover and refrigerate until serving.
3. Combine the chili powder, cumin, oregano and salt. Add chicken and toss to coat evenly. In a lightly greased nonstick skillet, saute chicken until no longer pink.
4. Spread each tortilla with 2 Tbsp. guacamole; top with chicken and ¼ cup salsa. Fold tortillas in half.
2 tacos: 465 cal., 16g fat (2g sat. fat), 63mg chol., 1351mg sod., 49g carb. (5g sugars, 8g fiber), 33g pro.

SAUCY SKILLET FISH

The main industry here on Kodiak Island is fishing, so I'm always on the lookout for new seafood recipes. This is my favorite way to fix halibut or salmon, since it's quick and tasty. I often get requests for the recipe when I serve it to guests.
—*Merle Powell, Kodiak, AK*

TAKES: 20 min. • **MAKES:** 8 servings

- ½ cup all-purpose flour
- 1¼ tsp. salt
- 1 tsp. paprika
- ⅛ tsp. pepper
- 2 lbs. halibut, haddock or salmon fillets or steaks
- 1 medium onion, sliced
- ⅓ cup butter, cubed
- 1½ cups sour cream
- 1 tsp. dried basil
- 1 Tbsp. minced fresh parsley

1. In a large bowl, combine the flour, salt, paprika and pepper. Add fish and toss to coat (if using fillets, cut into serving-size pieces first).
2. In a large cast-iron or other heavy skillet, saute onion in butter until tender; remove and set aside. Add fish to the skillet, cook over medium heat until fish just begins to flake easily with a fork, 3-5 minutes on each side. Remove fish to a serving plate and keep warm.
3. Add the sour cream, basil and onion to the skillet; heat through (do not boil). Serve with fish. Garnish with parsley.
1 serving: 319 cal., 18g fat (10g sat. fat), 87mg chol., 531mg sod., 9g carb. (3g sugars, 1g fiber), 26g pro.

CHICKEN CUTLET

I love this combination of chicken and cheese. Parmesan cheese, garlic powder and onion powder flavor the golden chicken cutlet, which is coated with seasoned bread crumbs.
—*Marie Hoyer, Lewistown, MT*

TAKES: 20 min. • **MAKES:** 1 serving

- 1 tsp. all-purpose flour
  Dash each garlic powder,
  onion powder and pepper
- 2 Tbsp. grated Parmesan cheese
- 2 Tbsp. buttermilk
- 3 Tbsp. seasoned bread crumbs
- 1 boneless skinless chicken breast
  half (6 oz.)
- 2 tsp. canola oil

1. In a shallow bowl, combine flour, garlic powder, onion powder and pepper. In another bowl, combine cheese and buttermilk. Place the bread crumbs in a third shallow bowl.
2. Flatten chicken to ¼-in. thickness. Coat chicken with flour mixture; dip in buttermilk, then coat with crumbs.
3. In a skillet over medium heat, cook chicken in oil for 5-7 minutes on each side or until no longer pink.
1 serving: 405 cal., 17g fat (4g sat. fat), 104mg chol., 636mg sod., 19g carb. (3g sugars, 1g fiber), 41g pro. **Diabetic Exchanges:** 5 lean meat, 2 fat, 1 starch.

COOL-KITCHEN TIP
You can make these cutlets ahead of time. Just be sure to store them in an airtight container in the fridge and use them within 3-4 days. They'd be great in a sandwich, or cut into strips to top a salad.

RAMEN NOODLE STIR-FRY

This mildly flavored stir-fry combines tender strips of chicken with vegetables and popular ramen noodles. I came up with this recipe when I wanted a quick-fix meal for myself. Sometimes I change the vegetables or substitute ground turkey for the chicken.
—*Dawn Boothe, Lynn Haven, FL*

TAKES: 15 min. • **MAKES:** 2 servings

- 1 pkg. (3 oz.) ramen noodles
- 8 oz. boneless skinless chicken breasts, cut into 2-in. strips
- 2 tsp. canola oil, divided
- 1 large green pepper, cubed
- ⅔ cup chopped onion
- 1 garlic clove, minced
- ½ cup reduced-sodium chicken broth
- 2 tsp. reduced-sodium soy sauce
- 1 tsp. salt-free seasoning blend
- 1 small tomato, cut into wedges

1. In a bowl, place noodles in 1½ cups hot water for 2 minutes; drain and set aside. Discard seasoning packet or save for future use.
2. In a large nonstick skillet, stir-fry chicken in 1 tsp. oil until no longer pink. Remove and keep warm.
3. Stir-fry the green pepper, onion and garlic in the remaining 1 tsp. oil until crisp-tender. Add the chicken, broth, soy sauce, seasoning blend and noodles; toss gently. Add tomato; heat through.
2 cups: 410 cal., 15g fat (5g sat. fat), 63mg chol., 548mg sod., 38g carb. (6g sugars, 3g fiber), 30g pro. **Diabetic Exchanges:** 3 lean meat, 2 starch, 1 vegetable, 1 fat.

SALMON WITH VEGETABLE SALSA

This recipe is delightful. You can pair the salsa with grilled chicken breasts or barbecued shrimp kabobs too. The only fresh ingredient not available in my son's garden was the avocado! Make a double batch of the salsa to serve with crisp tortilla chips.

—Priscilla Gilbert, Indian Harbour Beach, FL

TAKES: 30 min. • **MAKES:** 4 servings

- 1½ cups grape tomatoes, halved
- 1½ cups chopped peeled cucumber
- 1 medium ripe avocado, peeled and cubed
- 1 small red onion, chopped
- 2 Tbsp. minced fresh cilantro
- 1 jalapeno pepper, seeded and minced
- 2 Tbsp. lime juice
- ½ tsp. salt

FISH
- 4 salmon fillets (6 oz. each)
- 1 Tbsp. lime juice
- ½ tsp. salt
- ¼ tsp. cayenne pepper
- 1 Tbsp. butter

1. For the salsa, combine the tomatoes, cucumber, avocado, onion, cilantro, jalapeno, lime juice and salt; set aside.

2. Drizzle salmon with lime juice. Sprinkle with salt and cayenne pepper. In a large skillet, cook the fillets in butter until fish flakes easily with a fork, 3-4 minutes on each side. Serve with salsa.

Note: Wear disposable gloves when cutting hot peppers; the oils can burn skin. Avoid touching your face.

1 fillet with 1 cup salsa: 438 cal., 28g fat (6g sat. fat), 108mg chol., 721mg sod., 11g carb. (3g sugars, 4g fiber), 36g pro.

SHRIMP PASTA PRIMAVERA

They say the way to a man's heart is through his stomach. So when I invite that special guy to dinner, I like to prepare something equally wonderful. This well-seasoned pasta dish has tons of flavor.
—Shari Neff, Takoma Park, MD

TAKES: 15 min. • **MAKES:** 2 servings

- 4 oz. uncooked angel hair pasta
- 8 jumbo shrimp, peeled and deveined
- 6 fresh asparagus spears, trimmed and cut into 2-in. pieces
- ¼ cup olive oil
- 2 garlic cloves, minced
- ½ cup sliced fresh mushrooms
- ½ cup chicken broth
- 1 small plum tomato, peeled, seeded and diced
- ¼ tsp. salt
- ⅛ tsp. crushed red pepper flakes
- 1 Tbsp. each minced fresh basil, oregano, thyme and parsley
- ¼ cup grated Parmesan cheese

1. Cook pasta according to package directions. Meanwhile, in a large skillet, saute shrimp and asparagus in oil until shrimp turn pink, 3-4 minutes. Add garlic; cook 1 minute longer. Add the mushrooms, broth, tomato, salt and red pepper flakes; simmer, uncovered, for 2 minutes.
2. Drain pasta. Add the pasta and fresh herbs to skillet; toss to coat. Sprinkle with cheese.
1 serving: 581 cal., 32g fat (6g sat. fat), 89mg chol., 783mg sod., 49g carb. (4g sugars, 3g fiber), 24g pro.

MANDARIN-BERRY STEAK SALAD

Here's a salad that even meat lovers will ask for time and again. Sirloin steak, strawberries, pecans and goat cheese work extremely well together. Give it a try!
—Taste of Home *Test Kitchen*

TAKES: 25 min.
MAKES: 4 servings (1 cup vinaigrette)

- 3 Tbsp. olive oil
- ¼ cup cider vinegar
- ¼ cup orange juice
- 2 Tbsp. minced fresh parsley
- 2 Tbsp. honey
- 1 garlic clove, minced
- 1 tsp. chili sauce
- ½ tsp. salt
- 8 cups torn romaine
- ½ lb. cooked beef sirloin steak, sliced
- 3 cups sliced fresh strawberries
- 1 small red onion, sliced
- 1 can (11 oz.) mandarin oranges, drained
- ½ cup chopped pecans, toasted
- 2 oz. fresh goat cheese, crumbled

In a small bowl, whisk first 8 ingredients; set aside. Divide romaine among 4 plates; top with steak, strawberries, onion, oranges, pecans and cheese. Serve with vinaigrette.
1 serving: 443 cal., 24g fat (4g sat. fat), 46mg chol., 367mg sod., 40g carb. (31g sugars, 7g fiber), 21g pro.

PAN-FRIED SCALLOPS WITH WHITE WINE REDUCTION

I learned the art of reduction from a cooking class—the flavor is fabulous! Despite the fancy title, this special-occasion entree is easy to prepare.
—*Katherine Robinson, Glenwood Springs, CO*

TAKES: 30 min. • **MAKES:** 8 servings

- 2 lbs. sea scallops
- 1 tsp. salt
- ¼ tsp. pepper
- 2 Tbsp. olive oil

WHITE WINE REDUCTION

- ½ cup white wine or chicken broth
- ⅓ cup orange juice
- ¼ cup finely chopped onion
- 1 tsp. dried oregano
- 1 tsp. Dijon mustard
- 1 garlic clove, minced
- 3 Tbsp. cold butter, cubed

1. Sprinkle scallops with salt and pepper. In a large skillet, saute scallops in oil until firm and opaque. Remove and keep warm.
2. Add wine to the skillet, stirring to loosen browned bits from pan. Stir in the orange juice, onion, oregano, mustard and garlic. Bring to a boil; cook and stir until reduced by half, 2-3 minutes. Remove from the heat; stir in butter until melted. Serve with scallops.

4 scallops with 2 Tbsp. sauce: 181 cal., 9g fat (3g sat. fat), 49mg chol., 524mg sod., 5g carb. (1g sugars, 0 fiber), 19g pro.
Diabetic Exchanges: 3 lean meat, 2 fat.
Scallops with Citrus Herb Sauce: Omit White Wine Reduction. Cook scallops as directed. Wipe skillet clean if necessary. Saute 3 minced garlic cloves in 2 Tbsp. butter until tender; stir in ⅓ cup dry sherry. Cook until liquid is almost evaporated; stir in 2 Tbsp. lemon juice, ½ tsp. minced fresh oregano and ½ tsp. minced fresh tarragon. Serve with scallops.

EASY CITRUS SEAFOOD SALAD

This super simple, deceptively delicious recipe was inspired by a seafood salad I had in the Bahamas that featured conch. Conch is hard to get where I live, so I substituted crab and shrimp—and I like it even more!
—*Cindy Heyd, Edmond, OK*

TAKES: 15 min. • **MAKES:** 4 servings

- 1 medium orange
- 1 medium lemon
- 1 medium lime
- ½ lb. peeled and deveined cooked shrimp, coarsely chopped
- ½ lb. refrigerated fresh or imitation crabmeat, coarsely chopped
- 2 Tbsp. finely chopped sweet onion
- 2 Tbsp. finely chopped sweet red pepper
  Shredded lettuce
  Assorted crackers

Finely grate zest from orange. Cut orange crosswise in half; squeeze juice from orange. Transfer zest and juice to a large bowl. Repeat with lemon and lime. Add shrimp, crab, onion and pepper; toss to coat. Serve on lettuce with crackers.
¾ cup: 128 cal., 2g fat (0 sat. fat), 141mg chol., 309mg sod., 6g carb. (3g sugars, 1g fiber), 22g pro. **Diabetic Exchanges:** 3 lean meat.

PINEAPPLE SHRIMP TACOS

Taste the tropics with our cool and crispy take on shrimp tacos. Wrapping the shells in lettuce adds even more crunch, while keeping the tacos tidy after you take a bite.
—Taste of Home *Test Kitchen*

TAKES: 25 min. • **MAKES:** 4 servings

- 1 lb. uncooked shrimp (26-30 per lb.), peeled and deveined
- 3 tsp. olive oil, divided
- 1 large sweet orange pepper, sliced
- 1 large sweet red pepper, sliced
- 1 small onion, halved and sliced
- 1 cup pineapple tidbits
- 1 envelope fajita seasoning mix
- ⅓ cup water
- 8 corn tortillas (6 in.), warmed
- ½ cup crumbled Cotija or shredded mozzarella cheese
- 8 large romaine lettuce leaves

1. Cook shrimp in 2 tsp. oil in a large cast-iron or other heavy skillet over medium heat until shrimp turn pink, 4-6 minutes. Remove and keep warm.
2. In the same skillet, saute peppers, onion and pineapple in remaining 1 tsp. oil until vegetables are tender. Add seasoning mix and the water. Bring to a boil; cook and stir 2 minutes.
3. Return shrimp to skillet; heat through. Spoon mixture onto tortillas; top with cheese. Wrap tacos in lettuce to serve.
2 tacos: 382 cal., 11g fat (4g sat. fat), 153mg chol., 1123mg sod., 44g carb. (13g sugars, 6g fiber), 27g pro.

READER RAVE

"Oh my word, we are so in love with these tacos!"

—LEIGHPARKINSON, TASTEOFHOME.COM

COOL-KITCHEN TIP
Don't preheat the skillet when making this recipe. You'll be pressing the dough into the skillet with your hands, so you don't want it to be hot. You can also use frozen dough for this recipe; just let it thaw before rolling it out.

SKILLET PIZZA

I created this recipe during a hot spell one summer. With the temperature in the 90s every day, I didn't want to turn on the oven. So I decided to make our favorite pizza in a skillet instead! If you have an electric skillet, this is a great dish to take along to get-togethers—prepare it at home, then plug in the skillet when you arrive.
—*Darlene Brenden, Salem, OR*

TAKES: 30 min. • **MAKES:** 6 servings

- 1 pkg. (6½ oz.) pizza crust mix
- 1 can (8 oz.) tomato sauce
- 1 tsp. Italian seasoning
- ½ cup pepperoni slices
- ¼ cup chopped onion
- ¼ cup chopped green pepper
- ¼ cup sliced ripe olives
- 2 cups shredded mozzarella cheese

1. Grease a 12-in. electric or stovetop skillet. Prepare pizza crust according to package directions.
2. Line bottom and ½ in. up the side of the skillet with dough. Combine tomato sauce and Italian seasoning; spread over dough. Layer pepperoni, onion, green pepper and olives over sauce; sprinkle with cheese.
3. Cover and cook over medium heat (set electric skillet to 375°) until crust is brown on bottom and cheese is melted, about 15 minutes. Slide pizza onto a cutting board. Serve immediately.
1 piece: 298 cal., 16g fat (7g sat. fat), 40mg chol., 847mg sod., 26g carb. (3g sugars, 2g fiber), 15g pro.

QUICK APRICOT CHICKEN

This is one of my favorite ways to fix chicken in a hurry. Everybody just loves it, and leftovers are always just as good the next day. For variation, I've used pork instead of chicken and added ingredients like pineapple, mandarin oranges, snow peas and broccoli.
—*Vicki Ruiz, Twin Falls, ID*

TAKES: 15 min. • **MAKES:** 4 servings

- ½ cup apricot preserves
- 2 Tbsp. reduced-sodium soy sauce
- 1 Tbsp. chicken broth or sherry
- 1 Tbsp. canola oil
- 1 Tbsp. cornstarch
- 1 tsp. minced garlic
- ¼ tsp. ground ginger
- 1 lb. boneless skinless chicken breasts, cut into strips
- 1 medium green pepper, chopped
- ½ cup salted cashews
  Hot cooked rice
  Crushed red pepper flakes, optional

1. In a shallow microwave-safe dish, combine the first 7 ingredients; stir in chicken. Cover and microwave on high for 3 minutes, stirring once.
2. Add green pepper and cashews. Cover and microwave on high for 2-4 minutes or until chicken is no longer pink, stirring once. Let stand for 3 minutes. Serve with rice and, if desired, sprinkle with red pepper flakes.
1 cup: 391 cal., 16g fat (3g sat. fat), 63mg chol., 673mg sod., 34g carb. (26g sugars, 2g fiber), 28g pro.

TURKEY SCALLOPINI

Quick-cooking turkey breast slices make it easy to prepare a satisfying meal in minutes. I've also flattened boneless skinless chicken breast halves to use in place of the turkey.
—*Karen Adams, Cleveland, TN*

TAKES: 20 min. • **MAKES:** 4 servings

- 1 pkg. (17.6 oz.) turkey breast cutlets
- ¼ cup all-purpose flour
- ⅛ tsp. salt
- ⅛ tsp. pepper
- 1 large egg
- 2 Tbsp. water
- 1 cup soft bread crumbs
- ½ cup grated Parmesan cheese
- ¼ cup butter, cubed
  Minced fresh parsley

1. Flatten turkey to ¼-in. thickness. In a shallow bowl, combine the flour, salt and pepper. In another bowl, beat egg and water. In a third shallow bowl, combine bread crumbs and cheese.
2. Dredge turkey in flour mixture, then dip in egg mixture and coat with crumbs. Let stand for 5 minutes.
3. Melt butter in a large skillet over medium-high heat; cook turkey until the meat is no longer pink and the coating is golden brown, 2-3 minutes on each side. Sprinkle with parsley.
Note: To make soft bread crumbs, tear bread into pieces and place in a food processor or blender. Cover and pulse until crumbs form. One slice of bread yields ½-¾ cup crumbs.
4 oz. cooked turkey: 358 cal., 17g fat (10g sat. fat), 169mg chol., 463mg sod., 12g carb. (1g sugars, 0 fiber), 38g pro.
Chicken Scallopini: Substitute 4 boneless skinless chicken breast halves for the turkey; flatten to ¼-in. thickness and proceed as directed.

HERBED TUNA SALAD

Cooking for two is a challenge for us, since my husband and I do not care for leftovers. This well-seasoned salad with a distinctive dill flavor is my favorite lunch recipe.
—*Rebecca Schweizer, Chesapeake, VA*

TAKES: 15 min. • **MAKES:** 2 servings

- 1 can (6 oz.) light water-packed tuna, drained and flaked
- 2 Tbsp. finely chopped red onion
- 1 tsp. minced fresh parsley
- 1½ tsp. dill weed
- ⅛ tsp. garlic salt
- ⅛ tsp. dried thyme
- ⅛ tsp. pepper
- Pinch cayenne pepper
- 2 Tbsp. fat-free mayonnaise
- 1 Tbsp. reduced-fat sour cream
- 3 cups Boston lettuce leaves
- 6 grape tomatoes, sliced
  Optional: Sliced cucumber and fresh dill

1. In a small bowl, combine the first 8 ingredients. Combine the mayonnaise and sour cream; stir into the tuna mixture.
2. Divide the salad greens between 2 plates. Top with tuna mixture and tomatoes and, if desired, cucumbers and dill.
1 serving: 170 cal., 2g fat (1g sat. fat), 30mg chol., 452mg sod., 14g carb. (0 sugars, 4g fiber), 25g pro. **Diabetic Exchanges:** 3 lean meat, 2 vegetable.

TURKEY & APPLE ARUGULA SALAD

Try turkey anytime and not just at the holidays. Enjoy its flavor year-round in this refreshing salad with fresh fruit and salad greens.
—*Nancy Heishman, Las Vegas, NV*

TAKES: 20 min. • **MAKES:** 6 servings

- ½ cup orange juice
- 3 Tbsp. red wine vinegar
- 3 Tbsp. sesame oil
- 2 Tbsp. minced fresh chives
- ¼ tsp. salt
- ¼ tsp. coarsely ground pepper

SALAD

- 4 cups cubed cooked turkey
- 4 tsp. curry powder
- ½ tsp. freshly ground pepper
- ¼ tsp. salt
- 1 large apple, chopped
- 1 cup green grapes, halved
- 3 cups fresh arugula or baby spinach
- 1 can (11 oz.) mandarin oranges, drained
- ½ cup chopped walnuts
- ½ cup pomegranate seeds

1. For dressing, whisk together the first 6 ingredients.

2. Place turkey in a large bowl; sprinkle with seasonings and toss to combine. Stir in apple and grapes. Add arugula and mandarin oranges. Drizzle with dressing; toss lightly to combine.

3. Sprinkle with walnuts and pomegranate seeds. Serve immediately.

1½ cups: 354 cal., 17g fat (3g sat. fat), 94mg chol., 301mg sod., 22g carb. (17g sugars, 3g fiber), 30g pro.

SIMPLE SESAME CHICKEN WITH COUSCOUS

I created this dish after my three kids tried Chinese takeout and asked for more. To make things easy for myself, I typically use a rotisserie chicken from the deli.
—Naylet LaRochelle, Miami, FL

TAKES: 25 min. • **MAKES:** 4 servings

- 1½ cups water
- 1 cup uncooked whole wheat couscous
- 1 Tbsp. olive oil
- 2 cups coleslaw mix
- 4 green onions, sliced
- 2 Tbsp. plus ½ cup reduced-fat Asian toasted sesame salad dressing, divided
- 2 cups shredded cooked chicken breast
- 2 Tbsp. minced fresh cilantro Chopped peanuts, optional

1. In a small saucepan, bring water to a boil. Stir in couscous. Remove from heat; let stand, covered, 5-10 minutes or until water is absorbed. Fluff with a fork.
2. In a large nonstick skillet, heat oil over medium heat. Add coleslaw mix; cook and stir 3-4 minutes or just until tender. Add green onions, 2 Tbsp. dressing and couscous; heat through. Remove couscous mixture from pan; keep warm.
3. In same skillet, add chicken and the remaining ½ cup dressing; cook and stir over medium heat until heated through. Serve over couscous mixture; top with cilantro and, if desired, peanuts.
1 cup couscous with ½ cup chicken:
320 cal., 9g fat (1g sat. fat), 54mg chol., 442mg sod., 35g carb. (9g sugars, 5g fiber), 26g pro. **Diabetic Exchanges:** 3 lean meat, 2 starch, 1 fat.

GARLIC LIME SHRIMP

Our son, a restaurant owner, showed me how to make this quick shrimp and noodle dish zipped up with garlic and cayenne. It's also tasty served over rice.
—Gertraud Casbarro, Summerville, SC

TAKES: 20 min. • **MAKES:** 4 servings

- 1 lb. uncooked shrimp (31-40 per lb.), peeled and deveined
- 5 garlic cloves, minced
- ½ tsp. salt
- ¼ to ½ tsp. cayenne pepper
- ½ cup butter
- 3 Tbsp. lime juice
- 1 Tbsp. minced fresh parsley Hot cooked pasta

In a large skillet, saute the shrimp, garlic, salt and cayenne in butter until the shrimp turn pink, about 5 minutes. Stir in lime juice and parsley. Serve with pasta.
1 cup shrimp: 309 cal., 25g fat (15g sat. fat), 199mg chol., 613mg sod., 3g carb. (0 sugars, 0 fiber), 19g pro.

CHICKEN FEATS

Rotisserie chicken—already cooked, tender and delicious—makes these summertime dishes a snap.

SPICY PEANUT CHICKEN & NOODLES

This simple recipe tastes like it took hours to make. Everybody says it has the perfect levels of heat and spice.
—*Sharon Collison, Newark, DE*

TAKES: 30 min. • **MAKES:** 4 servings

- 1 pkg. (10.8 oz.) frozen broccoli, carrot and sugar snap pea blend
- ¾ cup reduced-sodium chicken broth
- ⅓ cup creamy peanut butter
- ¼ cup teriyaki sauce
- ¼ tsp. pepper
- ¼ tsp. cayenne pepper
- 1 cup coarsely shredded rotisserie chicken
- 1 pkg. (8.8 oz.) thick rice noodles
- 3 green onions, thinly sliced on a diagonal
  Additional chicken broth, optional

1. Microwave frozen vegetables according to package directions.
2. Place broth, peanut butter, teriyaki sauce, pepper and cayenne in a large skillet; cook and stir over medium heat until blended. Stir in chicken; heat through. Stir in vegetables.
3. Prepare noodles according to package directions. Drain and immediately add to chicken mixture, tossing to combine. Sprinkle with green onions. If desired, moisten with additional broth. Serve immediately.

1 serving: 489 cal., 14g fat (3g sat. fat), 31mg chol., 971mg sod., 68g carb. (8g sugars, 4g fiber), 22g pro.

THAI CHICKEN COLESLAW

My love of Thai peanut sauce inspired this salad creation that always has me going back for seconds. It also makes a delicious side when made without chicken.
—*Jodi Ollerman, Bigfork, MT*

PREP: 20 min. + chilling
MAKES: 4 servings

- ¼ cup lime juice
- ¼ cup reduced-sodium soy sauce
- ¼ cup creamy peanut butter
- 2 Tbsp. honey
- 1 Tbsp. Sriracha chili sauce
- 1 garlic clove, minced
- 1 tsp. minced fresh gingerroot or ¼ tsp. ground ginger
- 1 tsp. sesame oil

SALAD
- 1 pkg. (14 oz.) coleslaw mix
- 1½ cups shredded rotisserie chicken, chilled
- 4 green onions, chopped
- ¼ cup chopped fresh cilantro
  Chopped honey-roasted peanuts, optional

1. For dressing, whisk first 8 ingredients until blended.
2. Place first 4 salad ingredients in a large bowl; toss with dressing. Refrigerate, covered, 1 hour. If desired, sprinkle each serving with peanuts.

1 cup: 286 cal., 13g fat (3g sat. fat), 47mg chol., 835mg sod., 23g carb. (15g sugars, 4g fiber), 21g pro.

POMEGRANATE, CHICKEN & FARRO SALAD

This salad recipe is special—simple, yet sophisticated—and never fails to win raves. I use quick-cooking farro, which takes only 10 minutes on the stovetop. Many stores now carry packaged pomegranate seeds in the refrigerated produce section year-round.
—*David Dahlman, Chatsworth, CA*

PREP: 15 min. • **COOK:** 25 min. + cooling
MAKES: 8 servings

- 1½ cups uncooked farro, rinsed, or wheat berries
- 2 medium ripe avocados, peeled, pitted and chopped
- 3 cups shredded rotisserie chicken
- ¾ cup chopped dried apricots
- ½ cup thinly sliced green onions
- ½ cup chopped walnuts, toasted
- 1 Tbsp. chopped seeded jalapeno pepper, optional
- ¾ cup pomegranate seeds
- ⅓ cup olive oil
- ¼ cup orange juice
- 3 Tbsp. white wine vinegar
- 1 Tbsp. Dijon mustard
- ½ tsp. salt
- ½ tsp. pepper

1. Place farro in large saucepan; add water to cover. Bring to a boil. Reduce heat; cook, covered, until tender, 25-30 minutes. Drain and cool.
2. Arrange farro, avocados, chicken, apricots, green onions, walnuts and, if desired, jalapeno on a platter. Sprinkle with pomegranate seeds. In a small bowl, whisk remaining ingredients until blended. Serve dressing with salad.
Note: Wear disposable gloves when cutting hot peppers; the oils can burn skin. Avoid touching your face.
1 serving: 482 cal., 24g fat (3g sat. fat), 47mg chol., 251mg sod., 44g carb. (9g sugars, 9g fiber), 23g pro.

P. 150

STRESS-FREE SIDE DISHES

What are you looking for in a side? A quick and tasty dish that will complement your main course without fading into the background? Look no further!

CHILLED ASPARAGUS WITH BASIL CREAM

This recipe is an all-time family favorite that has been served at most of our holiday meals. I like it because it's simple and can be prepared ahead of time.
—*Melissa Puccetti, Rohnert Park, CA*

TAKES: 20 min. • **MAKES:** 8 servings

- 2 lbs. fresh asparagus, trimmed
- 1 cup mayonnaise
- ¼ cup heavy whipping cream
- 4 Tbsp. minced fresh basil, divided
- 2 garlic cloves, peeled and halved
- ½ tsp. salt
- ¼ tsp. pepper
- 2 Tbsp. pine nuts, toasted
- 1 Tbsp. grated lemon zest

1. In a large saucepan, bring 8 cups water to a boil. Add half the asparagus; cook, uncovered, just until crisp-tender, 2-4 minutes. Remove and immediately drop into ice water. Drain and pat dry. Repeat with remaining asparagus. Arrange on a serving platter.
2. Place mayonnaise, cream, 3 Tbsp. basil, garlic, salt and pepper in a food processor; cover and process until blended. Spoon over asparagus (or serve on the side). Garnish with pine nuts, lemon zest and the remaining 1 Tbsp. minced basil.
1 serving: 235 cal., 24g fat (5g sat. fat), 10mg chol., 296mg sod., 3g carb. (1g sugars, 1g fiber), 2g pro.

MISO-BUTTERED SUCCOTASH

The miso paste used in this super simple recipe gives depth and a hint of savoriness to canned or fresh vegetables. To brighten the flavor profile even more, you could add a splash of your favorite white wine.
—*William Milton III, Clemson, SC*

TAKES: 20 min. • **MAKES:** 6 servings

- 2 tsp. canola oil
- 1 small red onion, chopped
- 2 cans (15¼ oz. each) whole-kernel corn, drained
- 1½ cups frozen shelled edamame, thawed
- ½ medium sweet red pepper, chopped (about ½ cup)
- 2 Tbsp. unsalted butter, softened
- 1 tsp. white miso paste
- 3 green onions, thinly sliced
  Coarsely ground pepper

1. In a large skillet, heat oil over medium-high heat. Add red onion; cook and stir until crisp-tender, 2-3 minutes. Add corn, edamame and red pepper. Cook until vegetables reach desired tenderness, 4-6 minutes longer.
2. In a small bowl, mix butter and miso paste until combined; stir into pan until melted. Sprinkle with green onions and pepper before serving.
¾ cup: 193 cal., 9g fat (3g sat. fat), 10mg chol., 464mg sod., 20g carb. (11g sugars, 6g fiber), 8g pro.

COOL-KITCHEN TIP
White miso paste has a subtle, salty flavor. You can increase the amount in this recipe for more flavor. Miso is delicious in soups or mixed into cold spreads—mayonnaise, cream cheese or sour cream. It can give salad dressings and marinades a lift, too.

SQUASH RIBBONS

Steamed and well seasoned, these pretty vegetable ribbons will dress up your dinner plate. The strips of yellow summer squash and zucchini are easy to cut using a vegetable peeler or cheese slicer.
—*Taste of Home Test Kitchen*

TAKES: 15 min. • **MAKES:** 2 servings

- 1 small yellow summer squash
- 1 small zucchini
- 1 Tbsp. butter, melted
- ¼ tsp. onion powder
- ¼ tsp. dried rosemary, crushed
- ⅛ tsp. salt
- ⅛ tsp. dried thyme
- ⅛ tsp. pepper

1. With a vegetable peeler or metal cheese slicer, cut very thin slices down the length of each squash, making long ribbons. Place in a steamer basket; place in a saucepan over 1 in. boiling water. Cover and steam until tender, 2-3 minutes.
2. In a small bowl, combine the butter, onion powder, rosemary, salt, thyme and pepper. Add squash and toss to coat.
¾ cup: 80 cal., 6g fat (4g sat. fat), 15mg chol., 206mg sod., 5g carb. (4g sugars, 2g fiber), 2g pro. **Diabetic exchanges:** 1½ fat, 1 vegetable.

SPINACH RICE

I like to serve this Greek-style rice dish alongside steaks with mushrooms. It makes an elegant meal that can easily be doubled for guests.
—*Jeanette Cakouros, Brunswick, ME*

TAKES: 20 min. • **MAKES:** 2 servings

- 2 Tbsp. olive oil
- ½ cup chopped onion
- ¾ cup water
- 1 Tbsp. dried parsley flakes
- ¼ to ½ tsp. salt
- ⅛ tsp. pepper
- ½ cup uncooked instant rice
- 2 cups fresh baby spinach

1. In a saucepan, heat oil over medium-high heat; saute onion until tender. Stir in water, parsley, salt and pepper; bring to a boil. Stir in rice; top with spinach.
2. Cover; remove from heat. Let stand until the rice is tender, 7-10 minutes. Stir to combine.

¾ cup: 235 cal., 14g fat (2g sat. fat), 0 chol., 326mg sod., 25g carb. (2g sugars, 2g fiber), 3g pro. **Diabetic exchanges:** 3 fat, 1½ starch, 1 vegetable.

READER RAVE

"Really tasty, simple but clever ... it lends well to adaptations. Thanks so much!"

—KIMFORKES, TASTEOFHOME.COM

SUMMER SQUASH & ZUCCHINI SIDE DISH

I'm trying to cut my risk for cardiac disease by changing the way I eat. This colorful side dish is packed with as much nutrition as fresh-picked flavor.
—*Marlene Agnelly, Ocean Springs, MS*

TAKES: 30 min. • **MAKES:** 6 servings

- 1 Tbsp. olive oil
- 1 medium yellow summer squash, quartered and sliced
- 1 medium zucchini, quartered and sliced
- 1 medium onion, chopped
- 1 medium sweet red pepper, cut into 1-in. pieces
- 2 garlic cloves, minced
- ½ tsp. salt-free spicy seasoning blend
- ¼ tsp. salt
- ⅛ tsp. pepper
- 1 medium tomato, chopped

In a large skillet, heat oil over medium heat; add yellow squash, zucchini, onion and red pepper. Cook and stir 5 minutes. Add garlic and seasonings; cook until vegetables are crisp-tender, 2-3 minutes. Stir in tomato; heat through.

⅔ cup: 50 cal., 3g fat (0 sat. fat), 0 chol., 106mg sod., 6g carb. (4g sugars, 2g fiber), 1g pro. **Diabetic exchanges:** 1 vegetable, ½ fat.

COOL-KITCHEN TIP
Feel free to play with this recipe—add corn, peas or whatever your garden is growing. Skip the seasoning blend and use fresh herbs from the garden or your favorite dried herbs from the pantry. Add a squeeze of lemon for a bright finish.

STIR-FRIED GREEN BEANS

In no time at all, I can stir-fry everyday green beans with garlic and a variety of herbs and spices for this flavorful side dish.
—*Heidi Wilcox, Lapeer, MI*

TAKES: 20 min. • **MAKES:** 2 servings

- 1 Tbsp. butter
- ½ lb. fresh green beans, trimmed
- 1 garlic clove, minced
- 1 tsp. minced fresh parsley
- ½ tsp. dried basil
- ¼ tsp. salt
- ¼ tsp. dried oregano
- ⅛ tsp. cayenne pepper

In a large nonstick skillet, melt butter over medium heat; add beans. Cook and stir until crisp-tender, 5-7 minutes. Add garlic; cook and stir 1 minute longer. Stir in parsley, basil, salt, oregano and cayenne.

¾ cup: 77 cal., 6g fat (4g sat. fat), 15mg chol., 358mg sod., 6g carb. (2g sugars, 3g fiber), 2g pro. **Diabetic exchanges:** 1 vegetable, 1 fat.

COOL-KITCHEN TIP
Since this recipe relies on so few ingredients, we don't recommend using frozen green beans—they lose their crisp-tender texture and will yield a soggy side dish. Save your frozen beans for soups, casseroles and other recipes that specifically call for them.

BEST BEETS

I enjoy preparing this recipe because it gives me a chance to use the tender, fresh beets from our garden. It's so good and very colorful!
—*Lucille Terry, Frankfort, KY*

TAKES: 20 min. • **MAKES:** 8 servings

- ¾ cup sugar
- 2 tsp. cornstarch
- ⅓ cup vinegar
- ⅓ cup water or beet liquid
- 1 tsp. ground mustard
- 1 tsp. onion powder
- 4 cups cooked, sliced beets
- 3 Tbsp. butter
- ¼ tsp. salt
  Dash white pepper

In a saucepan, combine the sugar and cornstarch. Add vinegar and water or beet liquid; bring to a boil. Add all remaining ingredients; reduce heat to simmer. Heat through.
¾ cup: 142 cal., 4g fat (3g sat. fat), 11mg chol., 282mg sod., 26g carb. (23g sugars, 2g fiber), 1g pro.

SPANISH RICE

You'll find my Spanish rice is so much better than any boxed variety in grocery stores. Best of all, it can be prepared in about the same time as those so-called convenience foods and uses items you already have in your pantry.
—*Anne Yaeger, Washington DC*

TAKES: 25 min. • **MAKES:** 6 servings

- ¼ cup butter, cubed
- 2 cups uncooked instant rice
- 1 can (14½ oz.) diced tomatoes, undrained
- 1 cup boiling water
- 2 beef bouillon cubes
- 1 medium onion, chopped
- 1 garlic clove, minced
- 1 bay leaf
- 1 tsp. sugar
- 1 tsp. salt
- ¼ tsp. pepper

In a saucepan, melt butter over medium heat. Add rice; cook and stir until lightly browned. Add remaining ingredients; bring to a boil. Reduce heat; cover and simmer until the liquid is absorbed and rice is tender, 10-15 minutes. Remove bay leaf before serving.
¾ cup: 217 cal., 8g fat (5g sat. fat), 20mg chol., 886mg sod., 33g carb. (4g sugars, 2g fiber), 4g pro.

FRIED ASPARAGUS

This battered asparagus is a favorite at events. It's fun to eat with a side of ranch dressing for dipping.
—*Lori Kimble, Montgomery, AL*

TAKES: 30 min. • **MAKES:** 2½ dozen

- 1 cup all-purpose flour
- ¾ cup cornstarch
- 1¼ tsp. salt
- 1¼ tsp. baking powder
- ¾ tsp. baking soda
- ¾ tsp. garlic salt
- ½ tsp. pepper
- 1 cup beer or nonalcoholic beer
- 3 large egg whites
- 2½ lbs. fresh asparagus, trimmed
  Oil for deep-fat frying
  Ranch salad dressing

1. In a large bowl, combine the first 7 ingredients. Combine beer and egg whites; stir into the dry ingredients just until moistened. Dip asparagus into batter.
2. In a deep cast-iron or electric skillet, heat 1½ in. oil to 375°. Fry asparagus in batches until golden brown, 2-3 minutes on each side. Drain on paper towels. Serve immediately with ranch dressing.
1 piece: 70 cal., 4g fat (0 sat. fat), 0 chol., 207mg sod., 7g carb. (1g sugars, 0 fiber), 1g pro.

BOK CHOY & RADISHES

This is such a great-tasting, good-for-you recipe. With bok choy and radishes, the simple dish capitalizes on the fresh flavors of spring.
—*Ann Baker, Texarkana, TX*

TAKES: 25 min. • **MAKES:** 8 servings

- 1 head bok choy
- 2 Tbsp. butter
- 1 Tbsp. olive oil
- 12 radishes, thinly sliced
- 1 shallot, sliced
- 1 tsp. lemon-pepper seasoning
- ¾ tsp. salt

1. Cut off and discard root end of the bok choy, leaving stalks with leaves. Cut green leaves from stalks and cut the leaves into 1-in. slices; set aside. Cut white stalks into 1-in. pieces.
2. In a large cast-iron or other heavy skillet, cook stalks in butter and oil until crisp-tender, 3-5 minutes. Add radishes, shallot, lemon pepper, salt and reserved leaves; cook and stir until heated through, about 3 minutes.
¾ cup: 59 cal., 5g fat (2g sat. fat), 8mg chol., 371mg sod., 3g carb. (2g sugars, 1g fiber), 2g pro. **Diabetic exchanges:** 1 vegetable, 1 fat.

COOL-KITCHEN TIP

A thrifty alternative to purchased garlic salt is to mix up your own. Just combine 1 tsp. garlic powder with 3 tsp. table salt or other fine-grained salt. The ratio works the same for onion salt.

COLORFUL COUSCOUS

We love it when side dishes pop with color, like the pepper accents you'll see in this light and fluffy couscous. It's a scrumptious switch from baked potatoes or rice and cooks in record time.
—Taste of Home *Test Kitchen*

TAKES: 25 min. • **MAKES:** 6 servings

- 2 Tbsp. olive oil
- 5 miniature sweet peppers, julienned
- ⅓ cup finely chopped onion
- 2 garlic cloves, minced
- 1 can (14½ oz.) chicken broth
- ¼ cup water
- ½ tsp. salt
- ¼ tsp. pepper
- 1 pkg. (10 oz.) couscous

In a large saucepan, heat oil over medium-high heat; saute peppers, onion and garlic until tender, 2-3 minutes. Stir in broth, water, salt and pepper; bring to a boil. Stir in couscous. Remove from heat; let stand, covered, 5 minutes. Fluff with a fork.
¾ cup: 220 cal., 5g fat (1g sat. fat), 2mg chol., 498mg sod., 37g carb. (2g sugars, 2g fiber), 7g pro.

READER RAVE
"Very tasty! I added sliced zucchini."

—MZIVICH, TASTEOFHOME.COM

SPICY HONEY MUSTARD GREEN BEANS

I love fresh beans but was getting tired of just steaming and eating them plain. So I whipped up this easy honey-mustard combination for a simple side.
—*Carol Traupman-Carr, Breinigsville, PA*

TAKES: 20 min. • **MAKES:** 2 servings

- ½ lb. fresh green beans, trimmed
- ¼ cup thinly sliced red onion
- 2 Tbsp. spicy brown mustard
- 2 Tbsp. honey
- 1 Tbsp. snipped fresh dill or 1 tsp. dill weed

1. In a large saucepan, bring 6 cups water to a boil. Add beans; cook, uncovered, just until crisp-tender, 3-4 minutes. Drain beans and immediately drop into ice water. Drain and pat dry; transfer to a small bowl.
2. In a second bowl, combine the onion, mustard, honey and dill. Pour over beans; toss to coat.
1 serving: 122 cal., 0 fat (0 sat. fat), 0 chol., 159mg sod., 27g carb. (21g sugars, 4g fiber), 2g pro.

CHERRY TOMATO MOZZARELLA SAUTE

This side is fast to fix and full of flavor. It's perfect with almost any main dish.
—*Summer Jones, Pleasant Grove, UT*

TAKES: 25 min. • **MAKES:** 4 servings

- 2 tsp. olive oil
- ¼ cup chopped shallots
- 1 tsp. minced fresh thyme
- 1 garlic clove, minced
- 2½ cups cherry tomatoes, halved
- ¼ tsp. salt
- ¼ tsp. pepper
- 4 oz. fresh mozzarella cheese, cut into ½-in. cubes

In a large skillet, heat oil over medium-high heat; saute shallots with thyme until tender. Add garlic; cook and stir 1 minute. Stir in tomatoes, salt and pepper; heat through. Remove from heat; stir in cheese.
⅔ cup: 127 cal., 9g fat (4g sat. fat), 22mg chol., 194mg sod., 6g carb. (4g sugars, 2g fiber), 6g pro.

ASPARAGUS & GREEN BEANS WITH TARRAGON LEMON DIP

Tarragon balances the tangy flavor from lemon in the creamy sauce covering fresh asparagus and green beans. I serve this as a side dish as well as an appetizer.
—*Bonnie Hawkins, Elkhorn, WI*

TAKES: 20 min. • **MAKES:** 10 servings

- 1 lb. fresh asparagus, trimmed
- 1 lb. fresh green beans, trimmed
- 1 cup mayonnaise
- ¼ cup lemon juice
- 1 shallot, finely chopped
- 2 Tbsp. minced fresh tarragon or 2 tsp. dried tarragon
- 2 Tbsp. minced fresh parsley or 2 tsp. dried parsley flakes
- 2 tsp. grated lemon zest
  Dash pepper

1. Place 1 in. of water in a Dutch oven; add asparagus and beans. Bring to a boil. Reduce heat; cover and simmer for 3-5 minutes or until crisp-tender.
2. Meanwhile, in a small bowl, combine the remaining ingredients. Drain the vegetables; transfer to a serving platter. Drizzle with dip.

1 serving: 183 cal., 18g fat (2g sat. fat), 8mg chol., 126mg sod., 5g carb. (2g sugars, 2g fiber), 1g pro.

SAUTEED BROCCOLI

When I needed a new recipe for cooking broccoli, I came up with my own. It makes a nice side dish for most entrees.
—*Jim MacNeal, Waterloo, NY*

TAKES: 20 min. • **MAKES:** 10 servings

1	cup chopped onion
1	cup julienned sweet red pepper
¼	cup olive oil
12	cups fresh broccoli florets
1⅓	cups water
3	tsp. minced garlic
½	tsp. salt
½	tsp. pepper

In a Dutch oven, saute onion and red pepper in oil for 2-3 minutes or until crisp-tender. Stir in the broccoli, water, garlic, salt and pepper. Cover and cook over medium heat for 5-6 minutes or until the broccoli is crisp-tender.
¾ cup: 82 cal., 6g fat (1g sat. fat), 0 chol., 142mg sod., 7g carb. (2g sugars, 2g fiber), 3g pro. **Diabetic exchanges:** 1 vegetable, 1 fat.

CORN WITH HERBS

A pleasant blend of herbs enhances this fast, easy and yummy side dish. It's our family's favorite way to eat fresh corn.
—*Tania Bikerman, Pittsburgh, PA*

TAKES: 25 min. • **MAKES:** 8 servings

8	cups fresh or frozen corn, thawed
1	cup finely chopped red onion
¾	cup butter, cubed
12	garlic cloves, minced
4	to 6 tsp. herbes de Provence or Italian seasoning
1	tsp. salt

In a Dutch oven over medium-high heat, cook and stir corn and onion in butter for 5 minutes. Add garlic; cook 1 minute longer. Add herbes de Provence and salt; cook 2-4 minutes or until the vegetables are tender.
¾ cup: 302 cal., 19g fat (11g sat. fat), 45mg chol., 441mg sod., 33g carb. (6g sugars, 5g fiber), 6g pro.

COOL-KITCHEN TIP

It's easy to customize this recipe to your liking or adapt the flavors to match your main dish. Try adding lemon, Parmesan cheese and red pepper flakes. Or, give your vegetables an Asian twist by using teriyaki or soy sauce. You can also use the sauteed brococoli as an ingredient in your main dish instead of as a side—try tossing it into a pasta recipe or using it in a stir-fry.

ASIAN SNOW PEA TOSS

My love for Asian flavors sparked the idea for this easy, healthy side dish. I use just-picked peas from our garden for this salad and serve it alongside grilled chicken.
—Mary Ann Dell, Phoenixville, PA

TAKES: 20 min. • **MAKES:** 12 servings

- ¼ cup orange marmalade
- ¼ cup seasoned rice vinegar
- 2 Tbsp. sesame oil
- 4 tsp. minced fresh gingerroot
- 1 pkg. (12 oz.) frozen shelled edamame
- 1 lb. fresh snow peas
- 1 can (15 oz.) black beans, rinsed and drained
- 1 small sweet red pepper, cut into thin strips
- 3 green onions, chopped
- 1 can (11 oz.) mandarin oranges, drained
- ¼ tsp. salt
- ¼ tsp. pepper

1. In a small bowl, whisk the marmalade, vinegar, sesame oil and ginger.

2. Cook the edamame according to package directions, adding the snow peas during the last minute of cooking. Drain and rinse in cold water.

3. Place in a large bowl. Stir in the black beans, red pepper and green onions. Add the marmalade mixture, mandarin oranges, salt and pepper; toss to coat.

Note: Edamame is a popular Asian food produced by harvesting soybeans early, before they become hard. The young beans are parboiled and frozen to retain their freshness and can be found in the freezer of grocery and health food stores.

¾ cup: 148 cal., 4g fat (1g sat. fat), 0 chol., 304mg sod., 22g carb. (13g sugars, 4g fiber), 6g pro. **Diabetic exchanges:** 1 starch, 1 lean meat.

RAW CAULIFLOWER TABBOULEH

This recipe is super easy and fast to make. I love that I can offer it to my guests with special dietary restrictions.
—Maiah Miller, Montclair, VA

PREP: 10 min. + chilling • **MAKES:** 6 cups

- 1 medium head cauliflower
- ½ cup oil-packed sun-dried tomatoes
- 12 pitted Greek olives
- 2 cups fresh parsley leaves
- 1 cup fresh cilantro leaves
- 1 Tbsp. white wine vinegar or cider vinegar
- ¼ tsp. salt
- ¼ tsp. pepper

Core and coarsely chop cauliflower. In batches, pulse cauliflower in a food processor until it resembles rice (do not overprocess). Transfer to a large bowl. Add remaining ingredients to food processor; pulse until finely chopped. Add to cauliflower; toss to combine. Refrigerate for 1 hour before serving to allow the flavors to blend.

¾ cup: 55 cal., 3g fat (0 sat. fat), 0 chol., 215mg sod., 7g carb. (2g sugars, 2g fiber), 2g pro. **Diabetic exchanges:** 1 vegetable, ½ fat.

COOL-KITCHEN TIP

Tabbouleh is a Middle Eastern herb salad and is usually made with bulgar, a nutritious whole grain. This lighter spin on the classic salad features cauliflower instead, which cuts calories and carbs by more than half.

SLICED BRUSSELS SPROUTS WITH PECANS

Brussels sprouts cook quickly when they are thinly sliced. Chicken broth, sugar and pecans sweeten up their taste.
—Taste of Home *Test Kitchen*

TAKES: 20 min. • **MAKES:** 6 servings

- ½ cup chopped onion
- 2 tsp. butter
- 1 lb. fresh Brussels sprouts, thinly sliced
- ⅓ cup chicken broth
- 1 Tbsp. sugar
- ½ tsp. salt
- 3 Tbsp. chopped pecans, toasted

In a large skillet, saute onion in butter until tender. Add Brussels sprouts; saute for 2 minutes. Add the broth, sugar and salt; cover and cook until Brussels sprouts are tender, about 5 minutes longer, stirring occasionally. Sprinkle with pecans.
½ cup: 83 cal., 4g fat (1g sat. fat), 3mg chol., 280mg sod., 11g carb. (5g sugars, 3g fiber), 3g pro.

READER RAVE
"I made this tonight for dinner at my sister's house. She told me she wasn't letting me take any of the Brussels sprouts home, and she meant it!"

—JOANOLMSTEAD, TASTEOFHOME.COM

MASHED CAULIFLOWER

This side dish is lower in carbs than mashed potatoes but just as flavorful and satisfying. If you want to add some color, chopped green onions make a nice garnish.
—Tina Martini, Sparks, NV

TAKES: 25 min. • **MAKES:** 2½ cups

- 1 medium head cauliflower, broken into florets
- ½ cup shredded Swiss cheese
- 1 Tbsp. butter
- ¾ tsp. salt
- ¼ tsp. pepper
- ⅛ tsp. garlic powder
- 2 to 3 Tbsp. 2% milk

1. In a large saucepan, bring 1 in. water to a boil. Add cauliflower; cook, covered, until very tender, 8-12 minutes. Drain.
2. Mash cauliflower, adding cheese, butter, seasonings and enough milk to reach desired consistency.
¾ cup: 160 cal., 10g fat (6g sat. fat), 28mg chol., 718mg sod., 11g carb. (4g sugars, 4g fiber), 9g pro.

LEMON-SCENTED BROCCOLINI

Even the most finicky eaters will eagerly eat this vegetable seasoned with lemon pepper, lemon zest and lemon juice. If you prefer, use broccoli instead.
—*Kim Champion, Phoenix, AZ*

TAKES: 30 min. • **MAKES:** 12 servings

- 2½ **lbs. Broccolini or broccoli spears**
- 6 **Tbsp. butter**
- 1 **Tbsp. plus 1½ tsp. lemon juice**
- 1 **Tbsp. lemon-pepper seasoning**
- 1 **tsp. grated lemon zest**
- ¼ **tsp. salt**

1. In a large saucepan, bring 4 cups water to a boil. Add Broccolini; cook, uncovered, until just tender, 5-7 minutes. Drain and immediately place Broccolini in ice water. Drain and pat dry.

2. In a large skillet, melt butter. Stir in the lemon juice, lemon pepper, grated lemon zest and salt. Add Broccolini; toss until heated through.

1 serving: 90 cal., 6g fat (4g sat. fat), 15mg chol., 232mg sod., 7g carb. (2g sugars, 1g fiber), 3g pro. **Diabetic exchanges:** 1 vegetable, 1 fat.

Zesty Broccolini: Cook Broccolini as directed. Saute 3 minced garlic cloves and 1 tsp. grated fresh ginger in ¼ cup olive oil for 1 minute. Add Broccolini and ¼ tsp. crushed pepper flakes; saute for 1-2 minutes or until heated through.

MICROWAVE RICE PILAF

This speedy side dish complements almost any main dish. It's just the right amount for my husband and me but also easy to double for a larger group.
—*Norma Jean Koelmel, Shattuc, IL*

TAKES: 30 min. • **MAKES:** 2 servings

- ¼ cup each chopped onion, celery and green pepper
- 1 Tbsp. butter
- ½ cup hot water
- 1 jar (4½ oz.) sliced mushrooms, drained
- ⅓ cup uncooked instant rice
- 1½ tsp. chicken bouillon granules

1. In a 1-qt. microwave-safe dish, combine the onion, celery, green pepper and butter. Microwave, uncovered, on high until the vegetables are crisp-tender, 2-4 minutes.
2. Stir in the remaining ingredients. Cook on high until rice is tender, 7-10 minutes longer.

1 cup: 145 cal., 6g fat (4g sat. fat), 16mg chol., 960mg sod., 20g carb. (3g sugars, 3g fiber), 3g pro.

SAUTEED GARLIC MUSHROOMS

These mushrooms are so delicious served with steak, chicken or pork. So simple—but you just can't beat mushrooms, garlic and butter together!
—*Joan Schroeder, Mesquite, NV*

TAKES: 15 min. • **MAKES:** 6 servings

- ¾ lb. sliced fresh mushrooms
- 2 to 3 tsp. minced garlic
- 1 Tbsp. seasoned bread crumbs
- ⅓ cup butter, cubed

In a large cast-iron or other heavy skillet, saute the mushrooms, garlic and bread crumbs in butter until the mushrooms are tender, 3-5 minutes.
½ cup: 109 cal., 10g fat (6g sat. fat), 27mg chol., 123mg sod., 3g carb. (1g sugars, 1g fiber), 2g pro.

INDIAN GINGER POTATOES

This easy ginger potato dish is so tasty. You can make it even faster by cooking the potatoes ahead of time or using leftover spuds.
—*Erin Kelkar, Norcross, GA*

TAKES: 30 min. • **MAKES:** 4 servings

- 4 medium potatoes (about 1½ lbs.), peeled and cut into 1-in. pieces
- 2 Tbsp. canola oil
- 1 medium onion, coarsely chopped
- 1 jalapeno pepper, seeded and finely chopped
- 1 Tbsp. minced fresh gingerroot
- ½ tsp. ground turmeric
- ¼ cup water
- ½ tsp. salt
- ¼ tsp. garlic powder
- ⅛ tsp. cayenne pepper
- 2 Tbsp. chopped fresh cilantro

1. Place potatoes in a large saucepan; add enough water to cover. Bring to a boil. Reduce heat; cook, uncovered, until tender, 8-12 minutes. Drain.

2. Meanwhile, in a large skillet, heat oil over medium-high heat. Add onion, jalapeno and ginger; cook and stir until onion is lightly browned, 3-4 minutes. Add turmeric; cook 1 minute longer.

3. Reduce heat to low; add potatoes, water, salt, garlic powder and cayenne pepper. Cook, covered, until potatoes are heated through, 4-6 minutes; stir occasionally. Sprinkle with cilantro before serving.

Note: Wear disposable gloves when cutting hot peppers; the oils can burn skin. Avoid touching your face.

¾ cup: 201 cal., 7g fat (1g sat. fat), 0 chol., 301mg sod., 32g carb. (4g sugars, 3g fiber), 3g pro. **Diabetic exchanges:** 2 starch, 1½ fat.

FRIED CABBAGE

When I was young, my family grew our own cabbages. It was fun to put them to use in the kitchen, just like I did with this comforting side. It's so good with potatoes, deviled eggs and cornbread.
—*Bernice Morris, Marshfield, MO*

TAKES: 20 min. • **MAKES:** 6 servings

- 2 Tbsp. butter
- 1 tsp. sugar
- ½ tsp. salt
- ¼ tsp. crushed red pepper flakes
- ⅛ tsp. pepper
- 6 cups coarsely chopped cabbage
- 1 Tbsp. water

In a large skillet, melt butter over medium heat. Stir in the sugar, salt, pepper flakes and pepper. Add the cabbage and water. Cook for 5-6 minutes or until tender, stirring occasionally.

1 cup: 59 cal., 4g fat (2g sat. fat), 10mg chol., 251mg sod., 6g carb. (3g sugars, 2g fiber), 1g pro. **Diabetic exchanges:** 1 vegetable, 1 fat.

ZUCCHINI PASTA

The taste of this rich and creamy zucchini pasta dish will have people convinced it's not low-fat, but it is! Garlicky and fresh-flavored, this will be a hit.
—*Maria Regakis, Saugus, MA*

TAKES: 25 min. • **MAKES:** 6 servings

- 8 oz. uncooked linguine
- 4 cups coarsely shredded zucchini (about 3 medium)
- 4 tsp. olive oil
- 2 garlic cloves, thinly sliced
- ¼ cup fat-free plain yogurt
- ¾ cup shredded reduced-fat cheddar cheese
- ¾ tsp. salt
- ¼ tsp. pepper

1. Cook linguine according to package directions. In a sieve or colander, drain the zucchini, squeezing to remove excess liquid. Pat dry.
2. In a large nonstick skillet, saute zucchini in oil for 2 minutes. Add garlic; cook and stir until zucchini is tender, 1-2 minutes longer. Transfer to a large bowl. Add yogurt, cheese, salt and pepper.
3. Drain linguine; add to zucchini mixture and toss to coat.

¾ cup: 225 cal., 7g fat (2g sat. fat), 10mg chol., 403mg sod., 32g carb. (4g sugars, 2g fiber), 10g pro. **Diabetic exchanges:** 1½ starch, 1½ fat, 1 vegetable.

COOL-KITCHEN TIP

There are different ways to shred zucchini, depending on the tools you have. This recipe calls for the zucchini to be coarsely shredded, but you can experiment with various methods of chopping or shredding— try a peeler, a spiralizer, a box grater or even a food processor.

SZECHUAN SUGAR SNAP PEAS

Simple seasonings transform crisp, sweet sugar snap peas into an unbeatable side dish your family will love. You can use chopped walnuts in place of the cashews if you prefer.
—*Jeanne Holt, St. Paul, MN*

TAKES: 25 min. • **MAKES:** 8 servings

- 6 cups fresh sugar snap peas
- 2 tsp. peanut oil
- 1 tsp. sesame oil
- 3 Tbsp. thinly sliced green onions
- 1 tsp. grated orange zest
- ½ tsp. minced garlic
- ½ tsp. minced fresh gingerroot
- ⅛ tsp. crushed red pepper flakes
- 1 Tbsp. minced fresh cilantro
- ¼ tsp. salt
- ⅛ tsp. pepper
- ⅓ cup salted cashew halves

1. In a Dutch oven, saute peas in peanut oil and sesame oil until crisp-tender. Add the onions, orange zest, garlic, ginger and pepper flakes; saute 1 minute longer.
2. Remove from heat; stir in the cilantro, salt and pepper. Sprinkle with cashews just before serving.
¾ cup: 107 cal., 5g fat (1g sat. fat), 0 chol., 121mg sod., 10g carb. (5g sugars, 4g fiber), 5g pro. **Diabetic exchanges:** 2 vegetable, 1 fat.

GARLIC OREGANO ZUCCHINI

I've found that this flavorful side dish goes with practically anything, but is especially good with chicken and fish. For a colorful variation, use half yellow summer squash.
—*Teresa Kraus, Cortez, CO*

TAKES: 15 min. • **MAKES:** 4 servings

- 2 Tbsp. canola oil
- 1 tsp. minced garlic
- 4 medium zucchini, sliced
- 1 tsp. dried oregano
- ½ tsp. salt
- ⅛ tsp. pepper

In a large skillet, heat oil over medium heat; add garlic. Cook and stir 1 minute. Add zucchini, oregano, salt and pepper. Cook and stir until zucchini is crisp-tender, 4-6 minutes.
1 cup: 97 cal., 8g fat (1g sat. fat), 0 chol., 311mg sod., 7g carb. (4g sugars, 2g fiber), 2g pro. **Diabetic exchanges:** 1½ fat, 1 vegetable.
Zucchini & Pepper Saute: Omit oregano. Cut 1 medium sweet orange pepper into thin strips. Saute zucchini and orange pepper in oil until crisp-tender. Add garlic; saute 1 minute. Stir in 2 tsp. brown sugar, 2 tsp. lemon juice, ½ tsp. dried basil and salt and pepper to taste. Cook until sugar is dissolved.

FRITTERS AWAY!

Fritters—or vegetable pancakes—are a quick way to whip up a fun and healthy side.

HARISSA SWEET POTATO FRITTERS

I had leftover sweet potatoes and had to think up a new way to use them. We love spice, so I seasoned these fun fritters with harissa, which added just enough flavor without making them too spicy. If you want more heat, you can always adjust the spice to please your taste buds.
—Teri Rasey, Cadillac, MI

PREP: 20 min. + standing
COOK: 5 min./batch • **MAKES:** 6 servings

- 6 cups boiling water
- 3 cups shredded and peeled sweet potatoes, slightly packed (about 2 medium)
- 2 large eggs
- ¼ cup all-purpose flour
- 1 tsp. baking powder
- 1 tsp. cornstarch
- 1 tsp. seasoned salt
- 2 to 3 tsp. harissa
- 1 small onion, grated
- ¼ cup coconut oil
- ½ cup crumbled queso fresco
  Optional: Sliced avocado, sliced tomato and minced fresh cilantro

1. Pour boiling water over sweet potatoes in a large bowl; let stand 20 minutes. Drain, squeezing to remove excess liquid. Pat dry.
2. In a large bowl, whisk the eggs, flour, baking powder, cornstarch, seasoned salt and harissa. Add the sweet potatoes and onion; toss to coat.
3. In a large nonstick skillet, heat 2 Tbsp. coconut oil over medium heat. Working in batches, drop sweet potato mixture by ¼ cupfuls into oil; press slightly to flatten. Fry for 1-2 minutes on each side until golden brown, using remaining oil as needed. Drain on paper towels. Serve with crumbled queso fresco and optional toppings as desired.
2 fritters: 217 cal., 13g fat (10g sat. fat), 69mg chol., 421mg sod., 20g carb. (3g sugars, 2g fiber), 6g pro.

COOL-KITCHEN TIP
Mix some harissa with mayonnaise for a great dipping sauce.

ZUCCHINI PANCAKES

Made with zucchini, these are a tasty change of pace from ordinary potato pancakes. Add a little shredded onion to give them a savory kick.
—Charlotte Goldberg, Honey Grove, PA

TAKES: 20 min. • **MAKES:** 2 servings

- 1½ cups shredded zucchini
- 1 large egg, lightly beaten
- 3 Tbsp. grated Parmesan cheese
- 2 Tbsp. biscuit/baking mix
  Dash pepper
- 1 Tbsp. canola oil
  Sour cream, optional

1. Place zucchini in a colander over a plate; let stand to drain. Squeeze and blot dry with paper towels.
2. In a bowl, mix egg, cheese, baking mix and pepper. Add zucchini; toss to coat.
3. In a large skillet, heat oil over medium heat. Drop 4 pancakes into skillet; press lightly to flatten. Cook until golden brown, about 2 minutes per side. If desired, serve with sour cream.
2 pancakes: 174 cal., 13g fat (3g sat. fat), 99mg chol., 256mg sod., 9g carb. (2g sugars, 1g fiber), 7g pro.

ONION POTATO PANCAKES

When Grandma prepared potato pancakes, she used an old-fashioned grater—great for potatoes but not for knuckles! With homemade applesauce, this side dish complements a meal so well. I made these pancakes for my family and often served them as a main dish for light suppers.
—*Joan Hutter, Warwick, RI*

TAKES: 20 min. • **MAKES:** 6 servings

- 2 **large eggs**
- 1 **medium onion, quartered**
- 2 **tablespoons all-purpose flour**
- ¾ **tsp. salt**
- ¼ **tsp. pepper**
- ¼ **tsp. baking powder**
- 4 **medium potatoes, peeled and cubed (about 1½ pounds)**
- 2 **Tbsp. chopped fresh parsley**
- 3 **to 4 Tbsp. vegetable oil**

1. In a blender or food processor, place the eggs, onion, flour, salt, pepper, baking powder and ½ cup of potatoes. Cover and process on high until smooth. Add parsley and remaining potatoes; cover and pulse 2-4 times until potatoes are chopped.
2. Pour 1-2 Tbsp. oil onto a hot griddle or skillet. Pour batter by ⅓ cupfuls onto griddle; flatten slightly to a 4- to 5-in. diameter. Cook over medium heat until golden, 2-3 minutes on each side. Add oil to griddle as needed.
2 pancakes: 159 cal., 6g fat (1g sat. fat), 47mg chol., 262mg sod., 22g carb. (2g sugars, 3g fiber), 4g pro. **Diabetic exchanges:** 1½ starch, 1 fat.

BROCCOLI FRITTERS

These cute cakes offer a fun and kid-friendly way to use broccoli. They're perfect as a side dish or an appetizer.
—*Tracy Eubanks, Ewing, KY*

PREP: 20 min. • **COOK:** 10 min./batch
MAKES: 12 servings

- 1 **bunch broccoli, cut into florets**
- 2 **large eggs, lightly beaten**
- 2 **large egg whites**
- ⅓ **cup grated Parmesan cheese**
- 2 **Tbsp. all-purpose flour**
- ½ **tsp. salt**
- ½ **tsp. garlic powder**
- ½ **tsp. pepper**
- 2 **Tbsp. canola oil**
     Salsa, optional

1. Place broccoli in a steamer basket; place in a small saucepan over 1 in. of water. Bring to a boil; cover and steam until crisp-tender, 3-4 minutes. Coarsely chop broccoli and set aside.
2. In a large bowl, combine the eggs, egg whites, cheese, flour, salt, garlic powder and pepper. Stir in the broccoli.
3. Heat 1 Tbsp. oil in a large cast-iron or other heavy skillet over medium heat. Drop battered broccoli by heaping ⅛ cupfuls into oil; press lightly to flatten. Cook in batches until golden brown, 3-4 minutes on each side, using the remaining 1 Tbsp. oil as needed. Drain on paper towels. If desired, serve with salsa .
1 fritter: 67 cal., 4g fat (1g sat. fat), 33mg chol., 176mg sod., 5g carb. (1g sugars, 1g fiber), 4g pro.

COOL-KITCHEN TIP
Store cooled fritters in a sealed container in the refrigerator for up to 3 days. To extend their freshness, freeze cooled fritters in single layers; thaw as needed. To use, place on a greased sheet pan and bake at 350° for 10 minutes or until hot.

P. 176

SLOW-COOKED SENSATIONS

The slow cooker is the magic answer to creating hearty, slow-simmered dishes without generating a lot of hot air.

SLOW-COOKED CARNITAS

Simmer succulent pork the easy slow-cooker way. Instead of using tortillas, I'll often put the meat on top of shredded lettuce for a tasty salad.
—*Lisa Glogow, Aliso Viejo, CA*

PREP: 20 min. • **COOK:** 6 hours
MAKES: 12 servings

- 1 boneless pork shoulder butt roast (3 to 4 lbs.)
- 3 garlic cloves, thinly sliced
- 2 tsp. olive oil
- ½ tsp. salt
- ½ tsp. pepper
- 1 bunch green onions, chopped
- 1½ cups minced fresh cilantro
- 1 cup salsa
- ½ cup chicken broth
- ½ cup tequila or additional chicken broth
- 2 cans (4 oz. each) chopped green chiles
- 12 flour tortillas (8 in.) or corn tortillas (6 in.), warmed
  Optional: Fresh cilantro leaves, sliced red onion and chopped tomatoes

1. Cut roast in half; place in a 5-qt. slow cooker. Sprinkle with the garlic, oil, salt and pepper. Add onions, cilantro, salsa, broth, tequila and chiles. Cover; cook on low until meat is tender, 6-8 hours.

2. Remove meat; cool slightly. Shred with 2 forks and return to the slow cooker; heat through. Spoon about ⅔ cup meat mixture onto each tortilla; serve with the toppings of your choice.

1 carnita: 363 cal., 15g fat (5g sat. fat), 67mg chol., 615mg sod., 28g carb. (1g sugars, 1g fiber), 24g pro.

COCONUT-MANGO MALVA PUDDING

My friend shared this amazing malva pudding recipe with me. Malva pudding is a dense, spongy cake drenched in a rich, sticky butter sauce. My slow-cooked tropical spin incorporates a creamy coconut sauce and juicy mangoes!
—*Carmell Childs, Orangeville, UT*

PREP: 20 min.
COOK: 2½ hours + standing
MAKES: 12 servings

- 4 large eggs
- 1½ cups sugar
- ¼ cup apricot preserves
- 2 Tbsp. butter, melted
- 1 can (13.66 oz.) coconut milk
- 2 tsp. vanilla extract
- 2 tsp. white vinegar
- 2 cups all-purpose flour
- 1¼ tsp. baking soda
- 1 tsp. salt

SAUCE

- 1 cup canned coconut milk
- ½ cup butter, melted
- ½ cup sugar
- 2 Tbsp. apricot preserves
- ½ tsp. coconut extract
- 2 medium mangoes, peeled and chopped
- ¼ cup sweetened shredded coconut, toasted
- 1 container (8 oz.) frozen whipped topping, thawed

1. In large bowl, beat eggs, sugar, apricot preserves and butter until combined. Add coconut milk, vanilla and vinegar; stir to combine (batter will be thin). In another bowl, whisk flour, baking soda and salt. Gradually stir flour mixture into the batter just until moistened. Transfer to a greased 5-qt. slow cooker. Cook, covered, on high until a toothpick inserted in cake comes out with moist crumbs, 2½-3 hours.

2. Meanwhile, for sauce, whisk together coconut milk, butter, sugar, apricot preserves and extract until smooth. Poke holes in warm cake with a skewer or chopstick. Pour mixture evenly over pudding; let stand to allow pudding to absorb sauce, 15-20 minutes. Serve with chopped mango, coconut and a dollop of whipped topping.

1 serving: 518 cal., 24g fat (19g sat. fat), 87mg chol., 452mg sod., 71g carb. (52g sugars, 2g fiber), 6g pro.

SECRET'S IN THE SAUCE BBQ RIBS

A sweet, rich sauce makes these ribs so tender that the meat literally falls off the bones. And the aroma is wonderful. Yum!
—*Tanya Reid, Winston-Salem, NC*

PREP: 10 min. • **COOK:** 6 hours
MAKES: 5 servings

- 4½ lbs. pork baby back ribs
- 1½ tsp. pepper
- 2½ cups barbecue sauce
- ¾ cup cherry preserves
- 1 Tbsp. Dijon mustard
- 1 garlic clove, minced

Cut ribs into serving-sized pieces; sprinkle with pepper. Place in a 5- or 6-qt. slow cooker. Combine the barbecue sauce, preserves, mustard and garlic; pour over ribs. Cook, covered, on low until meat is tender, 6-8 hours. Serve with sauce.

1 serving: 921 cal., 58g fat (21g sat. fat), 220mg chol., 1402mg sod., 50g carb. (45g sugars, 2g fiber), 48g pro.

SLOW-COOKED SOUTHWEST CHICKEN

This dish needs just 15 minutes of prep, so you'll be out of the kitchen in no time. The delicious low-fat chicken gets even better with a garnish of reduced-fat sour cream and fresh cilantro.
—*Brandi Castillo, Santa Maria, CA*

PREP: 15 min. • **COOK:** 3 hours
MAKES: 6 servings

- 2 cans (15 oz. each) black beans, rinsed and drained
- 1 can (14½ oz.) reduced-sodium chicken broth
- 1 can (14½ oz.) diced tomatoes with mild green chiles, undrained
- ½ lb. boneless skinless chicken breast
- 1 jar (8 oz.) chunky salsa
- 1 cup frozen corn
- 1 Tbsp. dried parsley flakes
- 1 tsp. ground cumin
- ¼ tsp. pepper
- 3 cups hot cooked rice
  Optional: Lime wedges and fresh cilantro leaves

1. In a 2- or 3-qt. slow cooker, combine beans, broth, tomatoes, chicken, salsa, corn and seasonings. Cover and cook on low for 3-4 hours or until a thermometer inserted in chicken reads 165°.

2. Shred chicken with 2 forks and return to slow cooker; heat through. Serve over rice. If desired, serve with lime wedges and fresh cilantro.

FREEZE OPTION: After shredding the chicken, freeze cooled mixture in freezer containers. To use, partially thaw in refrigerator overnight. Heat through in a saucepan, stirring occasionally; add broth or water if necessary.

1 cup: 320 cal., 1g fat (0 sat. fat), 21mg chol., 873mg sod., 56g carb. (7g sugars, 8g fiber), 19g pro.

THAI CHICKEN THIGHS

Thanks to the slow cooker, this traditional Thai dish becomes incredibly easy to make. If you want to crank up the spice a bit, use more jalapeno peppers.
—Taste of Home *Test Kitchen*

PREP: 25 min. • **COOK:** 5 hours
MAKES: 8 servings

- 8 bone-in chicken thighs (about 3 lbs.), skin removed
- ½ cup salsa
- ¼ cup creamy peanut butter
- 2 Tbsp. lemon juice
- 2 Tbsp. reduced-sodium soy sauce
- 1 Tbsp. chopped seeded jalapeno pepper
- 2 tsp. Thai chili sauce
- 1 garlic clove, minced
- 1 tsp. minced fresh gingerroot
- 2 green onions, sliced
- 2 Tbsp. sesame seeds, toasted
  Hot cooked basmati rice, optional

1. Place chicken in a 3-qt. slow cooker. In a small bowl, combine the salsa, peanut butter, lemon juice, soy sauce, jalapeno, Thai chili sauce, garlic and ginger; pour over chicken.

2. Cover and cook on low until chicken is tender, 5-6 hours. Sprinkle with green onions and sesame seeds. Serve with rice if desired.

Note: Wear disposable gloves when cutting hot peppers; the oils can burn skin. Avoid touching your face.

1 chicken thigh with ¼ cup sauce: 261 cal., 15g fat (4g sat. fat), 87mg chol., 350mg sod., 5g carb. (2g sugars, 1g fiber), 27g pro. **Diabetic exchanges:** 4 lean meat, 1 fat, ½ starch.

COCONUT CHICKEN & SWEET POTATO STEW

This stew tastes as if you spent hours in the kitchen. The flavors of coconut milk, sweet potato and coriander nicely complement the chicken. A garnish of cilantro and toasted coconut adds a bit of sophistication.
—*Nicole Filizetti, Stevens Point, WI*

PREP: 20 min. • **COOK:** 6 hours
MAKES: 8 servings (2½ qt.)

- 1½ lbs. boneless skinless chicken breasts, cubed
- 2 lbs. sweet potatoes (about 3 medium), peeled and cubed
- 3 cups canned coconut milk, divided
- 1 can (8 oz.) unsweetened pineapple tidbits, drained
- 1 small onion, chopped
- 1 tsp. ground coriander
- ½ tsp. salt
- ½ tsp. crushed red pepper flakes
- ¼ tsp. pepper
  Optional: Hot cooked basmati rice, toasted unsweetened shredded coconut, minced fresh cilantro and lime wedges

1. Combine chicken, sweet potatoes, 2 cups coconut milk, pineapple, onion and seasonings in a 4- or 5-qt. slow cooker. Cook, covered, on low until chicken and sweet potatoes are tender, 6-8 hours.
2. Stir in the remaining 1 cup coconut milk. If desired, serve stew with basmati rice and toppings of your choice.

1¼ cups: 365 cal., 16g fat (14g sat. fat), 47mg chol., 223mg sod., 34g carb. (17g sugars, 4g fiber), 21g pro.

SLOW-COOKED GINGERED PEARS

My slow cooker allows me to serve this special dessert without much effort. These tender pears feature a surprise filling of candied ginger and pecans.
—*Catherine Mueller, St. Paul, MN*

PREP: 35 min. • **COOK:** 4 hours
MAKES: 6 servings

- ½ cup finely chopped crystallized ginger
- ¼ cup packed brown sugar
- ¼ cup chopped pecans
- 1½ tsp. grated lemon zest
- 6 medium Bartlett or Anjou pears
- 2 Tbsp. butter, cubed
  Optional: Vanilla ice cream and caramel ice cream topping

1. In a small bowl, combine the ginger, brown sugar, pecans and lemon zest. Using a melon baller or long-handled spoon, core pears to within ¼ in. of bottom. Spoon ginger mixture into the center of each.
2. Place pears upright in a 5-qt. slow cooker. Top each with butter. Cover, covered, on low until tender, 4-5 hours. Serve with ice cream and caramel topping if desired.
1 filled pear: 263 cal., 8g fat (3g sat. fat), 10mg chol., 43mg sod., 52g carb. (32g sugars, 6g fiber), 1g pro.

TANGERINE CHICKEN TAGINE

My family and friends love foods from around the world, especially Moroccan entrees, so I created this flavorful dish. Cooking it in the slow cooker keeps each morsel moist and rich in flavor.
—*Brenda Watts, Gaffney, SC*

PREP: 20 min. • **COOK:** 6 hours
MAKES: 8 servings

- 2 Tbsp. brown sugar
- 1 tsp. curry powder
- 1 tsp. ground cinnamon
- 1 tsp. cumin seeds
- ½ tsp. ground ginger
- 1 roasting chicken (5 to 6 lbs.), patted dry
- 1 lb. carrots, peeled and thinly sliced
- 1 lb. parsnips, peeled and thinly sliced
- 2 large tangerines, peeled and sliced
- 1 cup chopped dried apricots
- ½ cup slivered almonds
- ½ cup chicken broth

1. Combine first 5 ingredients; rub spice mixture over chicken until well coated.
2. Arrange carrots, parsnips, tangerines, apricots and almonds in bottom of a 6-qt. slow cooker. Place chicken breast side up on vegetables; pour in broth. Cook, covered, on low until a thermometer inserted in thigh reads 170° and chicken is tender, 6-8 hours.
3. Remove chicken, vegetables and fruits to a serving platter; let stand 5-10 minutes before carving chicken.
1 serving: 503 cal., 24g fat (6g sat. fat), 112mg chol., 232mg sod., 35g carb. (20g sugars, 6g fiber), 39g pro.

SLOW-COOKER
AL PASTOR BOWLS

You'll love this easy version of a traditional Mexican favorite. It's easy to serve either over rice or in tortillas with your favorite toppings.
—Taste of Home *Test Kitchen*

PREP: 10 min. • **COOK:** 6 hours
MAKES: 8 cups

- 2 cans (7 oz. each) whole green chiles
- 1 can (20 oz.) pineapple chunks, drained
- 1 medium onion, chopped
- ½ cup orange juice
- ¼ cup white vinegar
- 3 garlic cloves, peeled
- 2 Tbsp. chili powder
- 2 tsp. salt
- 1½ tsp. smoked paprika
- 1 tsp. dried oregano
- 1 tsp. ground cumin
- ½ tsp. ground coriander
- 4 lbs. boneless pork loin roast
  Hot cooked rice
  Optional: Black beans, chopped avocado, corn, sliced radishes, lime and Mexican crema

1. Puree first 12 ingredients in a blender. In a 5- or 6-qt. slow cooker, combine pork and pineapple mixture. Cook, covered, on low until pork is very tender, 6-8 hours. Stir to break up pork.
2. Serve pork in bowls over rice. Add toppings as desired.
⅔ cup: 232 cal., 7g fat (3g sat. fat), 75mg chol., 512mg sod., 11g carb. (8g sugars, 1g fiber), 30g pro. **Diabetic exchanges:** 4 lean meat, ½ starch.

BARBECUE PORK
COBB SALAD

My lunchtime salad gets way more interesting topped with barbecue pork, cheddar cheese and creamy avocado. It's as satisfying as it is scrumptious.
—Shawn Carleton, San Diego, CA

PREP: 30 min. • **COOK:** 4 hours
MAKES: 6 servings

- 1¼ cups barbecue sauce
- ½ tsp. garlic powder
- ¼ tsp. paprika
- 1½ lbs. pork tenderloin
- 12 cups chopped romaine
- 3 plum tomatoes, chopped
- 2 avocados, peeled and chopped
- 2 small carrots, thinly sliced
- 1 medium sweet red or green pepper, chopped
- 3 hard-boiled large eggs, chopped
- 1½ cups shredded cheddar cheese
  Salad dressing of your choice

1. In a greased 3-qt. slow cooker, mix barbecue sauce, garlic powder and paprika. Add pork; turn to coat. Cook, covered, on low 4-5 hours or until pork is tender.
2. Remove pork from slow cooker; shred into bite-sized pieces. In a bowl, toss shredded pork with 1 cup of the barbecue sauce mixture.
3. Place romaine on a large serving platter; arrange pork, tomatoes, avocado, carrots, chopped pepper, eggs and cheese over romaine. Drizzle with dressing.
FREEZE OPTION: Place shredded pork in freezer containers. Cool and freeze. To use, partially thaw in refrigerator overnight. Heat through in a covered saucepan, stirring gently. Add broth or water if necessary.
1 serving: 492 cal., 24g fat (9g sat. fat), 185mg chol., 868mg sod., 35g carb. (23g sugars, 7g fiber), 35g pro.

COOL-KITCHEN TIP
Because this pork is just as delicious served cold, it can also be the centerpiece of a great make-ahead lunch.

SLOW-COOKER BEEF & BROCCOLI

I love introducing my kids to all kinds of flavors. This Asian-inspired slow-cooker meal is one of their favorites, so I serve it often.
—*Brandy Stansbury, Edna, TX*

PREP: 20 min. • **COOK:** 6½ hours
MAKES: 4 servings

- 2 cups beef broth
- ½ cup reduced-sodium soy sauce
- ⅓ cup packed brown sugar
- 1½ tsp. sesame oil
- 1 garlic cloves, minced
- 1 beef top sirloin steak (1½ lbs.), cut into ½-in.-thick strips
- 2 Tbsp. cornstarch
- ¼ cup cold water
- 4 cups fresh broccoli florets
  Hot cooked rice
  Optional: Sesame seeds and thinly sliced green onions

1. In a 5-qt. slow cooker, combine the first 5 ingredients. Add beef; stir to coat. Cover and cook on low 6 hours or until tender.
2. In a small bowl, whisk cornstarch and cold water until smooth; stir into slow cooker. Cover and cook on high until thickened, about 30 minutes.
3. Meanwhile, in a large saucepan, place a steamer basket over 1 in. of water. Place broccoli in basket. Bring water to a boil. Reduce heat to maintain a simmer; steam, covered, until crisp-tender, 3-4 minutes. Stir broccoli into slow cooker. Serve over rice. If desired, garnish with sesame seeds and green onions.

1 cup: 366 cal., 9g fat (3g sat. fat), 69mg chol., 1696mg sod., 28g carb. (19g sugars, 2g fiber), 42g pro.

COOL-KITCHEN TIP

To make this recipe healthier, try adding more veggies and serving over hot cooked brown rice or even quinoa.

SLOW-COOKER JERKED SHORT RIBS

Sweet and spicy jerk seasonings give these saucy ribs an unforgettable taste! They're great in the summer because they don't heat up the kitchen.
—Susan Hein, Burlington, WI

PREP: 15 min. • **COOK:** 6 hours
MAKES: 10 servings

- 1   Tbsp. ground coriander
- 2   tsp. ground ginger
- 2   tsp. onion powder
- 2   tsp. garlic powder
- 1   tsp. salt
- 1   tsp. pepper
- 1   tsp. dried thyme
- ¾   tsp. ground allspice
- ¾   tsp. ground nutmeg
- ½   tsp. ground cinnamon
- 10 bone-in beef short ribs (about 5 lbs.)
- 1   large sweet onion, chopped
- ½   cup beef broth
- 1   jar (10 oz.) apricot preserves
- 3   Tbsp. cider vinegar
- 3   garlic cloves, minced

1. Combine first 10 ingredients. Reserve 2 Tbsp. of the seasoning mixture; rub the remaining mixture over ribs. Place onion and broth in a 6-qt. slow cooker; cover with ribs. Cook, covered, on low until ribs are tender, 6-8 hours.
2. Meanwhile, combine preserves, vinegar, garlic and the 2 Tbsp. reserved seasoning mixture. Serve with ribs.
1 short rib with 3 Tbsp. sauce: 265 cal., 11g fat (5g sat. fat), 55mg chol., 330mg sod., 23g carb. (14g sugars, 1g fiber), 19g pro.

SLOW-COOKED CORNED BEEF

A great result is not luck; it's just an amazing Irish recipe. With this meal in the slow cooker at sunrise, you can definitely fill the seats at the dinner table by sundown. Plus, by making two briskets at once, you'll be all set for another meal!
—Heather Parraz, Rochester, WA

PREP 20 MIN. • **COOK:** 9 hours
MAKES: 6 servings (plus about 14 oz. cooked corned beef leftovers)

- 6   medium red potatoes, quartered
- 2   medium carrots, cut into chunks
- 1   large onion, sliced
- 2   corned beef briskets with spice packets (3 lbs. each)
- ¼   cup packed brown sugar
- 2   Tbsp. sugar
- 2   Tbsp. coriander seeds
- 2   Tbsp. whole peppercorns
- 4   cups water

1. In a 6-qt. slow cooker, combine the potatoes, carrots and onion. Add briskets (discard spice packets from corned beef or save for another use). Sprinkle the brown sugar, sugar, coriander and peppercorns over meat. Pour water over top.
2. Cook, covered, on low until meat and vegetables are tender, 9-11 hours.
3. Remove meat and vegetables to a serving platter. Thinly slice 1 brisket across the grain and serve with vegetables. Save the remaining brisket for another use.
4 oz. cooked corned beef with ¾ cup vegetables: 557 cal., 31g fat (10g sat. fat), 156mg chol., 1825mg sod., 38g carb. (16g sugars, 4g fiber), 32g pro.

SOUTHWEST CHICKEN CHILI

Chicken thighs are a nice change of pace in this easy chili. I also add a smoked ham hock and fresh cilantro to add flavor and keep the dish interesting.
—*Phyllis Beatty, Chandler, AZ*

PREP: 15 min. • **COOK:** 6 hours
MAKES: 5 servings

- 1½ lbs. boneless skinless chicken thighs, cut into 1-in. cubes
- 1 Tbsp. olive oil
- 1 smoked ham hock
- 1 can (15½ oz.) great northern beans, rinsed and drained
- 1 can (14½ oz.) chicken broth
- 1 can (4 oz.) chopped green chiles
- ¼ cup chopped onion
- 2 Tbsp. minced fresh cilantro
- 1 tsp. garlic powder
- 1 tsp. ground cumin
- ½ tsp. dried oregano
- ⅛ to ¼ tsp. crushed red pepper flakes
  Optional: Sour cream and sliced jalapeno chile pepper

1. In a large skillet, brown chicken in oil over medium-high heat. Transfer to a 3-qt. slow cooker. Add the ham hock, beans, broth, chiles, onion and seasonings. Cover and cook on low until ham is tender, 6-8 hours.

2. Remove ham bone. When cool enough to handle, remove meat from bone; discard bone. Cut meat into bite-sized pieces and return to slow cooker. If desired, serve with sour cream and sliced jalapeno.

Note: Wear disposable gloves when cutting hot peppers; the oils can burn skin. Avoid touching your face.

1 cup: 343 cal., 16g fat (4g sat. fat), 104mg chol., 735mg sod., 16g carb. (1g sugars, 5g fiber), 33g pro.

CHILI MAC

This recipe has regularly appeared on my family menus for more than 40 years, and it's never failed to please at potlucks and bring-a-dish gatherings. Sometimes I turn it into a soup by adding a can of beef broth.
—*Marie Posavec, Berwyn, IL*

PREP: 15 min. • **COOK:** 6 hours
MAKES: 6 servings

- 1 lb. lean ground beef (90% lean), cooked and drained
- 2 cans (16 oz. each) hot chili beans, undrained
- 2 large green peppers, chopped
- 1 large onion, chopped
- 4 celery ribs, chopped
- 1 can (8 oz.) no-salt-added tomato sauce
- 2 Tbsp. chili seasoning mix
- 2 garlic cloves, minced
- 1 pkg. (7 oz.) elbow macaroni, cooked and drained
  Salt and pepper to taste
  Optional: Shredded pepper jack cheese and sliced jalapeno pepper

1. In a 5-qt. slow cooker, combine the first 8 ingredients. Cover and cook on low for 6 hours or until heated through.
2. Stir in macaroni. Season with salt and pepper. If desired, top individual servings with cheese and sliced jalapenos.
Note: Wear disposable gloves when cutting hot peppers; the oils can burn skin. Avoid touching your face.
1 serving: 348 cal., 8g fat (3g sat. fat), 47mg chol., 713mg sod., 49g carb. (8g sugars, 12g fiber), 27g pro. **Diabetic exchanges:** 3 starch, 3 lean meat.

SLOW-COOKER CHIPOTLE PORK CHOPS

I love the tender texture of pork chops made in the slow cooker! The flavor of this sauce is similar to barbecue, but with a little extra kick. The crispy onions on top add a delectable crunch.
—*Elisabeth Larsen, Pleasant Grove, UT*

PREP: 15 min. • **COOK:** 4 hours
MAKES: 8 servings

- 8 bone-in pork loin chops (7 oz. each)
- 1 small onion, finely chopped
- ⅓ cup chopped chipotle peppers in adobo sauce
- ¼ cup packed brown sugar
- 2 Tbsp. red wine vinegar
- 2 garlic cloves, minced
- ½ tsp. salt
- ¼ tsp. pepper
- 1 can (15 oz.) tomato sauce
- 1 can (14½ oz.) fire-roasted diced tomatoes, undrained

TOPPINGS

- 1 can (6 oz.) French-fried onions
- ¼ cup minced fresh cilantro

Place all ingredients except toppings in a 5-qt. slow cooker. Cook, covered, on low until a thermometer inserted in pork reads at least 145°, 4-5 hours. Top with French-fried onions and cilantro just before serving.
1 pork chop: 408 cal., 20g fat (6g sat. fat), 86mg chol., 844mg sod., 24g carb. (10g sugars, 2g fiber), 32g pro.

MY BRAZILIAN FEIJOADA

A co-worker's mom used to make this dish for him and it was his favorite. So I made him my own version. Instead of sausage you can use ham hocks, or substitute lean white meat for the red meat if you prefer.
—*Christiane Counts, Webster, TX*

PREP: 20 min. + soaking • **COOK:** 7 hours
MAKES: 10 servings

- 8 oz. dried black beans (about 1 cup)
- 2 lbs. boneless pork shoulder butt roast, trimmed and cut into 1-in. cubes
- 3 bone-in beef short ribs (about 1½ lbs.)
- 4 bacon strips, cooked and crumbled
- 1¼ cups diced onion
- 3 garlic cloves, minced
- 1 bay leaf
- ¾ tsp. salt
- ¾ tsp. pepper
- 1½ cups chicken broth
- 1 cup water
- ½ cup beef broth
- 8 oz. smoked sausage, cut into ½-in. slices
  Orange sections
  Hot cooked rice, optional

1. Rinse and sort beans; soak according to package directions. Meanwhile, place pork roast, short ribs and bacon in a 6-qt. slow cooker. Add onion, garlic, bay leaf and seasonings; pour chicken broth, water and beef broth over the meat. Cook, covered, on high for 2 hours.
2. Stir in black beans and sausage. Cook, covered, on low until meat and beans are tender, 5-6 hours. Discard the bay leaf. Remove short ribs. When cool enough to handle, remove meat from bones; discard bones. Shred meat with 2 forks; return to slow cooker. Top servings with orange sections. If desired, serve with hot rice.
1 serving: 481 cal., 27g fat (11g sat. fat), 123mg chol., 772mg sod., 17g carb. (2g sugars, 4g fiber), 41g pro.

CASABLANCA CHUTNEY CHICKEN

If you enjoy Indian food, you'll love this dish. An array of spices and dried fruit slowly simmer with boneless chicken thighs for an aromatic and satisfying meal.
—*Roxanne Chan, Albany, CA*

PREP: 25 min. • **COOK:** 4 hours
MAKES: 4 servings

- 1 lb. boneless skinless chicken thighs, cut into ¾-in. pieces
- 1 can (14½ oz.) chicken broth
- ⅓ cup finely chopped onion
- ⅓ cup chopped sweet red pepper
- ⅓ cup chopped carrot
- ⅓ cup chopped dried apricots
- ⅓ cup chopped dried figs
- ⅓ cup golden raisins
- 2 Tbsp. orange marmalade
- 1 Tbsp. mustard seed
- 2 garlic cloves, minced
- ½ tsp. curry powder
- ¼ tsp. crushed red pepper flakes
- ¼ tsp. ground cumin
- ¼ tsp. ground cinnamon
- ¼ tsp. ground cloves
- 2 Tbsp. minced fresh parsley
- 2 Tbsp. minced fresh mint
- 1 Tbsp. lemon juice
- 4 Tbsp. chopped pistachios
  Cooked pearl (Israeli) couscous, optional

1. In a 3-qt. slow cooker, combine the first 16 ingredients. Cover and cook on low for 4 hours or until chicken is tender.
2. Stir in the parsley, mint and lemon juice; heat through. Sprinkle each serving with pistachios; if desired, serve with cooked Israeli couscous.
1 cup: 389 cal., 13g fat (3g sat. fat), 78mg chol., 567mg sod., 44g carb. (31g sugars, 6g fiber), 26g pro.

COOL-KITCHEN TIP

Feijoada is a versatile stew of beans, various meats and sausages typically served over rice. The word *feijao* translates to *bean* in Portuguese. Brazil's version specifically uses black beans, although different regions also use brown or red beans.

COOL-KITCHEN TIP
Browning sauce is used to add flavor and color to recipes. It's used here to enhance the color traditionally provided by brown sugar. You can make it at home or find it in the grocery store near the broth and gravy.

CARIBBEAN CHICKEN STEW

I lived with a West Indian family for a while and enjoyed watching them cook. I lightened up this recipe by leaving out the oil and sugar, removing the skin from the chicken and using chicken sausage.
—*Joanne Iovino, Kings Park, NY*

PREP: 25 min. + marinating
COOK: 6 hours • **MAKES:** 8 servings

- ¼ cup ketchup
- 3 garlic cloves, minced
- 1 Tbsp. sugar
- 1 Tbsp. hot pepper sauce
- 1 tsp. browning sauce, optional
- 1 tsp. dried basil
- 1 tsp. dried thyme
- 1 tsp. paprika
- ½ tsp. salt
- ½ tsp. dried oregano
- ½ tsp. ground allspice
- ½ tsp. pepper
- 8 bone-in chicken thighs (about 3 lbs.), skin removed
- 1 lb. fully cooked andouille chicken sausage links, sliced
- 1 medium onion, finely chopped
- 2 medium carrots, finely chopped
- 2 celery ribs, finely chopped
  Hot cooked rice, optional

1. In a bowl, combine ketchup, garlic, sugar, pepper sauce and, if desired, browning sauce; stir in seasonings. Add chicken thighs, sausage and vegetables. Cover; refrigerate 8 hours or overnight.
2. Transfer chicken mixture to a 4- or 5-qt. slow cooker. Cook, covered, on low until chicken is tender, 6-8 hours. If desired, serve with rice.

1 serving: 309 cal., 14g fat (4g sat. fat), 131mg chol., 666mg sod., 9g carb. (6g sugars, 1g fiber), 35g pro. **Diabetic exchanges:** 5 lean meat, ½ starch.

PINEAPPLE RUMCHATA SHORTCAKES

This deliciously different dessert is made in the slow cooker in jars instead of in the oven. When done, add final touches to the cooled shortcake jars and serve.
—*Joan Hallford, North Richland Hills, TX*

PREP: 20 min. • **COOK:** 1½ hours + cooling
MAKES: 6 servings

- 1½ cups all-purpose flour
- ¼ cup sugar
- 1 tsp. baking powder
- ½ tsp. salt
- ¼ tsp. baking soda
- ⅓ cup cold butter
- 1 large egg, room temperature
- ¾ cup sour cream
- 3 Tbsp. RumChata liqueur

TOPPING
- 1½ cups fresh pineapple, cut into ½-in. pieces
- 3 Tbsp. sugar, divided
- 1 to 2 Tbsp. RumChata liqueur
- 1 tsp. grated lime zest
- ½ cup heavy whipping cream
- 1 medium lime, thinly sliced, optional

1. In a large bowl, whisk flour, sugar, baking powder, salt and baking soda. Cut in butter until mixture resembles coarse crumbs. In another bowl, whisk egg, sour cream and RumChata. Add to the flour mixture; stir just until moistened.
2. Spoon mixture into 6 greased half-pint jars. Center lids on jars and screw on bands until fingertip tight. Place jars in a 6- or 7-qt. oval slow cooker; add enough hot water to reach halfway up the jars, about 5 cups. Cook, covered, on high 1½-2 hours or until a toothpick inserted in center of shortcake comes out clean.
3. Meanwhile, for the topping, combine pineapple, 2 Tbsp. sugar, RumChata and lime zest. Refrigerate, covered, at least 1 hour.
4. Remove jars from slow cooker to wire racks to cool completely. In a large bowl, beat cream until it begins to thicken. Add the remaining 1 Tbsp. sugar; beat until soft peaks form.
5. Top shortcakes with pineapple mixture, whipped cream and, if desired, lime slices.

1 shortcake: 463 cal., 28g fat (17g sat. fat), 101mg chol., 442mg sod., 47g carb. (20g sugars, 1g fiber), 6g pro.

LOUISIANA RED BEANS & RICE

Smoked turkey sausage and red pepper flakes add zip to this slow-cooked version of the New Orleans classic. For extra heat, add red pepper sauce.
—*Julia Bushree, Menifee, CA*

PREP: 20 min. • **COOK:** 3 hours
MAKES: 8 servings

- 4 cans (16 oz. each) kidney beans, rinsed and drained
- 1 can (14½ oz.) diced tomatoes, undrained
- 1 pkg. (14 oz.) smoked turkey sausage, sliced
- 3 celery ribs, chopped
- 1 large onion, chopped
- 1 cup chicken broth
- 1 medium green pepper, chopped
- 1 small sweet red pepper, chopped
- 6 garlic cloves, minced
- 1 bay leaf
- ½ tsp. crushed red pepper flakes
- 2 green onions, chopped
  Hot cooked rice

1. In a 4- or 5-qt. slow cooker, combine the first 11 ingredients. Cook, covered, on low until vegetables are tender, 3-4 hours.
2. Stir before serving. Remove bay leaf. Serve with green onions and rice.
FREEZE OPTION: Discard bay leaf and freeze cooled bean mixture in freezer containers. To use, partially thaw in refrigerator overnight. Heat through in a saucepan, stirring occasionally; add broth or water if necessary. Serve as directed.
1 cup: 291 cal., 3g fat (1g sat. fat), 32mg chol., 1070mg sod., 44g carb. (8g sugars, 13g fiber), 24g pro.

SPICY SEAFOOD STEW

The hardest part of this quick and easy recipe is peeling and dicing the potatoes—and you can even do that the night before. Just place the potatoes in water and store them in the refrigerator overnight to speed up assembly the next day.
—Bonnie Marlow, Ottoville, OH

PREP: 30 min. • **COOK:** 4¾ hours
MAKES: 9 servings (about 2 qt.)

  2 lbs. potatoes, peeled and diced
  1 lb. carrots, sliced
  1 jar (24 oz.) pasta sauce
  2 jars (6 oz. each) sliced mushrooms, drained
1½ tsp. ground turmeric
1½ tsp. minced garlic
  1 tsp. cayenne pepper
 ¼ tsp. salt
1½ cups water
  1 lb. sea scallops
  1 lb. uncooked shrimp (31-40 per lb.), peeled and deveined

1. In a 5-qt. slow cooker, combine the first 8 ingredients. Cook, covered, on low until potatoes are tender, 4½-5 hours.
2. Stir in water, scallops and shrimp. Cook, covered, until scallops are opaque and shrimp turn pink, 15-20 minutes longer.
1 cup: 229 cal., 2g fat (0 sat. fat), 73mg chol., 803mg sod., 34g carb. (10g sugars, 6g fiber), 19g pro.

NORTH AFRICAN CHICKEN & RICE

I'm always looking to try recipes from different cultures and this one is a huge favorite. We love the spice combinations. This cooks equally well in a slow cooker or pressure cooker.
—Courtney Stultz, Weir, KS

PREP: 10 min. • **COOK:** 4 hours
MAKES: 8 servings

  1 medium onion, diced
  1 Tbsp. olive oil
  8 boneless skinless chicken thighs (about 2 lbs.)
  1 Tbsp. minced fresh cilantro
  1 tsp. ground turmeric
  1 tsp. paprika
  1 tsp. sea salt
 ½ tsp. pepper
 ½ tsp. ground cinnamon
 ½ tsp. chili powder
  1 cup golden raisins
 ½ to 1 cup chopped pitted green olives
  1 medium lemon, sliced
  2 garlic cloves, minced
 ½ cup chicken broth or water
  4 cups hot cooked brown rice

In a 3- or 4-qt. slow cooker, combine onion and oil. Place chicken thighs on top of onion; sprinkle with next 7 ingredients. Top with raisins, olives, lemon and garlic. Add broth. Cook, covered, on low until chicken is tender, 4-5 hours. Serve with hot cooked rice.
1 serving: 386 cal., 13g fat (3g sat. fat), 76mg chol., 556mg sod., 44g carb. (12g sugars, 3g fiber), 25g pro.

SLOW-COOKER JAMBALAYA RISOTTO

I love risotto, so I was thrilled when I found a slow-cooker recipe for it. I then adapted a jambalaya recipe for this dish.
—Angela Westra, Cambridge, MA

PREP: 20 min. • **COOK:** 2 hours
MAKES: 6 servings

- 2½ cups chicken broth
- 1 can (14½ oz.) diced tomatoes, undrained
- 1½ cups tomato sauce
- 1¼ cups uncooked arborio rice
- 3 Tbsp. finely chopped onion
- 1 Tbsp. dried parsley flakes
- 1 Tbsp. olive oil
- ½ tsp. garlic powder
- ½ tsp. dried thyme
- ½ tsp. pepper
- ¼ tsp. salt
- ¼ tsp. cayenne pepper
- 1 bay leaf
- ½ lb. uncooked shrimp (31-40 per lb.), peeled, deveined and tails removed
- ½ lb. fully cooked andouille sausage links, sliced
- ⅔ cup shredded Parmesan cheese, optional
  Sliced green onions, optional

1. In a 4- or 5-qt. slow cooker, combine the first 13 ingredients. Cook, covered, on high for 1¾ hours.
2. Stir in shrimp, sausage and, if desired, cheese. Cook until shrimp turn pink and rice is tender, 10-15 minutes longer. Remove bay leaf. Top with green onions if desired.
1½ cups: 335 cal., 11g fat (3g sat. fat), 97mg chol., 1276mg sod., 42g carb. (4g sugars, 3g fiber), 19g pro.

ZA'ATAR CHICKEN

It's hard to find a dinner both my husband and kids will enjoy—and even harder to find one that's fast and easy. This is it! No matter how much I make of this dish, it's gone to the last bite.
—Esther Erani, Brooklyn, NY

PREP: 20 min. • **COOK:** 5 hours
MAKES: 6 servings

- ¼ cup za'atar seasoning
- ¼ cup olive oil
- 3 tsp. dried oregano
- 1 tsp. salt
- ½ tsp. ground cumin
- ½ tsp. ground turmeric
- 3 lbs. bone-in chicken thighs
- 1 cup pimiento-stuffed olives
- ½ cup dried apricots
- ½ cup pitted dried plums (prunes)
- ¼ cup water
  Hot cooked basmati rice, optional

1. In a large bowl, combine the first 6 ingredients. Add chicken; toss to coat.
2. Arrange olives, apricots and plums on the bottom of a 4- or 5-qt. slow cooker. Add water; top with chicken. Cook, covered, on low until chicken is tender, 5-6 hours. If desired, serve with rice.
1 serving: 484 cal., 32g fat (7g sat. fat), 107mg chol., 1367mg sod., 18g carb. (10g sugars, 2g fiber), 30g pro.

SATAY-STYLE PORK STEW

Thai cuisine features flavors that are hot, sour, salty and sweet. This one-dish pork satay balances all of them using ginger and red pepper flakes, rice vinegar, garlic and creamy peanut butter.
—*Nicole Werner, Ann Arbor, MI*

PREP: 25 min. • **COOK:** 8 hours
MAKES: 6 servings

- 1 boneless pork shoulder butt roast (3 to 4 lbs.), cut into 1½-in. cubes
- 2 medium parsnips, peeled and sliced
- 1 small sweet red pepper, thinly sliced
- 1 cup chicken broth
- ¼ cup reduced-sodium teriyaki sauce
- 2 Tbsp. rice vinegar
- 1 Tbsp. minced fresh gingerroot
- 1 Tbsp. honey
- 2 garlic cloves, minced
- ½ tsp. crushed red pepper flakes
- ¼ cup creamy peanut butter
  Hot cooked rice, optional
- 2 green onions, chopped
- 2 Tbsp. chopped dry roasted peanuts

1. In a 3-qt. slow cooker, combine the first 10 ingredients. Cover and cook on low until pork is tender, 8-10 hours.

2. Skim fat; stir in peanut butter. Serve with rice if desired; top servings with onions and peanuts.

FREEZE OPTION: Before adding toppings, freeze cooled stew in freezer containers. To use, partially thaw in refrigerator overnight. Heat through in a saucepan, stirring occasionally; add broth or water if necessary.

1 cup: 519 cal., 30g fat (10g sat. fat), 135mg chol., 597mg sod., 19g carb. (9g sugars, 3g fiber), 44g pro.

COOL-KITCHEN TIP

Satay, popular in many Southeast Asian countries, is marinated meat served on skewers with a spicy soy and peanut sauce.

ASPARAGUS TUNA NOODLE CASSEROLE

I updated a traditional tuna casserole using fresh asparagus and asparagus soup. This is so different and delicious. Use frozen asparagus when fresh is not in season.

—*Nancy Heishman, Las Vegas, NV*

PREP: 20 min. • **COOK:** 5 hours
MAKES: 8 servings

- 2 cups uncooked elbow macaroni
- 2 cans (10½ oz. each) condensed cream of asparagus soup, undiluted
- 2 cups sliced fresh mushrooms
- 1 medium sweet red pepper, chopped
- 1 small onion, chopped
- ¼ cup lemon juice
- 1 Tbsp. dried parsley flakes, divided
- 1½ tsp. smoked paprika, divided
- 1 tsp. garlic salt
- ½ tsp. pepper
- 2 lbs. fresh asparagus, cut into 1-in. pieces
- 2 pouches (6.4 oz. each) light tuna in water
- 1½ cups shredded Colby cheese
- 1 cup multigrain snack chips, crushed
- 4 bacon strips, cooked and crumbled

1. Cook macaroni according to package directions for al dente; drain. Transfer to a 4- or 5-qt. greased slow cooker. Stir in soup, mushrooms, red pepper, onion, lemon juice, 1½ tsp. parsley, 1 tsp. paprika, the garlic salt and pepper. Cook, covered, on low for 4 hours.
2. Stir in asparagus and tuna. Cook, covered, on low until the asparagus is crisp-tender, about 1 hour longer. Sprinkle with the remaining 1½ tsp. parsley and ½ tsp. paprika. Serve with cheese, crushed chips and bacon.

1⅓ cups: 338 cal., 15g fat (6g sat. fat), 44mg chol., 1110mg sod., 30g carb. (5g sugars, 5g fiber), 22g pro.

SOUTHERN POT ROAST

Cajun seasoning adds kick to this tender beef roast that's served with a corn and tomato mixture. It is an unusual dish, but it's full of flavor.

—*Amber Zurbrugg, Alliance, OH*

PREP: 10 min. • **COOK:** 5 hours
MAKES: 5 servings

- 1 boneless beef chuck roast (2½ lbs.)
- 1 Tbsp. Cajun seasoning
- 1 pkg. (9 oz.) frozen corn, thawed
- ½ cup chopped onion
- ½ cup chopped green pepper
- 1 can (14½ oz.) diced tomatoes, undrained
- ½ tsp. pepper
- ½ tsp. hot pepper sauce

1. Cut roast in half; place in a 5-qt. slow cooker. Sprinkle with Cajun seasoning. Top with corn, onion and green pepper. Combine the tomatoes, pepper and hot pepper sauce; pour over vegetables.
2. Cover and cook on low until meat is tender, 5-6 hours. Serve corn mixture with a slotted spoon.
FREEZE OPTION: Freeze cooled beef mixture in freezer containers. To use, partially thaw in refrigerator overnight. Microwave, covered, on high in a microwave-safe dish until heated through, stirring gently; add broth or water if necessary. .

1 serving: 455 cal., 22g fat (8g sat. fat), 147mg chol., 601mg sod., 17g carb. (5g sugars, 3g fiber), 47g pro.

SLOW-COOKER PAD THAI

I love pad thai, but I hate standing over a hot stir-fry—especially in the summer. This slow-cooker version lets me keep my cool and enjoy pad thai, too.
—Shawn Barto, Palmetto, FL

PREP: 20 min. • **COOK:** 4 hours
MAKES: 4 servings

- 3 boneless skinless chicken breast halves (5 to 6 oz. each)
- ¼ cup packed brown sugar
- ¼ cup lime juice
- 2 Tbsp. soy sauce
- 2 garlic cloves, minced
- 1 tsp. fish sauce or additional soy sauce
- ¼ tsp. crushed red pepper flakes
- 8 oz. uncooked Asian lo mein noodles
- 2 tsp. butter
- 2 large eggs, beaten
- 3 green onions, thinly sliced
- ¼ cup chopped salted peanuts
- ¼ cup chopped fresh cilantro

1. Place chicken in a 1½- or 3-qt. slow cooker. Combine the next 6 ingredients; pour over chicken. Cook, covered, on low until a thermometer inserted in chicken reads 165°, about 4 hours. Remove chicken; cool slightly. Shred chicken with 2 forks and return to slow cooker.
2. In a large saucepan, cook noodles according to package directions. In a small nonstick skillet, heat butter over medium heat. Pour in eggs; cook and stir until eggs are thickened and no liquid egg remains.
3. Drain noodles. Stir eggs and noodles into slow cooker. Top with green onions, peanuts and cilantro.
FREEZE OPTION: Freeze cooled chicken mixture in freezer containers. To use, partially thaw in refrigerator overnight. Heat through in a saucepan, stirring occasionally; add water or broth if necessary. Prepare noodles and eggs as directed; stir into chicken mixture. Garnish as directed.
1 serving: 482 cal., 12g fat (3g sat. fat), 157mg chol., 891mg sod., 59g carb. (14g sugars, 2g fiber), 34g pro.

SLOW-COOKER VEGGIE LASAGNA

This veggie-licious alternative to traditional lasagna makes use of slow-cooker convenience. I suggest using chunky spaghetti sauce.
—Laura Davister, Little Suamico, WI

PREP: 25 min. • **COOK:** 3½ hours
MAKES: 2 servings

- ½ cup shredded part-skim mozzarella cheese
- 3 Tbsp. 1% cottage cheese
- 2 Tbsp. grated Parmesan cheese
- 2 Tbsp. egg substitute
- ½ tsp. Italian seasoning
- ⅛ tsp. garlic powder
- ¾ cup meatless spaghetti sauce, divided
- ½ cup sliced zucchini, divided
- 2 no-cook lasagna noodles
- 4 cups fresh baby spinach
- ½ cup sliced fresh mushrooms

1. Cut two 18x3-in. strips of heavy-duty foil; crisscross so they resemble an "X". Place strips on bottom and up side of a 1½-qt. slow cooker. Coat strips with cooking spray.
2. In a small bowl, combine the first 6 ingredients. Spread 1 Tbsp. spaghetti sauce on the bottom of prepared slow cooker. Top with half the zucchini and a third of the cheese mixture.
3. Break noodles into 1-in. pieces; sprinkle half of the noodles over cheese mixture. Spread with 1 Tbsp. sauce. Top with half the spinach and half the mushrooms. Repeat layers. Top with remaining cheese mixture and remaining spaghetti sauce.
4. Cover and cook on low until noodles are tender, 3½-4 hours.
1 serving: 259 cal., 8g fat (4g sat. fat), 23mg chol., 859mg sod., 29g carb. (9g sugars, 4g fiber), 19g pro. **Diabetic exchanges:** 2 lean meat, 2 medium-fat meat, 1½ starch, 1 vegetable, ½ fat.

STARTER PACK

Use your slow cooker to precook ingredients for the week's meals! These recipes make enough for sandwiches, salads and other tasty dishes.

BUTTER & HERB TURKEY

My kids love turkey for dinner, and this easy recipe lets me make it whenever I want. No special occasion required!
—Rochelle Popovic, South Bend, IN

PREP: 10 min. • **COOK:** 5 hours
MAKES: 12 servings (3 cups gravy)

- 1 bone-in turkey breast (6 to 7 lbs.)
- 2 Tbsp. butter, softened
- ½ tsp. dried rosemary, crushed
- ½ tsp. dried thyme
- ¼ tsp. garlic powder
- ¼ tsp. pepper
- 1 can (14½ oz.) chicken broth

- 3 Tbsp. cornstarch
- 2 Tbsp. cold water

1. Rub turkey with butter. Combine the rosemary, thyme, garlic powder and pepper; sprinkle over turkey. Place in a 6-qt. slow cooker. Pour broth over top. Cover and cook on low until tender, 5-6 hours.
2. Remove turkey to a serving platter; keep warm. Skim fat from cooking juices; transfer to a small saucepan. Bring to a boil. Combine cornstarch and water until smooth. Gradually stir into the pan. Bring to a boil; cook and stir until thickened, about 2 minutes. Serve with turkey.

5 oz. cooked turkey with ¼ cup gravy: 339 cal., 14g fat (5g sat. fat), 128mg chol., 266mg sod., 2g carb. (0 sugars, 0 fiber), 48g pro.

BEST EVER ROAST BEEF

This is the best roast beef I've ever had, and it's great for family dinners! Cube leftover meat and save any extra sauce to add to fried rice.
—Caroline Flynn, Troy, NY

PREP: 15 min. • **COOK:** 7 hours
MAKES: 12 servings

- 1 boneless beef chuck roast (4 lbs.), trimmed
- 1 large sweet onion, chopped
- 1⅓ cups plus 3 Tbsp. water, divided
- 1 can (10½ oz.) condensed French onion soup
- ½ cup packed brown sugar
- ⅓ cup reduced-sodium soy sauce
- ¼ cup cider vinegar
- 6 garlic cloves, minced
- 1 tsp. ground ginger
- ¼ tsp. pepper
- 3 Tbsp. cornstarch

1. Cut roast in half. Transfer to a 5-qt. slow cooker; add onion and 1⅓ cups water. In a small bowl, combine the soup, brown sugar, soy sauce, vinegar, garlic, ginger and pepper; pour over top. Cover and cook on low until meat is tender, 7-8 hours.
2. Remove meat to a serving platter and keep warm. Skim fat from cooking juices; transfer to a small saucepan. Bring liquid to a boil. Combine cornstarch and remaining 3 Tbsp. water until smooth; gradually stir into the pan. Bring to a boil; cook and stir until thickened, about 2 minutes. Serve with roast.

FREEZE OPTION: Freeze cooled beef mixture in freezer containers. To use, partially thaw in refrigerator overnight. Microwave, covered, on high in a microwave-safe dish until heated through, stirring gently.

4 oz. cooked beef with ¼ cup gravy: 324 cal., 15g fat (6g sat. fat), 99mg chol., 451mg sod., 15g carb. (11g sugars, 1g fiber), 31g pro.

HONEY-GLAZED HAM

Here's an easy solution for feeding a large group. The simple ham is perfect for family dinners where time in the kitchen is as valuable as space in the oven.
—*Jacquie Stolz, Little Sioux, IA*

PREP: 10 min. • **COOK:** 4½ hours
MAKES: 14 servings

- 1 boneless fully cooked ham (4 lbs.)
- 1½ cups ginger ale
- ¼ cup honey
- ½ tsp. ground mustard
- ½ tsp. ground cloves
- ¼ tsp. ground cinnamon

1. Cut ham in half; place in a 5-qt. slow cooker. Pour ginger ale over ham. Cover and cook on low until heated through, 4-5 hours.
2. Combine the honey, mustard, cloves and cinnamon; stir until smooth. Spread over ham; cook 30 minutes longer.
3 oz. cooked ham: 165 cal., 5g fat (2g sat. fat), 66mg chol., 1348mg sod., 8g carb. (7g sugars, 0 fiber), 24g pro.

COOL-KITCHEN TIP
If you don't have ginger ale, you can use any other white soda.

EASY LEMON-ROSEMARY CHICKEN

This slow-cooker chicken is perfect for spring gatherings with its light and fresh lemon and rosemary flavor. It also pairs well with a variety of sides. Plus, the slow cooker does most of the work!
—*Courtney Stultz, Weir, KS*

PREP: 15 min. • **COOK:** 4 hours + standing
MAKES: 6 servings

- 1 broiler/fryer chicken (3 to 4 lbs.)
- 2 celery ribs, cut into 1-in. pieces
- 1 medium onion, chopped
- 1 medium apple, sliced
- 1 Tbsp. olive oil
- 1 Tbsp. minced fresh rosemary or 1 tsp. dried rosemary, crushed
- 2 tsp. sea salt
- 1½ tsp. minced fresh thyme or ½ tsp. dried thyme
- 1½ tsp. paprika
- 1 garlic clove, minced
- 1 tsp. pepper
- 1 medium lemon, sliced

1. Fill chicken cavity with celery, onion and apple. Tuck wings under chicken; tie drumsticks together. Place in a 6-qt. slow cooker, breast side up. Rub chicken with oil; rub with rosemary, salt, thyme, paprika, garlic and pepper. Top with lemon slices.
2. Cook, covered, on low until a thermometer inserted in thickest part of a thigh reads at least 170°-175°, 4-5 hours. Remove chicken from slow cooker; tent with foil. Discard vegetables and apple. Let chicken stand 15 minutes before carving.
5 oz. cooked chicken: 318 cal., 19g fat (5g sat. fat), 104mg chol., 730mg sod., 1g carb. (0 sugars, 0 fiber), 33g pro.

P. 204

INSTANT POT®, AIR FRYER & MORE

Convenient kitchen gadgets let you cook apps, sides, mains and desserts without ever turning on your oven.

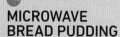

MICROWAVE BREAD PUDDING

I came up with this warm dessert one night while babysitting. The kids were asking for something sweet, and I was craving bread pudding.
—*Victoria Kvassay, Covina, CA*

TAKES: 20 min. • **MAKES:** 8 servings

- ¾ cup heavy whipping cream
- ½ cup semisweet chocolate chips
- ¼ cup whipped cream cheese
- ¼ cup sugar
- 1 Tbsp. butter
- 10 slices white bread, cut into 1-in. cubes
- 15 miniature peanut butter cups, quartered
  Creamy peanut butter, melted, optional

1. In a large microwave-safe bowl, combine cream, chocolate chips, cream cheese, sugar and butter. Cover and microwave on high until the chips are melted, 2-3 minutes; stir until smooth. Add bread cubes; toss to coat.

2. Place half the bread mixture in a greased 8-in. square microwave-safe dish. Sprinkle with peanut butter cups; top with remaining bread mixture. Microwave, uncovered, on high until peanut butter cups are melted, about 1½ minutes. Serve warm and if desired, drizzle with peanut butter.

1 piece: 346 cal., 20g fat (11g sat. fat), 35mg chol., 259mg sod., 39g carb. (21g sugars, 2g fiber), 6g pro.

JALAPENO POPPER STUFFED CHICKEN BREASTS

My husband is not crazy about chicken, but one of his favorite snacks are jalapeno poppers, so I created this dinnertime recipe to give our chicken plenty of flavor. He loves it cooked this way. Best of all is the quick cooking with little cleanup!
—*Donna Gribbins, Shelbyville, KY*

PREP: 15 min. • **COOK:** 15 min./batch
MAKES: 4 servings

- 4 oz. cream cheese, softened
- 1 cup shredded cheddar cheese
- 1 jalapeno pepper, seeded and finely chopped
- 4 boneless skinless chicken breast halves (6 oz. each)
- ½ tsp. salt
- ½ tsp. pepper
- 8 thick-sliced bacon strips

1. Preheat air fryer to 375°. In a small bowl, mix the cream cheese, cheddar cheese and jalapeno pepper. Cut a pocket horizontally in the thickest part of each chicken breast. Fill with cheese mixture. Sprinkle chicken with salt and pepper. Wrap 2 bacon strips around each chicken breast; secure with toothpicks.
2. In batches, place chicken in greased air fryer, seam side down. Cook until a thermometer inserted into the chicken reads 165°, 14-16 minutes, turning once. Let stand 5 minutes. Discard toothpicks before serving.
Note: Wear disposable gloves when cutting hot peppers; the oils can burn skin. Avoid touching your face.
1 stuffed chicken breast: 518 cal., 33g fat (15g sat. fat), 171mg chol., 1150mg sod., 3g carb. (1g sugars, 0 fiber), 51g pro.

AIR-FRYER PORK TENDERLOIN

I originally developed this pork tenderloin recipe to cook on the stove and finish in the oven, but I now make it even quicker in an air fryer—and it's just as tasty.
—*Lynn Faria, Southington, CT*

PREP: 10 min. • **COOK:** 20 min. + standing
MAKES: 2 servings

- 1 pork tenderloin (¾ lb.)
- 1 Tbsp. spicy brown mustard
- 2 tsp. canola oil
- 1 tsp. garlic powder
- 1 tsp. onion powder
- ½ tsp. pepper

Preheat air fryer to 375°. Trim silver skin from tenderloin if desired; pat dry. In a bowl, stir together remaining ingredients; spread over tenderloin. Place on greased tray in the air-fryer basket. Cook until a thermometer reads 145°, 18-20 minutes. Let stand 10 minutes before slicing.
5 oz. cooked pork: 257 cal., 11g fat (2g sat. fat), 95mg chol., 145mg sod., 2g carb. (0 sugars, 0 fiber), 34g pro. **Diabetic exchanges:** 5 lean meat, 1 fat.

AIR-FRYER PEANUT BUTTER COOKIES

An iconic American cookie, this version is so easy to mix up and bakes even faster in the air fryer. Cookie cravings can now be satisfied in mere minutes!
—*Maggie Schimmel, Wauwatosa, WI*

PREP: 15 min. • **COOK:** 5 min./batch
MAKES: 3 dozen

- 1 large egg, room temperature, beaten
- 1 cup sugar
- 1 cup creamy peanut butter

1. In a large bowl, mix all the ingredients. Roll level Tbsp. of dough into balls. Flatten with a fork.
2. Preheat air fryer to 400°. In batches, place 1 in. apart in greased air fryer. Cook until lightly browned, 3-4 minutes. Allow to cool slightly on the pan and remove to wire racks to cool.
1 cookie: 66 cal., 4g fat (1g sat. fat), 5mg chol., 32mg sod., 7g carb. (6g sugars, 0 fiber), 2g pro.

COOL-KITCHEN TIP

After the cookies have cooled completely, place them in an airtight container or resealable bag and store at room temperature. To freeze, store them in an airtight container in the freezer for up to 2 months.

EASY SWEDISH MEATBALLS

This recipe relies on ingredients we always have on hand. While the tender meatballs cook in the microwave, make your favorite noodles on the stovetop to get this saucy entree on the table in just half an hour.
—*Sheryl Ludeman, Kenosha, WI*

TAKES: 30 min. • **MAKES:** 4 servings

- 1 small onion, chopped
- 1 large egg
- ¼ cup seasoned bread crumbs
- 2 Tbsp. 2% milk
- ½ tsp. salt
- ⅛ tsp. pepper
- 1 lb. ground beef

SAUCE
- 1 can (10¾ oz.) condensed cream of mushroom soup, undiluted
- ½ cup sour cream
- ¼ cup 2% milk
- 1 Tbsp. dried parsley flakes
- ¼ tsp. ground nutmeg, optional
  Hot cooked noodles
  Minced fresh parsley, optional

1. In a large bowl, combine onion, egg, bread crumbs, milk, salt and pepper. Crumble beef over mixture; mix lightly but thoroughly. Shape into 1-in. meatballs, about 24.
2. Place meatballs in a shallow 1½-qt. microwave-safe dish. Cover; microwave on high until the meat is no longer pink, 7½ minutes; drain.
3. Combine the soup, sour cream, milk, parsley and, if desired, nutmeg; pour over meatballs. Cover and cook on high until heated through, 5-6 minutes. Serve with noodles and, if desired, top with parsley.
6 meatballs with sauce: 366 cal., 21g fat (10g sat. fat), 135mg chol., 1055mg sod., 15g carb. (4g sugars, 1g fiber), 26g pro.

AIR-FRIED AVOCADO

Ordinary avocado just got even more exciting! These juicy, flavorful, easy and healthy appetizers are for those who are huge fans of avocado. They even go well on tacos!
—*Julie Peterson, Crofton, MD*

PREP: 10 min. • **COOK:** 10 min./batch
MAKES: 28 servings

- 1 large egg, beaten
- ¼ cup cornmeal
- ½ tsp. salt
- ½ tsp. garlic powder
- ½ tsp. ground chipotle pepper
- 2 medium avocados, peeled and sliced
  Cooking spray
  Optional: Lime wedges, salsa, pico de gallo or spicy ranch dressing

1. Preheat air fryer to 400°. Place egg in a shallow bowl. In another shallow bowl, mix cornmeal, salt, garlic powder and chipotle pepper. Dip avocado slices in egg, then into cornmeal mixture, gently patting to help adhere.
2. In batches, place avocado slices in a single layer on greased tray in air-fryer basket; spritz with cooking spray. Cook until golden brown, 4 minutes. Turn; spritz with cooking spray. Cook until golden brown, 3-4 minutes longer. If desired, serve avocado slices with lime wedges, salsa, pico de gallo or ranch dressing.
1 piece: 22 cal., 2g fat (0 sat. fat), 5mg chol., 25mg sod., 1g carb. (0 sugars, 1g fiber), 0 pro.

COOL-KITCHEN TIP

These avocado fries are a fantastic way to use avocados that are not yet quite ripe enough for guacamole. Stick with ones that are still slightly firm.

AIR-FRYER HONEY SWEET POTATOES

The flavors of sweet potatoes, cinnamon and honey are such classics. Try this side dish with roast chicken or pork.
—*Laura Mifsud, Northville, MI*

PREP: 10 min. • **COOK:** 20 min.
MAKES: 6 servings

- 3 Tbsp. honey
- 2 Tbsp. olive oil
- ¾ tsp. ground cinnamon
- ½ tsp. salt
- ¼ tsp. pepper
- 3 medium sweet potatoes, peeled and cut into ½-in. cubes

Preheat air fryer to 350°. In a large bowl, whisk together the honey, oil, cinnamon, salt and pepper; add potatoes and toss to coat. Transfer to greased tray in air-fryer basket. Cook until potatoes are tender, 20-25 minutes, stirring every 5 minutes.
¾ cup: 169 cal., 5g fat (1g sat. fat), 0 chol., 207mg sod., 32g carb. (18g sugars, 3g fiber), 2g pro. **Diabetic Exchanges:** 2 starch, ½ fat.

AIR-FRYER FUDGY BROWNIES

Don't heat up your kitchen! These small-batch air-fryer brownies come together so quickly, and no oven is required. Top with nuts or powdered sugar for a quick homemade treat.
—*Rashanda Cobbins, Milwaukee, WI*

PREP: 10 min. • **BAKE:** 45 min.
MAKES: 9 servings

- ⅓ cup butter, cubed
- 1½ cups 60% cacao bittersweet chocolate baking chips, divided
- 2 large eggs, room temperature
- ¾ cup sugar
- 2 Tbsp. water
- 1 tsp. vanilla extract
- ¾ cup all-purpose flour
- ¼ tsp. baking soda
- ¼ tsp. salt

1. Preheat air fryer to 325°. Line a 6-in. square or round cake pan with parchment, letting ends extend up sides. In a small microwave-safe bowl, melt butter and 1 cup chocolate chips; stir until smooth. Cool slightly. In a small bowl, beat sugar and eggs. Stir in the water and vanilla. Combine flour, baking soda and salt; gradually add to the chocolate mixture. Fold in remaining ½ cup chocolate chips.
2. Pour batter into prepared pan. Bake for 40-45 minutes or until a toothpick inserted in center comes out with moist crumbs (do not overbake). Tent with foil as needed to prevent overbrowning. Cool on a wire rack.
3. Lifting with parchment, remove the brownies from pan. Cut into squares.
1 brownie: 315 cal., 16g fat (10g sat. fat), 59mg chol., 174mg sod., 43g carb. (32g sugars, 2g fiber), 4g pro.

AIR-FRYER PIZZA PUFFS

I love pizza in any form, so it seemed only logical to turn my pizza love into an appetizer. These little bundles can be made ahead of time and chilled until you're ready to pop them into the air fryer.
—Vivi Taylor, Middleburg, FL

PREP: 20 min. • **COOK:** 10 min./batch
MAKES: 20 servings

- 1   loaf (1 lb.) frozen pizza dough, thawed
- 20   slices pepperoni
- 8   oz. part-skim mozzarella cheese, cut into 20 cubes
- ¼   cup butter
- 2   small garlic cloves, minced
     Dash salt
     Marinara sauce, warmed
     Optional: Crushed red pepper flakes and grated Parmesan cheese

1. Preheat the air fryer to 350°. Shape the dough into 1½-in. balls; flatten into ⅛-in.-thick circles. Place 1 pepperoni slice and 1 cheese cube in center of each circle; wrap dough around pepperoni and cheese. Pinch edges to seal; shape into a ball. Repeat with remaining dough, cheese and pepperoni.
2. In batches, place balls seam side up in a single layer on greased tray in air-fryer basket; cook 6-8 minutes or until light golden brown. Cool slightly.
3. Meanwhile, in a small saucepan, melt butter over low heat. Add garlic and salt, taking care not to brown butter or garlic; brush over puffs. Serve with marinara sauce; if desired, sprinkle with red pepper flakes and Parmesan.
Freeze option: Cover and freeze unbaked pizza puffs on waxed paper-lined baking sheets until firm. Transfer to a freezer container; seal and return to freezer. To use, preheat air fryer to 350°; bake pizza puffs on greased tray in air-fryer basket as directed, increasing time as necessary until golden brown.
1 pizza puff: 120 cal., 6g fat (3g sat. fat), 15mg chol., 189mg sod., 11g carb. (1g sugars, 0 fiber), 5g pro.

AIR-FRYER CRUMB-TOPPED SOLE

Looking for a low-carb supper that's ready in a flash? These buttery fillets are covered with a rich sauce and topped with toasty bread crumbs.
—Taste of Home *Test Kitchen*

PREP: 10 min. • **COOK:** 10 min./batch
MAKES: 4 servings

- 3   Tbsp. reduced-fat mayonnaise
- 3   Tbsp. grated Parmesan cheese, divided
- 2   tsp. mustard seed
- ¼   tsp. pepper
- 4   sole fillets (6 oz. each)
- 1   cup soft bread crumbs
- 1   green onion, finely chopped
- ½   tsp. ground mustard
- 2   tsp. butter, melted
     Cooking spray
     Additional chopped green onion, optional

1. Preheat air fryer to 375°. Combine mayonnaise, 2 Tbsp. cheese, mustard seed and pepper; spread over the tops of the fillets.
2. In batches, place fish in a single layer on greased tray in air-fryer basket. Cook until fish flakes easily with a fork, 3-5 minutes.
3. Meanwhile, in a small bowl, combine the bread crumbs, onion, ground mustard and remaining 1 Tbsp. cheese; stir in butter. Spoon over fillets, patting gently to adhere; spritz topping with cooking spray. Cook until golden brown, 2-3 minutes longer. If desired, sprinkle with additional onions.
1 fillet: 233 cal., 11g fat (3g sat. fat), 89mg chol., 714mg sod., 8g carb. (1g sugars, 1g fiber), 24g pro.

COOL-KITCHEN TIP
Red snapper, tilapia and cod can be substituted for the sole.

AIR-FRYER SCALLOPS

I never liked seafood until my husband urged me to try scallops, and now I love it. With the crunchy breading, my air-fryer scallops are the best you'll ever have.
—*Martina Preston, Willow Grove, PA*

TAKES: 25 min. • **MAKES:** 2 servings

- 1 **large egg**
- ⅓ **cup mashed potato flakes**
- ⅓ **cup seasoned bread crumbs**
- ⅛ **tsp. salt**
- ⅛ **tsp. pepper**
- 6 **sea scallops (about ¾ lb.), patted dry**
- 2 **Tbsp. all-purpose flour**
  Butter-flavored cooking spray

1. Preheat air fryer to 400°. In a shallow bowl, lightly beat egg. In another bowl, toss together the potato flakes, bread crumbs, salt and pepper. In a third bowl, toss the scallops with flour to coat lightly. Dip in the egg, then in the potato mixture, patting to adhere.

2. Arrange scallops in a single layer on greased tray in air-fryer basket; spritz with cooking spray. Cook until golden brown, 3-4 minutes. Turn; spritz with cooking spray. Cook until breading is golden brown and scallops are firm and opaque, 3-4 minutes longer.

3 scallops: 298 cal., 5g fat (1g sat. fat), 134mg chol., 1138mg sod., 33g carb. (2g sugars, 2g fiber), 28g pro.

COOL-KITCHEN TIP
To soak up any excess oil, put the cooked scallops on a paper towel-lined plate.

AIR-FRYER CHEESECAKE

This cheesecake is something I've been making and perfecting for years. My daughter insisted it be served at her wedding. I was happy to oblige.
—*Howard Koch, Lima, OH*

PREP: 20 min. • **COOK:** 45 min. + chilling
MAKES: 8 servings

- 1¼ cups graham cracker crumbs
- ⅓ cup butter, melted
- ¼ cup sugar
  FILLING/TOPPING
- 2 pkg. (8 oz. each) cream cheese, softened
- 2 large eggs, room temperature, lightly beaten
- ⅔ cup sugar, divided
- 2 tsp. vanilla extract, divided
  Dash salt
- 1 cup sour cream
  Whipped cream, optional

1. Preheat air fryer to 325°. In a bowl, combine the graham cracker crumbs, butter and sugar. Pat into bottom and 1 in. up sides of an 8-in. springform pan that fits into the air fryer. Chill while preparing filling.
2. For filling, beat cream cheese and eggs in a bowl on medium speed for 1 minute. Add ⅓ cup sugar, 1 tsp. vanilla and salt. Continue beating until well blended, about 1 minute. Pour into crust.
3. Cook for 25-30 minutes or until center is almost set. Cool 10 minutes. For topping, combine sour cream and remaining sugar and vanilla in a small bowl; spread over cheesecake. Cook 15 minutes longer. Cool on a wire rack 10 minutes. Loosen sides from pan with a knife. Cool 1 hour longer. Refrigerate for 3 hours or overnight. If desired, serve with whipped cream.
1 piece: 504 cal., 36g fat (20g sat. fat), 145mg chol., 357mg sod., 40g carb. (30g sugars, 1g fiber), 7g pro.

COOL-KITCHEN TIP
Instead of using graham cracker crumbs when making the crust, try using the crumbs of vanilla wafers.

QUICK POACHED SALMON WITH CUCUMBER SAUCE

There's no reason to fear cooking fish at home when you have this simple recipe. Besides basil, try using dill, fennel or coriander in the herby sauce.
—*Crystal Jo Bruns, Iliff, CO*

TAKES: 20 min. • **MAKES:** 4 servings

- 1 cup water
- ½ cup dry white wine or chicken broth
- 1 small onion, sliced
- 2 sprigs fresh parsley
- ¼ tsp. salt
- 5 peppercorns
- 4 salmon fillets (6 oz. each)
  SAUCE
- ½ cup sour cream
- ⅓ cup chopped seeded peeled cucumber
- 1 Tbsp. finely chopped onion
- ¼ tsp. salt
- ¼ tsp. dried basil

1. In an 11x7-in. microwave-safe dish coated with cooking spray, combine first 6 ingredients. Microwave, uncovered, on high until the mixture comes to a boil, 2-3 minutes.
2. Carefully add salmon to dish. Cover and microwave at 70% power until fish flakes easily with a fork, 5-5½ minutes.
3. Meanwhile, in a small bowl, combine the sour cream, cucumber, onion, salt and basil. Remove salmon from poaching liquid. Serve with sauce.
1 salmon fillet with 3 Tbsp. sauce: 361 cal., 21g fat (7g sat. fat), 105mg chol., 393mg sod., 4g carb. (2g sugars, 0 fiber), 30g pro.

AIR-FRYER CRAB RANGOON

I always order crab Rangoon when out to eat. The appetizer is one of my favorites. I decided to create a healthier version at home using my air fryer.
—*Emily Higgins, Wingdale, NY*

PREP: 30 min. • **COOK:** 5 min./batch
MAKES: about 3 dozen

- 1 pkg. (8 oz.) reduced-fat cream cheese
- ½ cup mayonnaise
- 2 green onions, sliced
- 1 tsp. paprika
- 1 Tbsp. lime juice
- 1 tsp. garlic powder
- 1 tsp. reduced-sodium soy sauce
- 8 oz. fresh crabmeat
- 40 wonton wrappers
   Cooking spray
   Chinese-style mustard

1. In a small bowl, beat cream cheese and mayonnaise. Stir in green onions, paprika, lime juice, garlic powder and soy sauce. Fold in crab.

2. Preheat air fryer to 350°. Spoon 2 tsp. filling in the center of a wonton wrapper. (Cover remaining wrappers with a damp paper towel until ready to use.) Moisten wrapper edges with water. Fold opposite sides over the filling, pressing centers together to seal. Repeat with remaining sides, making a 4-pointed star. Repeat.

3. In batches, place wontons in a single layer on greased tray in air-fryer basket; spritz with cooking spray. Cook until golden brown and crispy, 5-8 minutes. Serve with mustard.

1 appetizer: 62 cal., 3g fat (1g sat. fat), 11mg chol., 111mg sod., 5g carb. (0 sugars, 0 fiber), 2g pro.

COOL-KITCHEN TIP
Do you have leftover Rangoon? Refrigerate them and then reheat in the air fryer at 350° for 2-3 minutes.

PRESSURE-COOKER CHICKEN MARBELLA

This is sweet, briny, savory and herbal, and it packs a big punch of garlic. The Mediterranean flavors make me think of dinner on the patio with family or friends.
—*Beth Jacobson, Milwaukee, WI*

PREP: 30 min. • **COOK:** 10 min. + releasing
MAKES: 6 servings

- 1 cup reduced-sodium chicken broth
- 1 cup pitted green olives, divided
- 1 cup pitted dried plums (prunes), divided
- 2 Tbsp. dried oregano
- 2 Tbsp. packed brown sugar
- 2 Tbsp. capers, drained
- 2 Tbsp. olive oil
- 4 garlic cloves, minced
- ½ tsp. salt
- ½ tsp. pepper
- 6 bone-in chicken thighs, skin removed (about 2 lbs.)
- 1 Tbsp. minced fresh parsley
- 1 Tbsp. white wine
- 1 Tbsp. lemon juice
  Hot cooked couscous

1. Place broth, ½ cup olives, ½ cup dried plums, oregano, brown sugar, capers, oil, garlic, salt and pepper in a food processor; process until smooth. Transfer mixture to a 6-qt. electric pressure cooker. Place chicken in the pressure cooker. Lock lid; close pressure-release valve. Adjust to pressure-cook on high for 10 minutes. Allow pressure to naturally release for 10 minutes, then quick-release any remaining pressure.
2. Chop remaining olives and dried plums. Remove chicken; keep warm. Stir parsley, wine, lemon juice and remaining olives and plums into olive mixture. Serve with chicken and couscous.
1 chicken thigh: 352 cal., 17g fat (3g sat. fat), 77mg chol., 908mg sod., 26g carb. (13g sugars, 2g fiber), 23g pro.

PRESSURE-COOKER BUFFALO WING POTATOES

I was getting tired of mashed potatoes and baked spuds, so I decided to create something new. This potluck-ready recipe is an easy and delicious twist on the usual potato dish.
—*Summer Feaker, Ankeny, IA*

TAKES: 20 min. • **MAKES:** 6 servings

- 2 lbs. Yukon Gold potatoes, cut into 1-in. cubes
- 1 small sweet yellow pepper, chopped
- ½ small red onion, chopped
- ¼ cup Buffalo wing sauce
- ½ cup shredded cheddar cheese
  Optional: Crumbled cooked bacon, sliced green onions and sour cream

1. Place steamer basket and 1 cup water in a 6-qt. electric pressure cooker. Set potatoes, yellow pepper and onion in basket. Lock lid; close pressure-release valve. Adjust to pressure-cook on high for 3 minutes. Quick-release pressure.
2. Remove vegetables to a serving bowl; discard cooking liquid. Add Buffalo wing sauce to vegetables; gently stir to coat. Sprinkle with the cheese. Cover and let stand until cheese is melted, 1-2 minutes. If desired, top with bacon, green onions and sour cream.
¾ cup: 182 cal., 4g fat (2g sat. fat), 9mg chol., 382mg sod., 32g carb. (3g sugars, 3g fiber), 6g pro. **Diabetic Exchanges:** 2 starch, ½ fat.

PRESSURE-COOKER LAVA CAKE

Because I love chocolate, this decadent cake has long been a family favorite. It's even delicious cold the next day.
—Elizabeth Farrell, Hamilton, MT

PREP: 15 min. • **COOK:** 20 min. + standing
MAKES: 8 servings

- 1 cup all-purpose flour
- 1 cup packed brown sugar, divided
- 5 Tbsp. baking cocoa, divided
- 2 tsp. baking powder
- ¼ tsp. salt
- ½ cup fat-free milk
- 2 Tbsp. canola oil
- ½ tsp. vanilla extract
- ⅛ tsp. ground cinnamon
- 1¼ cups hot water
  Optional toppings: Fresh raspberries and ice cream

1. In a large bowl, whisk flour, ½ cup brown sugar, 3 Tbsp. cocoa, baking powder and salt. In another bowl, whisk milk, oil and vanilla until blended. Add to flour mixture; stir just until moistened.
2. Spread into a 1½-qt. baking dish coated with cooking spray. In a small bowl, mix cinnamon and remaining ½ cup brown sugar and 2 Tbsp. cocoa; stir in hot water. Pour over batter (do not stir).
3. Place trivet insert and 1 cup water in a 6-qt. electric pressure cooker. Cover baking dish with foil. Fold an 18x12-in. piece of foil lengthwise into thirds, making a sling. Use sling to lower the dish onto trivet. Lock lid; close pressure-release valve. Adjust to pressure-cook on high for 20 minutes. Quick-release pressure.
4. Using foil sling, carefully remove baking dish. Let stand 15 minutes. A toothpick inserted in cake portion should come out clean. If desired, serve with raspberries and ice cream.
1 serving: 208 cal., 4g fat (0 sat. fat), 0 chol., 208mg sod., 42g carb. (28g sugars, 1g fiber), 3g pro.

AIR-FRYER SOUTHWESTERN CHICKEN ENCHILADAS

These air-fryer enchiladas are not only quick and easy but are a perfect dinner for Taco Tuesday (or any day of the week). Use rotisserie chicken for a substitute for cooked chicken.
—Joan Hallford, North Richland Hills, TX

PREP: 20 min. • **COOK:** 10 min./batch
MAKES: 6 servings

- 2 cups shredded cooked chicken
- 1¼ cups shredded Monterey Jack cheese or pepper jack cheese, divided
- 1¼ cups shredded sharp cheddar cheese, divided
- ½ cup hominy or whole kernel corn, rinsed and drained
- ½ cup canned black beans, rinsed and drained
- 1 can (4 oz.) chopped green chiles
- 1 Tbsp. chili seasoning mix
- ¼ tsp. salt
- ¼ tsp. pepper
- 12 flour tortillas (6 in.), warmed
- 1 cup enchilada sauce
  Sour cream, guacamole, salsa, and limes

1. Do not preheat air fryer. In a large bowl, combine chicken, ½ cup Monterey Jack cheese, ½ cup cheddar cheese, hominy, beans, chiles and seasonings. Line air fryer basket with foil, letting ends extend up sides; grease foil. Place ¼ cup chicken mixture off center on each tortilla; roll up. In batches, place in air fryer, seam side down. Top with half the enchilada sauce; sprinkle with half the remaining Monterey Jack and cheddar cheeses.
2. Cook until heated through and cheeses are melted, 10-12 minutes. Repeat with the remaining ingredients. Serve with toppings of your choice.
2 enchiladas: 525 cal., 24g fat (12g sat. fat), 86mg chol., 1564mg sod., 43g carb. (3g sugars, 3g fiber), 33g pro.

AIR-FRYER PLANTAINS

Having grown up in Puerto Rico, I've had so much amazing Caribbean food, but tostones have always been a favorite of mine. Traditionally they are deep fried, but this version gives me the same fabulous taste without some of the calories.
—*Leah Martin, Gilbertsville, PA*

PREP: 15 min. + soaking
COOK: 15 min./batch • **MAKES:** 3 dozen

- 3 garlic cloves, minced
- 1 Tbsp. garlic salt
- ½ tsp. onion powder
- 6 green plantains, peeled and cut into 1-in. slices
  Cooking spray
  SEASONING MIX
- 1 Tbsp. garlic powder
- 1½ tsp. garlic salt
- ½ tsp. onion powder
- ½ tsp. kosher salt
  Optional: Guacamole and pico de gallo

1. In a large bowl, combine garlic, garlic salt and onion powder. Add plantains; cover with cold water. Soak 30 minutes. Drain plantains; place on paper towels and pat dry.
2. Preheat air fryer to 375°. In batches, place the plantains in a single layer on greased tray in air-fryer basket; spritz with cooking spray. Cook until lightly browned, 10-12 minutes. Place plantain pieces between 2 sheets of aluminum foil. With the bottom of a glass, flatten to ½-in. thickness. Increase air-fryer temperature to 400°. Return flattened plantains to air fryer; cook 2-3 minutes longer or until golden brown. Combine seasoning mix ingredients; sprinkle over tostones.
1 piece: 39 cal., 0 fat (0 sat. fat), 0 chol., 110mg sod., 10g carb. (4g sugars, 1g fiber), 0 pro.

PRESSURE-COOKER BUFFALO SHRIMP MAC & CHEESE

Rich, creamy and slightly spicy, this shrimp and pasta dish does it all. It's a nice new twist on popular Buffalo chicken dishes.
—*Robin Haas, Cranston, RI*

PREP: 15 min. • **COOK:** 10 min. + releasing
MAKES: 6 servings

- 2 cups 2% milk
- 1 cup half-and-half cream
- 1 Tbsp. unsalted butter
- 1 tsp. ground mustard
- ½ tsp. onion powder
- ¼ tsp. white pepper
- ¼ tsp. ground nutmeg
- 1½ cups uncooked elbow macaroni
- 2 cups shredded cheddar cheese
- 1 cup shredded Gouda or Swiss cheese
- ¾ lb. frozen cooked salad shrimp, thawed
- 1 cup crumbled blue cheese
- 2 Tbsp. Louisiana-style hot sauce
- 2 Tbsp. minced fresh chives
- 2 Tbsp. minced fresh parsley
  Additional Louisiana-style hot sauce, optional

1. In a 6-qt. electric pressure cooker, combine the first 7 ingredients; stir in macaroni. Lock the lid; close pressure-release valve. Adjust to pressure-cook on high for 3 minutes. Allow pressure to naturally release for 4 minutes, then quick-release any remaining pressure.
2. Select saute setting and adjust for medium heat. Stir in shredded cheeses, shrimp, blue cheese and hot sauce. Cook until heated through, 5-6 minutes. Just before serving, stir in chives, parsley and, if desired, additional hot sauce.
1 serving: 551 cal., 34g fat (20g sat. fat), 228mg chol., 1269mg sod., 22g carb. (7g sugars, 1g fiber), 38g pro.

AIR-FRYER ROSEMARY-LEMON CHICKEN THIGHS

These air-fryer chicken thighs remind me of Sunday dinner. The lemon and herb butter really makes the chicken flavorful and juicy!

—Alyssa Lang, North Scituate, RI

PREP: 10 min. • **COOK:** 25 min.
MAKES: 4 servings

- ¼ cup butter, softened
- 3 garlic cloves, minced
- 2 tsp. minced fresh rosemary or ½ tsp. dried rosemary, crushed
- 1 tsp. minced fresh thyme or ¼ tsp. dried thyme
- 1 tsp. grated lemon zest
- 1 Tbsp. lemon juice
- 4 bone-in chicken thighs (about 1½ lbs.)
- ⅛ tsp. salt
- ⅛ tsp. pepper

1. Preheat air fryer to 400°. In a small bowl, combine butter, garlic, rosemary, thyme, lemon zest and lemon juice. Spread 1 tsp. butter mixture under skin of each chicken thigh. Spread remaining butter over skin of each thigh. Sprinkle with salt and pepper.

2. Place chicken, skin side up, on greased tray in air-fryer basket. Cook 20 minutes, turning once. Turn chicken again (skin side up) and cook until a thermometer reads 170°-175°, about 5 minutes.

1 chicken thigh: 329 cal., 26g fat (11g sat. fat), 111mg chol., 234mg sod., 1g carb. (0 sugars, 0 fiber), 23g pro.

MICROWAVED CHICKEN KIEV

I fix these easy microwaved chicken breasts all the time and love the taste.
—Dorothy LaCombe, Hamburg, NY

TAKES: 30 min. • **MAKES:** 4 servings

5   Tbsp. butter, softened, divided
½   tsp. minced chives
¼   tsp. garlic powder
¼   tsp. white pepper
4   boneless skinless chicken breast
     halves (6 oz. each)
⅓   cup cornflake crumbs
1   Tbsp. grated Parmesan cheese
½   tsp. dried parsley flakes
¼   tsp. paprika

1. In a small bowl, combine 3 Tbsp. butter, chives, garlic powder and pepper; shape into 4 cubes. Cover and freeze until firm, about 10 minutes.
2. Meanwhile, flatten chicken breast halves to ¼-in. thickness. Place a seasoned butter cube in the center of each. Fold long sides over butter; fold ends up and secure with a toothpick.
3. In a shallow bowl, combine cornflakes, cheese, parsley and paprika. Melt the remaining 2 Tbsp. butter. Dip chicken into melted butter; coat evenly with cornflake mixture. Place seam side down in a microwave-safe dish.
4. Microwave, uncovered, on high for 5-6 minutes or until chicken juices run clear and a thermometer reads 170°. Remove toothpicks. Drizzle chicken with drippings if desired.
1 filled chicken breast half: 328 cal., 18g fat (10g sat. fat), 132mg chol., 226mg sod., 4g carb. (0 sugars, 0 fiber), 35g pro.

PRESSURE-COOKER ANDOUILLE RED BEANS & RICE

Once my husband's favorite New Orleans takeout closed, I challenged myself to develop a tasty red beans and rice recipe that I could make at home. This pressure-cooker version is hearty and satisfies his Cajun cravings.
—Jennifer Schwarzkopf, Oregon, WI

PREP: 20 min. • **COOK:** 40 min. + releasing
MAKES: 8 servings

6   cups water
1   lb. dried kidney beans
1   large onion, chopped
1   celery rib, sliced
½   medium sweet red pepper, chopped
½   medium green pepper, chopped
4   garlic cloves, minced
1   bay leaf
1   tsp. kosher salt
1   tsp. dried thyme
1   to 2 tsp. Louisiana-style hot sauce
½   tsp. pepper
1   lb. fully cooked andouille
     sausage links, sliced
     Hot cooked rice
     Thinly sliced green onions,
     optional

1. Place the first 12 ingredients in a 6-qt. electric pressure cooker. Lock lid; close the pressure-release valve. Adjust to pressure-cook on high for 20 minutes. Quick-release pressure.
2. Stir in the sausage. Lock the lid; close the pressure-release valve. Adjust to pressure-cook on high for 17 minutes. Let pressure release naturally. Remove bay leaf. Serve with rice and, if desired, sprinkle with green onions.
Freeze option: Freeze cooled bean mixture in freezer containers. To use, partially thaw in refrigerator overnight. Heat through in a saucepan, stirring occasionally; add water if necessary.
1¼ cups: 349 cal., 12g fat (4g sat. fat), 74mg chol., 774mg sod., 40g carb. (3g sugars, 9g fiber), 25g pro.

PRESSURE-COOKER CUBAN CHICKEN

I love the flavors of Cuban food. With lots of citrus, garlic, cilantro and spices, I could eat it every day. I found that I could create that slow-cooked flavor using my Instant Pot, and now my family is eating Cuban food a lot more!
—Courtney Stultz, Weir, KS

PREP: 15 min. • **COOK:** 10 min.
MAKES: 4 servings

- 1 lb. boneless skinless chicken breasts
- 1 cup chicken broth
- ½ cup fresh cilantro leaves, chopped
- ½ cup orange juice
- 2 Tbsp. lime juice
- 1 Tbsp. olive oil
- 3 garlic cloves, minced
- 1 tsp. smoked paprika
- 1 tsp. dried oregano
- ½ tsp. salt
- ½ tsp. ground cumin
- ¼ tsp. pepper
  Hot cooked rice, optional

1. Place chicken and broth in a 6-qt. electric pressure cooker. Lock lid; close the pressure-release valve. Adjust to pressure-cook on high for 6 minutes. Quick-release pressure. A thermometer inserted in the chicken should read at least 165°.
2. Remove chicken; shred with 2 forks. Drain cooking juices. Return chicken to pressure cooker. Add remaining ingredients except rice. Select saute setting and adjust for low heat; simmer uncovered, 3-4 minutes or until heated through, stirring occasionally. Press cancel. If desired, serve with rice.
Freeze option: Freeze the cooled meat mixture and juices in freezer containers. To use, partially thaw in the refrigerator overnight. Heat through in a saucepan, stirring occasionally; add water or broth if necessary.
⅔ cup: 175 cal., 6g fat (1g sat. fat), 63mg chol., 373mg sod., 5g carb. (3g sugars, 1g fiber), 24g pro. **Diabetic Exchanges:** 3 lean meat, 1 fat.

PRESSURE-COOKER GARLIC-DILL DEVILED EGGS

I like to experiment with my recipes and was pleasantly surprised with how the fresh dill really perked up the flavor of these irresistible appetizers.
—Kami Horch, Calais, ME

PREP: 20 min. + chilling • **COOK:** 5 min.
MAKES: 2 dozen

- 1 cup cold water
- 12 large eggs
- ⅔ cup mayonnaise
- 4 tsp. dill pickle relish
- 2 tsp. snipped fresh dill
- 2 tsp. Dijon mustard
- 1 tsp. coarsely ground pepper
- ¼ tsp. garlic powder
- ⅛ tsp. paprika or cayenne pepper
  Additional snipped fresh dill, optional

1. Pour water into 6-qt. electric pressure cooker. Place trivet in cooker; set eggs on trivet. Lock lid; close pressure-release valve. Pressure-cook on low 5 minutes. Allow pressure to naturally release for 5 minutes; quick-release any remaining pressure. Immediately place eggs in a bowl of ice water to cool.
2. Cut eggs lengthwise in half. Remove yolks, reserving whites. In a bowl, mash yolks. Stir in all remaining ingredients except paprika. Spoon or pipe mixture into egg whites.
3. Refrigerate eggs, covered, for at least 30 minutes before serving. Sprinkle with paprika and, if desired, additional dill.
1 stuffed egg half: 78 cal., 7g fat (1g sat. fat), 93mg chol., 86mg sod., 1g carb. (0 sugars, 0 fiber), 3g pro.

PRESSURE-COOKER CAPONATA

This Italian eggplant dip preps quickly and actually gets better as it stands. Serve it warm or at room temperature. Try adding a little leftover caponata to scrambled eggs for a savory breakfast.
—Nancy Beckman, Helena, MT

PREP: 20 min. • **COOK:** 5 min.
MAKES: 6 cups

- 2 medium eggplants, cut into ½-in. pieces
- 1 can (14½ oz.) diced tomatoes, undrained
- 1 medium onion, chopped
- ½ cup dry red wine
- 12 garlic cloves, sliced
- 3 Tbsp. extra virgin olive oil
- 2 Tbsp. red wine vinegar
- 4 tsp. capers, undrained
- 5 bay leaves
- 1½ tsp. salt
- ¼ tsp. coarsely ground pepper
  French bread baguette slices, toasted
  Optional toppings: Fresh basil leaves, toasted pine nuts and additional olive oil

1. Place the first 11 ingredients in a 6-qt. electric pressure cooker (do not stir). Lock lid; close pressure-release valve. Adjust to pressure-cook on high for
3 minutes. Quick-release pressure.
2. Cool slightly; discard the bay leaves. Serve with toasted baguette slices. If desired, serve with toppings.
¼ cup: 34 cal., 2g fat (0 sat. fat), 0 chol., 189mg sod., 5g carb. (2g sugars, 2g fiber), 1g pro.

PRESSURE-COOKER THAI SWEET CHILI PORK BOWLS

My family loves pork tenderloin as well as Thai food, so I decided to combine the two in this easy pressure-cooker dish. It's very simple to put together and is perfect for a weeknight. Don't forget the cilantro, lime and Sriracha sauce—they really make the dish stand out.
—Debbie Glasscock, Conway, AR

PREP: 20 min. • **COOK:** 20 min. + releasing
MAKES: 6 servings

- 2 pork tenderloins (1 lb. each)
- ½ lb. sliced fresh mushrooms
- 1 large sweet onion, cut into 1-in. pieces
- 1 large sweet red pepper, cut into 1-in. pieces
- 1 cup hoisin sauce
- ¾ cup sweet chili sauce
- ¼ cup reduced-sodium soy sauce
- 2 Tbsp. lime juice
- 2 garlic cloves, minced
- 1½ tsp. minced fresh gingerroot
- 1 tsp. rice vinegar
  Torn fresh cilantro leaves
  Hot cooked rice, julienned green onions, lime wedges and Sriracha chili sauce

1. Place pork in a 6-qt. electric pressure cooker. Top with mushrooms, onion and red pepper. Whisk together hoisin sauce, chili sauce, soy sauce, lime juice, garlic, ginger and rice vinegar; pour over the vegetables. Lock lid; close pressure-release valve. Adjust to pressure-cook on high for 20 minutes. Allow pressure to release naturally.
2. Remove the pork; shred with 2 forks. Return the pork to the pressure cooker; heat through. Sprinkle with cilantro and green onions; serve with the rice, lime wedges and Sriracha.
1 serving: 384 cal., 7g fat (2g sat. fat), 86mg chol., 1664mg sod., 44g carb. (33g sugars, 3g fiber), 34g pro.

PRESSURE-COOKER STEAMED MUSSELS WITH PEPPERS

Here's a worthy way to use your one-pot cooker. Serve French bread along with the mussels to soak up the deliciously seasoned broth. If you like your food spicy, add the jalapeno seeds.
—Taste of Home Test Kitchen

PREP: 30 min. • **COOK:** 5 min.
MAKES: 4 servings

- 2 lbs. fresh mussels, scrubbed and beards removed
- 2 Tbsp. olive oil
- 1 jalapeno pepper, seeded and chopped
- 3 garlic cloves, minced
- 1 bottle (8 oz.) clam juice
- ½ cup white wine or additional clam juice
- ⅓ cup chopped sweet red pepper
- 3 green onions, sliced
- ½ tsp. dried oregano
- 1 bay leaf
- 2 Tbsp. minced fresh parsley
- ¼ tsp. salt
- ¼ tsp. pepper
  French bread baguette, sliced, optional

1. Tap mussels; discard any that do not close. Set aside. Select saute setting on a 6-qt. electric pressure cooker. Adjust for medium heat; add oil. When oil is hot, cook and stir jalapeno for 2-3 minutes or until crisp-tender. Add garlic; cook 1 minute longer. Press cancel. Stir in the mussels, clam juice, wine, red pepper, green onions, oregano and bay leaf. Lock the lid; close the pressure-release valve. Adjust to pressure-cook on high for 2 minutes. Quick-release pressure.
2. Discard bay leaf and any unopened mussels. Sprinkle with the parsley, salt and pepper. If desired, serve with the baguette slices.
Note: Wear disposable gloves when cutting hot peppers; the oils can burn skin. Avoid touching your face.
12 mussels: 293 cal., 12g fat (2g sat. fat), 65mg chol., 931mg sod., 12g carb. (1g sugars, 1g fiber), 28g pro.

STUFFED PEPPERS FOR FOUR

Truly a meal in one, this quick supper has it all: veggies, meat, pasta and sauce, packed into tender peppers.
—Taste of Home *Test Kitchen*

TAKES: 30 min. • **MAKES:** 4 servings

- ½ cup uncooked orzo pasta
- 4 medium sweet peppers (any color)
- ¼ cup water
- 1 lb. ground beef
- ½ cup chopped onion
- 2 cups pasta sauce
- 1 cup frozen broccoli-cauliflower blend, thawed and chopped
- ½ cup grated Parmesan cheese, divided

1. Cook the orzo according to package directions; drain. Cut and discard tops from peppers; remove seeds. Place in a 3-qt. round microwave-safe dish. Add water; microwave, covered, on high until peppers are crisp-tender, 7-9 minutes.
2. In a large skillet, cook and crumble beef with onion over medium heat until no longer pink, 5-7 minutes; drain. Stir in pasta sauce, vegetables, ¼ cup cheese and orzo. Spoon into peppers. Sprinkle with remaining cheese.
3. Microwave, uncovered, on high until heated through, 1-2 minutes.
1 stuffed pepper: 448 cal., 18g fat (7g sat. fat), 79mg chol., 734mg sod., 41g carb. (15g sugars, 6g fiber), 30g pro.

READER RAVE
"Absolutely delicious and easy to make. I loved how pretty it appeared."

—GRAMMYDEBBIE, TASTEOFHOME.COM

PRESSURE-COOKER TUSCAN CHICKEN PASTA

After the chicken and pasta cooks and the milk and cream cheese is added, the mixture will look liquidy. Just continue to cook and stir.
—Amber Gaines, Colorado Springs, CO

TAKES: 25 minutes • **MAKES:** 4 servings

- 1 lb. boneless skinless chicken breasts, cut into 1-in. pieces
- 8 oz. cellentani or uncooked spiral pasta
- 2 cups chicken broth
- 2 Tbsp. butter
- ¾ cup 2% milk
- 4 oz. cream cheese, cubed
- ½ tsp. garlic powder
- 3 cups fresh baby spinach
- 1 cup grated Parmesan cheese
- 1 pkg. (3 oz.) julienned soft sun-dried tomatoes (not packed in oil)
- 2 Tbsp. chopped fresh basil
- ⅛ tsp. salt
- ⅛ tsp. pepper
  Additional chopped fresh basil

1. In a 6-qt. electric pressure cooker, combine the first 4 ingredients. Lock lid; close pressure-release valve. Adjust to pressure-cook on high for 3 minutes. Let the pressure release naturally for 5 minutes; quick-release any remaining pressure.
2. Select saute setting; adjust for medium heat. Add milk, cream cheese and garlic powder. Cook and stir until the cream cheese is melted, 3-5 minutes. Stir in spinach, Parmesan, sun-dried tomatoes, basil, salt and pepper. Cook and stir until the spinach is wilted. Press cancel. Serve immediately. Garnish with additional basil if desired.
1½ cups: 660 cal., 26g fat (14g sat. fat), 130mg chol., 1199mg sod., 62g carb. (14g sugars, 7g fiber), 41g pro.

PRESSURE-COOKER ULTIMATE BLACK BEANS

Beans are the key to a lot of my family's meals, whether it's for a weekend breakfast or taco salads and burritos throughout the week. So I've been trying, for years, to find a homemade recipe as creamy and tasty as Mexican restaurant beans. This is that recipe.
—Helen Nelander, Boulder Creek, CA

PREP: 5 min. • **COOK:** 30 min. + releasing
MAKES: 20 servings

- 2 lbs. dried black beans (about 4½ cups)
- 4 tsp. salt, divided
- 12 cups water, divided
- ½ cup lard
- 1 Tbsp. ground cumin
- 2 tsp. garlic powder
  Optional: Queso fresco and cilantro

1. Rinse and sort beans. Transfer to a 6-qt. electric pressure cooker. Add 2 tsp. salt and 7 cups water. Lock lid; close pressure-release valve. Adjust to pressure-cook on high for 2 minutes. Allow the pressure to naturally release for 20 minutes and then quick-release any remaining pressure.
2. Drain the beans; discard liquid. Return beans to pressure cooker. Add remaining salt and water, lard, cumin and garlic powder. Lock lid; close pressure-release valve. Adjust to pressure-cook on high for 25 minutes. Allow pressure to naturally release 10 minutes and then quick-release any remaining pressure; do not drain.
3. If desired, mash or puree the beans in the broth and sprinkle with queso fresco and cilantro.

½ cup: 203 cal., 6g fat (2g sat. fat), 5mg chol., 475mg sod., 29g carb. (1g sugars, 7g fiber), 10g pro.

COOL-KITCHEN TIP
Lard makes the tastiest beans, but vegetable shortening also works well. Just don't omit the fat entirely, as it changes the texture of the beans.

PRESSURE-COOKER PEACHY SUMMER CHEESECAKE

This is a cool and refreshing dessert that is fancy enough to take to a gathering. You can make this ahead of time and freeze it. Make sure you wrap it well so that it's airtight, and add the peaches and whipped cream only after it thaws.
—*Joan Engelhardt, Latrobe, PA*

PREP: 25 min. • **COOK:** 30 min. + chilling
MAKES: 6 servings

- 1 pkg. (8 oz.) reduced-fat cream cheese
- 4 oz. fat-free cream cheese
- ½ cup sugar
- ½ cup reduced-fat sour cream
- 2 Tbsp. unsweetened apple juice
- 1 Tbsp. all-purpose flour
- ½ tsp. vanilla
- 3 large eggs, room temperature, lightly beaten
- 2 medium ripe peaches, peeled and thinly sliced

1. Place trivet insert and 1 cup water in a 6-qt. electric pressure cooker. Grease a 6-in. springform pan; place on a double thickness of heavy-duty foil (about 12 in. square). Wrap securely around pan.
2. In a large bowl, beat cream cheeses and sugar until smooth. Beat in sour cream, apple juice, flour and vanilla. Add eggs; beat on low speed just until blended. Pour into prepared pan. Cover the pan with foil. Fold an 18x12-in. piece of foil lengthwise into thirds, making a sling. Use the sling to lower the pan onto the trivet.
3. Lock the lid; close pressure-release valve. Adjust to pressure-cook on high for 30 minutes. Let pressure release naturally for 10 minutes; quick-release any remaining pressure. Using foil sling, carefully remove springform pan. Let stand 10 minutes. Remove foil from pan. Cool cheesecake on a wire rack 1 hour.
4. Loosen the sides from the pan with a knife. Refrigerate overnight, covering when cooled. To serve, remove rim from springform pan. Serve with peaches.
1 piece: 262 cal., 12g fat (7g sat. fat), 124mg chol., 342mg sod., 27g carb. (25g sugars, 1g fiber), 12g pro.

PRESSURE-COOKER SMOKED SALMON & DILL PENNE

I love making one-pot pastas in my pressure cooker. Every noodle soaks up the flavors of the delicious ingredients. I tried this version with some leftover smoked fish and fresh dill, and boom—this was born. It's now a staple in our house because it's on the table in half an hour, and the kids love it!
—*Shannon Dobos, Calgary, AB*

TAKES: 20 min. • **MAKES:** 6 servings

- 2¼ cups chicken broth
- ½ lb. smoked salmon fillets, flaked
- ½ cup heavy whipping cream
- 2 Tbsp. snipped fresh dill
- ½ tsp. pepper
- 12 oz. uncooked penne pasta
  Optional: Additional dill and lemon slices

Place the broth, salmon, cream, dill and pepper in a 6-qt. electric pressure cooker; top with the penne (do not stir). Lock the lid; close pressure-release valve. Adjust to pressure-cook on high for 8 minutes. Quick-release pressure. Gently stir before serving. If desired, top with additional dill and lemon slices.
1¼ cups: 322 cal., 10g fat (5g sat. fat), 33mg chol., 672mg sod., 42g carb. (3g sugars, 2g fiber), 15g pro.

SWEET MUG SHOTS

The microwave stands in for the oven for these indulgent single-serving "baked" goods!

CHOCOLATE PEANUT BUTTER MUG CAKE

This is a delectable little cake in a coffee mug! Try it with almond milk, too.
—Angela Lively, Conroe, TX

TAKES: 15 min. • **MAKES:** 1 serving

- 6 Tbsp. 2% milk
- 2 Tbsp. canola oil
- 6 Tbsp. all-purpose flour
- 3 Tbsp. sugar
- 3 Tbsp. quick-cooking oats
- ½ tsp. baking powder
- ¼ tsp. salt
- 2 Tbsp. semisweet chocolate chips
- 1 Tbsp. creamy peanut butter

1. Spray a 12-oz. coffee mug with cooking spray. Combine milk and oil in mug. Add flour, sugar, oats, baking powder and salt; stir to combine. Add the chocolate chips; dollop center with peanut butter.
2. Microwave on high for 2½ minutes or until toothpick inserted in center comes out clean. Serve immediately.
1 mug cake: 862 cal., 46g fat (9g sat. fat), 7mg chol., 945mg sod., 105g carb. (56g sugars, 5g fiber), 14g pro.

PEANUT BUTTER COOKIE IN A MUG

This peanut butter cookie in a mug is perfect for when you have a sweet tooth but don't want to make an entire batch of cookies. So quick and easy!
—Rashanda Cobbins, Milwaukee, WI

TAKES: 15 min. • **MAKES:** 1 serving

- 1 Tbsp. butter, softened
- 3 Tbsp. creamy peanut butter
- 3 Tbsp. sugar
- 1 large egg yolk, room temperature
- ¼ cup all-purpose flour
- 3 Tbsp. 2% milk
- ⅛ tsp. vanilla extract
- 1 Tbsp. chopped unsalted peanuts

1. Spray 12-oz. mug with cooking spray. Add the butter; microwave on high until melted, about 10 seconds. Stir in peanut butter and sugar until combined. Add egg yolk; stir in the flour. Add milk and vanilla extract. Top with peanuts.
2. Microwave on high 1 to 1½ minutes or until set. Serve immediately.
1 cookie: 782 cal., 46g fat (15g sat. fat), 219mg chol., 327mg sod., 77g carb. (46g sugars, 4g fiber), 20g pro.

RASPBERRY RICOTTA MUG CAKE

Who wouldn't want to dig in to a personal cake? Mug cakes are such a fun, casual treat, and you can make as few or as many as you need. The raspberry and ricotta combination makes for a tender crumb that bursts with fresh flavor.
—*Shauna Havey, Roy, UT*

TAKES: 15 min. • **MAKES:** 1 serving

- 4 Tbsp. all-purpose flour
- 3 Tbsp. sugar
- ¾ tsp. baking powder
- ¼ cup whole-milk ricotta cheese
- 3 Tbsp. half-and-half cream, divided
- 1 Tbsp. canola oil
- 1 Tbsp. fresh lemon juice
- 6 fresh raspberries, chopped
- 2 Tbsp. confectioners' sugar
  Optional: Fresh basil or mint leaves and raspberries

1. In a small bowl, stir together the flour, sugar and baking powder. Stir in ricotta, 2 Tbsp. half-and-half, oil and lemon juice until just combined. Top with chopped raspberries; stir to combine. Spoon into a 16-oz. ramekin or microwave-safe mug.
2. Microwave on high for 2-3 minutes or until set. Stir together the confectioners' sugar and remaining 1 Tbsp. half-and-half; drizzle over warm cake. Garnish if desired. Serve immediately.

1 cake: 601 cal., 25g fat (8g sat. fat), 48mg chol., 459mg sod., 84g carb. (58g sugars, 2g fiber), 12g pro.

COOL-KITCHEN TIP
Refrigerate fresh raspberries in their original container for up to 2 days. Rinse just before using.

P. 234

FROSTY TREATS

There's nothing better on a hot summer day than a frozen sweet! Ice cream, gelato, sorbet and more—they're just what you need in your freezer for a cool break.

EASY CHOCOLATE ICE CREAM

This super simple chocolate ice cream is the perfect treat at a moment's notice. It's also a bonus that most of the ingredients are kitchen staples.

—Taste of Home *Test Kitchen*

PREP: 10 min.
PROCESS: 20 min. + freezing
MAKES: 1½ qt.

- 2 cups half-and-half cream
- 1½ cups sugar
- ½ cup baking cocoa
- 1 tsp. vanilla extract
- 2 cups heavy whipping cream

Combine the half-and-half, sugar, cocoa and vanilla in a blender; process on low until mixture is smooth. Stir in heavy cream. Freeze in an ice cream freezer according to the manufacturer's directions.

½ cup: 288 cal., 18g fat (12g sat. fat), 65mg chol., 31mg sod., 28g carb. (28g sugars, 0 fiber), 2g pro.

COOL-KITCHEN TIP

This recipe is all about the chocolate flavor, so go ahead and splurge on high-quality cocoa, either regular or Dutch-processed.

✳ RAINBOW SHERBET ANGEL FOOD CAKE

Talk about a dessert that pops off the plate! Sometimes, I make this cake even more eye-catching by coloring the whipped cream too. Use whatever sherbet flavor combination you like.
—*Bonnie Hawkins, Elkhorn, WI*

PREP: 25 min. + freezing
MAKES: 12 servings

- 1 prepared angel food cake (8 to 10 oz.)
- 3 cups rainbow sherbet, softened if necessary
  WHIPPED CREAM
- 2 cups heavy whipping cream
- ⅓ cup confectioners' sugar
- 1 tsp. vanilla extract

1. Using a long serrated knife, cut cake horizontally into 4 layers. Place bottom layer on a freezer-safe serving plate; spread with 1 cup sherbet. Repeat twice with the middle cake layers and remaining 2 cups sherbet. Top with the remaining cake layer. Freeze, covered, until sherbet is firm, about 1 hour.
2. In a large bowl, beat cream until it begins to thicken. Add confectioners' sugar and vanilla; beat until soft peaks form. Frost top and sides of cake. Freeze until firm.
3. Thaw in refrigerator 30 minutes before serving. Cut cake with a serrated knife.
1 piece: 253 cal., 16g fat (10g sat. fat), 54mg chol., 174mg sod., 27g carb. (12g sugars, 2g fiber), 2g pro.

READER RAVE

"I have been making this cake for years. [It is] my son's most requested birthday cake."

—PATELL, TASTEOFHOME.COM

✳ ALMOND BUTTER SWIRL ICE CREAM

Warm weather days require ice cream! However, dealing with dairy intolerances can be tricky. This dairy-free recipe is a favorite at our house, especially with kids!
—*Courtney Stultz, Weir, KS*

PREP: 5 min.
PROCESS: 20 min. + freezing
MAKES: 1 qt.

- 1 can (13.66 oz.) coconut milk
- 1 cup unsweetened almond milk
- ½ cup sugar
- ½ cup almond butter (or other nut butter)
- ½ tsp. sea salt
- ½ cup semisweet chocolate chips, melted

Mix first 5 ingredients until well blended. Fill cylinder of ice cream maker no more than two-thirds full. Freeze according to manufacturer's directions, slowly adding melted chocolate during the last 2 minutes of processing. Serve immediately, or transfer to freezer containers, allowing headspace for expansion. Freeze until firm, 2-4 hours.
½ cup: 288 cal., 21g fat (12g sat. fat), 0 chol., 195mg sod., 24g carb. (20g sugars, 2g fiber), 5g pro.

❄ ICE CREAM BALLS

This is a fun and easy dessert to fix for Christmas gatherings ... even the kids can help! The cereal adds a crunchy texture to the ice cream and makes an everyday treat something special.
—*Anne Marie Woodhull, Cedar Springs, MI*

PREP: 15 min. + freezing
MAKES: 4 servings

- 1½ cups Corn Chex, crushed
- ¼ cup packed brown sugar
- 2 Tbsp. butter, melted
- ¼ cup finely chopped walnuts
- 1 pint vanilla ice cream, softened
  Optional: Hot fudge or caramel ice cream topping, maraschino cherries

1. In a shallow bowl, combine cereal, sugar and butter. Add nuts. Shape ice cream into 1-in. balls; roll in cereal mixture until well coated.

2. Freeze for at least 1 hour. If desired, serve with fudge or caramel ice cream topping and cherries.

4 ice cream balls: 331 cal., 18g fat (9g sat. fat), 44mg chol., 186mg sod., 40g carb. (29g sugars, 2g fiber), 4g pro.

COOL-KITCHEN TIPS

As you shape the ice cream balls and coat them in cereal, pop them back in the freezer for a few minutes if they get too soft.

You can use any kind of cereal. Experiment with flavors—including cinnamon, fruit or peanut butter—with your favorite ice cream.

To store ice cream balls, freeze on a baking tray until firm. Transfer to a zip-top bag and freeze for up to 3 months.

❄ HONEYDEW GRANITA

Make this refreshing summer treat when melons are ripe and flavorful. I like to garnish each serving with a sprig of mint or a small slice of melon.
—*Bonnie Hawkins, Elkhorn, WI*

PREP: 10 min. • **COOK:** 5 min. + freezing
MAKES: 5½ cups

- 1 cup sugar
- 1 cup water
- 6 cups cubed honeydew melon
- 2 Tbsp. sweet white wine

1. In a small saucepan, bring sugar and water to a boil over medium-high heat. Cook and stir until sugar is dissolved. Cool.
2. Pulse honeydew, sugar syrup and wine in batches in a food processor until smooth, 1-2 minutes. Transfer to an 8-in. square dish. Freeze 1 hour.
3. Stir with a fork. Freeze, stirring every 30 minutes, until frozen, 2-3 hours longer. Stir again with a fork just before serving.

½ cup: 107 cal., 0 fat (0 sat. fat), 0 chol., 17mg sod., 27g carb. (26g sugars, 1g fiber), 1g pro. **Diabetic exchanges:** 1½ starch, ½ fruit.

Honeydew Sorbet: After processing honeydew mixture, pour into the cylinder of an ice cream maker; freeze according to manufacturer's directions. Transfer to a freezer container; freeze for 4 hours or until firm.

COOL-KITCHEN TIPS

Sugar helps keep it from freezing into hard cubes of ice and also helps produce its wonderfully smooth texture, so don't skimp.

Wash fruit before eating, including the rind on melons. If you cut an unwashed melon, any microorganisms on the rind will be transferred to the fruit as the knife passes through.

❄ LEMON SHERBET

Lemon juice provides the snappy flavor in this wonderful ice cream recipe. The make-ahead treat looks splendid served in individual boats made from scooped-out lemon halves.
—*Taste of Home Test Kitchen*

PREP: 10 min. + freezing
MAKES: 1½ cups

- 1 cup half-and-half cream
- ⅓ cup sugar
- 3 Tbsp. lemon juice
- 1 tsp. grated lemon zest

1. In a small bowl, stir cream and sugar until sugar is dissolved. Stir in lemon juice and zest (mixture will thicken slightly). Cover and freeze until firm, about 8 hours or overnight.
2. Remove from the freezer 10 minutes before serving. Spoon into lemon boats or dessert dishes.

¾ cup: 295 cal., 12g fat (8g sat. fat), 60mg chol., 61mg sod., 39g carb. (38g sugars, 0 fiber), 4g pro.

LEMON COCONUT STREUSEL ICE CREAM CAKE

My family loves this cake anytime, but it's especially refreshing on a hot summer day. Sweet coconut combines beautifully with tart lemon juice, and the streusel adds a nice crunch. Look for cream of coconut in the cocktail mixer section of your grocery store. You can substitute any crunchy sugar, lemon or coconut cookies, as long as they're about 2 inches.
—*Janet Gill, Canton, OH*

PREP: 30 min. + freezing
MAKES: 16 servings

- 1 pkg. (11.2 oz.) shortbread cookies
- ½ cup sweetened shredded coconut, toasted
- ¼ cup macadamia nuts, coarsely chopped and toasted
- 1 tsp. grated lemon zest
- 1 can (15 oz.) cream of coconut
- ½ cup lemon juice
- 1½ qt. vanilla ice cream, softened
- 1 carton (8 oz.) frozen whipped topping, thawed, divided
  Optional: Fresh blueberries, raspberries and strawberries

1. Reserve 10 cookies for decoration. Crush remaining cookies; transfer to a bowl. Stir in coconut, macadamia nuts and lemon zest. Reserve 2 Tbsp. crumb mixture for topping.

2. In a large bowl, whisk cream of coconut and lemon juice until combined. Stir in softened ice cream until smooth. Fold in 1 cup whipped topping.

3. Sprinkle 1 cup crumb mixture onto bottom of a greased 9-in. springform pan. Top with half the ice cream mixture. Layer with remaining crumbs and ice cream mixture. Place reserved whole cookies around edge of pan. Top with remaining 2½ cups whipped topping; sprinkle with reserved 2 Tbsp. crumb mixture. Freeze, covered, until firm, at least 8 hours or overnight. If desired, serve with berries.
Note: To toast nuts and coconut, bake in separate shallow pans in a 350° oven for 5-10 minutes or until golden brown, stirring occasionally.
1 piece: 384 cal., 21g fat (13g sat. fat), 29mg chol., 149mg sod., 45g carb. (35g sugars, 1g fiber), 4g pro.

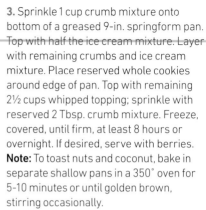

LEMON ICE

Pucker up for this sweet-tart treat. The delicious lemon dessert is a perfectly refreshing way to end a summer meal ... or any meal, for that matter.
—*Concetta Maranto Skenfield, Bakersfield, CA*

PREP: 15 min. + freezing
MAKES: 6 servings

- 2 cups sugar
- 1 cup water
- 2 cups lemon juice
  Optional: Lemon slices and fresh mint leaves

1. In a large saucepan over low heat, cook and stir sugar and water until sugar is dissolved. Remove from the heat; stir in lemon juice.
2. Pour into a freezer container. Freeze until mixture becomes slushy, about 8 hours, or overnight. If desired, top servings with lemon slices and mint.
½ cup: 278 cal., 0 fat (0 sat. fat), 0 chol., 1mg sod., 73g carb. (69g sugars, 0 fiber), 0 pro.

NO-CHURN BLUEBERRY GRAHAM CRACKER ICE CREAM

This sweet and creamy no-churn ice cream features a fresh blueberry jam swirl and graham cracker pieces. You can use raspberries instead of the blueberries for a different berry flavor.
—*Heather King, Frostburg, MD*

PREP: 25 min. + freezing • **MAKES:** 1¾ qt.

- ¾ cup fresh or frozen blueberries
- ¼ cup sugar
- 1 Tbsp. vanilla extract
- 2 cups heavy whipping cream
- 1 cup sweetened condensed milk
- 4 whole graham crackers, coarsely crushed

1. In a small saucepan, combine blueberries, sugar and vanilla. Bring to a boil; reduce heat. Simmer until mixture begins to thicken, about 5 minutes, stirring frequently. Cool completely. Refrigerate until chilled.

2. In a large bowl, beat cream until soft peaks form. Add condensed milk; beat until mixture thickens. Gently fold graham crackers into the cream mixture. Transfer to freezer containers, allowing headspace for expansion. Drop blueberry mixture by tablespoonfuls over ice cream. Cut through ice cream with a knife to swirl. Freeze for 8 hours or overnight before serving.

½ cup: 226 cal., 15g fat (9g sat. fat), 46mg chol., 64mg sod., 21g carb. (18g sugars, 0 fiber), 3g pro.

MANGO GLACE WITH PINEAPPLE POMEGRANATE SALSA

I'd like to say this dish was a brilliant idea that came from expert planning. But the truth is that between the quickly ripening fruit on my counter and the 100-degree heat, it pretty much invented itself! Very ripe fruit eliminates the need for added sugar.

—*Jodi Taffel, Altadena, CA*

PREP: 45 min. + freezing • **MAKES:** 1 dozen

- 4   medium ripe mangoes, peeled and chopped
- 1   fresh ripe pineapple, peeled and cut into ½-in. pieces
- 2   Tbsp. lime juice

FRUIT SALSA
- 1   cup finely chopped fresh pineapple
- 2   Tbsp. pomegranate seeds
- 1   Tbsp. minced fresh mint

1. Combine mangoes, pineapple and lime juice in a blender. Cover and process until smooth. Strain through a fine-mesh strainer into a large bowl. Pour into 1¾-in. silicone ice cube trays. Freeze until firm, 8 hours or overnight.

2. Combine fruit salsa ingredients; cover and refrigerate overnight.

3. Take cubes out of freezer 10 minutes before serving. Run a small spatula around the edge of each fruit cube to loosen; remove from trays. Serve with fruit salsa.

1 cube with 4 tsp. fruit salsa: 114 cal., 1g fat (0 sat. fat), 0 chol., 2mg sod., 29g carb. (24g sugars, 3g fiber), 1g pro.

SOUR CHERRY SORBET

My mother-in-law has a sour cherry tree in her yard that yields many quarts of cherries each June, and this frosty sweet-sour sorbet is a great way to use some up.

—*Carol Gaus, Elk Grove Village, IL*

PREP: 10 min. + freezing
MAKES: 6 servings

- 3   cups frozen pitted tart cherries
- 1   cup sugar
- ⅓   cup white wine or grape juice
- ½   tsp. almond extract
- ½   tsp. salt

Place cherries in a food processor; cover and process until smooth. Add remaining ingredients; cover and pulse until blended. Pour into a freezer container. Cover and freeze until firm.

⅓ cup: 175 cal., 0 fat (0 sat. fat), 0 chol., 198mg sod., 42g carb. (40g sugars, 1g fiber), 1g pro.

READER RAVE

"This is fabulous ... tastes just like cherry Life Savers! My family of nine loved it!"

—THERESE55, TASTEOFHOME.COM

NUTTY CARAMEL ICE CREAM CAKE

Tuck this dessert in the freezer for one of those anytime celebrations. This version is our favorite, but try it with other ice cream, cookie and syrup flavors. This cake can keep in the freezer for up to two months.
—David Stelzl, Waxhaw, NC

PREP: 30 min. + freezing
MAKES: 16 servings

- 4 cups crushed pecan shortbread cookies (about 33 cookies)
- ¼ cup butter, melted
- 6 cups butter pecan ice cream, softened
- 1 carton (8 oz.) frozen whipped topping, thawed
- ¾ cup slivered almonds, toasted
- ¾ cup milk chocolate English toffee bits
- ¼ cup caramel sundae syrup

1. Combine cookie crumbs and butter. Press 2 cups onto bottom of a greased 9-in. springform pan. Spoon half of ice cream into prepared pan. Freeze for 20 minutes.
2. Repeat layers with remaining cookie crumbs and ice cream. Spread with whipped topping. Sprinkle with almonds and toffee bits. Freeze, covered, overnight or until firm.
3. Remove from freezer 10 minutes before serving. Drizzle with syrup.
1 piece: 410 cal., 28g fat (11g sat. fat), 37mg chol., 232mg sod., 36g carb. (19g sugars, 1g fiber), 5g pro.

FROZEN LIME CAKE

We've got just the thing for block parties, cookouts or any time you need a cool dessert. The crust is a snap, and the ice cream and sherbet layers are so delicious. Everyone loves it!
—Kathy Gillogly, Sun City, CA

PREP: 15 min. + freezing
MAKES: 9 servings

- 1½ cups ground almonds
- ¾ cup crushed gingersnap cookies (about 15 cookies)
- ⅓ cup butter, melted
- 2 pints pineapple-coconut or vanilla ice cream, softened
- 2 pints lime sherbet, softened
  Whipped topping, optional

1. In a small bowl, combine almonds, cookies and butter. Press onto the bottom of a 9-in. square pan. Freeze 15 minutes.
2. Spread ice cream over crust. Cover and freeze at least 30 minutes.
3. Top with sherbet. Cover and freeze 4 hours or overnight.
4. Remove from the freezer 10 minutes before serving. Garnish pieces with whipped topping if desired.
1 piece: 499 cal., 29g fat (13g sat. fat), 98mg chol., 203mg sod., 54g carb. (40g sugars, 4g fiber), 8g pro.

EASY ICE CREAM SANDWICH CAKE

Here's a gooey, chocolaty dessert guests just can't resist. They'll never guess you simply dressed up ice cream sandwiches from the store!
—Taste of Home *Test Kitchen*

PREP: 20 min. + freezing
MAKES: 15 servings

- 19 ice cream sandwiches
- 1 jar (16 oz.) hot fudge ice cream topping
- 1½ cups salted peanuts
- 3 Heath candy bars (1.4 oz. each)
- 1 carton (8 oz.) frozen whipped topping, thawed (3 cups)

1. Cut 1 ice cream sandwich in half widthwise. Place one whole and one half sandwich along a short side of an ungreased 13x9-in. dish. Arrange 8 whole sandwiches in the opposite direction in the dish. Remove lid from fudge topping. Microwave 15-30 seconds to warm; stir. Spread half of fudge topping over the ice cream sandwiches.
2. In a food processor, combine peanuts and candy bars. Pulse until chopped; sprinkle half over fudge layer. Repeat layers of ice cream sandwiches and fudge topping. Spread whipped topping over top of cake. Sprinkle with the remaining peanut mixture.
3. Cover and freeze for up to 2 months. Remove from the freezer 20 minutes before serving.
1 piece: 422 cal., 19g fat (8g sat. fat), 26mg chol., 154mg sod., 54g carb. (33g sugars, 3g fiber), 9g pro.

BLACKBERRY DAIQUIRI SHERBET

The summer I decided to try making sherbet, which is one of my favorites, when blackberries were in season in my mom's garden. I love the flavor of daiquiris, and the two blend beautifully!
—*Shelly Bevington, Hermiston, OR*

PREP: 15 min.
PROCESS: 30 min./batch + freezing
MAKES: 1¼ qt.

- 3 cups fresh or frozen blackberries, thawed
- 1 cup sugar
- ¼ tsp. salt
- 1 can (12 oz.) evaporated milk
- 2 Tbsp. lime juice
- 1 tsp. rum extract
- ½ tsp. citric acid

1. Place blackberries, sugar and salt in a food processor; puree until smooth. Press through a fine-mesh strainer into a bowl; discard seeds and pulp. Stir remaining ingredients into puree.
2. Fill cylinder of ice cream maker no more than two-thirds full; freeze according to the manufacturer's directions. Transfer sherbet to freezer containers, allowing headspace for expansion. Freeze until firm, 8 hours or overnight.
½ cup: 147 cal., 3g fat (2g sat. fat), 12mg chol., 96mg sod., 28g carb. (26g sugars, 2g fiber), 3g pro.

COOL-KITCHEN TIP
Don't be tempted to substitute rum for the extract ... alcohol would keep the sherbet from freezing solid.

FRIED ICE CREAM DESSERT BARS

Fried ice cream is such a delicious treat, but it can be a hassle to make the individual servings. This recipe gives you the same fabulous flavor in an easy and convenient bar form.
—*Andrea Price, Grafton, WI*

PREP: 25 min. + freezing
COOK: 5 min. + cooling
MAKES: 16 servings

- ½ cup butter, cubed
- 2 cups crushed cornflakes
- 1½ tsp. ground cinnamon
- 3 Tbsp. sugar
- 1¾ cups heavy whipping cream
- ¼ cup evaporated milk
- ⅛ tsp. salt
- 1 can (14 oz.) sweetened condensed milk
- 2 tsp. vanilla extract
  Optional: Honey, whipped cream and maraschino cherries

1. In a large skillet, melt butter over medium heat. Add cornflakes and cinnamon; cook and stir until golden brown, about 5 minutes. Remove from heat; stir in sugar. Cool completely.
2. In a large bowl, beat cream, evaporated milk and salt until the mixture begins to thicken. Gradually beat in condensed milk and vanilla until thickened.
3. Sprinkle half the cornflakes onto the bottom of a greased 9-in. square baking pan. Pour creamy filling over the crust; sprinkle with remaining cornflakes. Cover and freeze overnight.
4. Cut into bars. If desired, serve with honey, whipped cream and cherries.
1 piece: 276 cal., 18g fat (11g sat. fat), 55mg chol., 187mg sod., 27g carb. (18g sugars, 0 fiber), 4g pro.

✽ PUMPKIN PECAN FROZEN YOGURT

I always keep fat-free frozen yogurt on hand. By combining it with just four other ingredients, I can quickly whip up this great-tasting treat.
—*Anne Smithson, Cary, NC*

PREP: 10 min. + freezing
MAKES: 8 servings

- 1 qt. fat-free frozen vanilla yogurt, softened
- ½ cup canned pumpkin
- ⅓ cup packed brown sugar
- ¾ tsp. pumpkin pie spice
- ¼ cup chopped pecans, toasted

In a large bowl, combine the first 4 ingredients. Transfer to a freezer container; freeze until serving. Sprinkle each serving with pecans.
½ cup: 161 cal., 3g fat (1g sat. fat), 2mg chol., 69mg sod., 30g carb., 1g fiber), 5g pro.

✽ STRAWBERRY SORBET

I first made a raspberry sorbet with an abundance of raspberries I had growing, but this simple recipe is amazing with any kind of berry. Strawberry is another of my go-tos.
—*Karen Bailey, Golden, CO*

TAKES: 5 min. + freezing
MAKES: 7 servings

- ¼ cup plus 1½ tsp. fresh lemon juice
- 3¾ cups fresh or frozen unsweetened chopped strawberries
- 2¼ cups confectioners' sugar

Place all ingredients in a blender or food processor; cover and process until smooth. Transfer to a freezer-safe container; freeze until firm.
½ cup: 181 cal., 0 fat (0 sat. fat), 0 chol., 2mg sod., 46g carb. (42g sugars, 2g fiber), 1g pro.

COOL-KITCHEN TIP
Homemade sorbet lasts for about 2-3 months when properly stored in the freezer. Ice crystals may develop after a month, so don't wait too long to enjoy it!

TRIPLE CHOCOLATE RICOTTA ICE CREAM

You're going to fall in love with this thick, rich ice cream made with ricotta cheese. It has a creamy texture that can't be beat.
—*Colleen Delawder, Herndon, VA*

PREP: 20 min.
PROCESS: 20 min. + freezing
MAKES: 1½ qt.

- 1 carton (15 oz.) whole-milk ricotta cheese
- 1¼ cups whole milk
- 1 cup sugar
- 4 oz. cream cheese, softened
- ½ cup baking cocoa
- ½ tsp. instant espresso powder
- ¼ tsp. salt
- 1 cup heavy whipping cream
- 3½ oz. milk chocolate, melted and cooled
- 3½ oz. dark chocolate candy bar, chopped

1. Place first 7 ingredients in a blender; cover and blend until combined, about 1 minute. Add cream and cooled melted chocolate; cover and blend until slightly thickened, about 30 seconds.
2. Fill cylinder of ice cream maker no more than two-thirds full; freeze according to manufacturer's directions, adding dark chocolate during the last 5 minutes of processing in proportion to the amount of the mixture in the cylinder. (Refrigerate any remaining mixture until ready to freeze.)
3. Transfer ice cream to freezer containers, allowing headspace for expansion. Freeze until firm, 2-4 hours.
½ cup: 321 cal., 20g fat (12g sat. fat), 53mg chol., 141mg sod., 33g carb. (30g sugars, 2g fiber), 8g pro.

FROSTY GINGER PUMPKIN SQUARES

My family loves getting together to sample good food. While pumpkin makes it perfect for the holidays, this ice cream dessert is requested year-round.
—*Kathryn Reeger, Shelocta, PA*

PREP: 30 min. + freezing
MAKES: 15 servings

- ¼ cup butter, melted
- 1 cup crushed graham cracker (about 16 squares)
- 1 cup crushed gingersnaps (about 18 cookies)
- 2 cups canned pumpkin
- 1 cup sugar
- ½ to 1 tsp. ground cinnamon
- ½ tsp. salt
- ½ tsp. ground ginger
- ¼ tsp. ground nutmeg
- 1 cup chopped walnuts
- ½ gallon vanilla ice cream, slightly softened

1. In a large bowl, combine the butter, graham crackers and gingersnaps. Press two-thirds of the crumb mixture into an ungreased 13x9-in. dish.
2. In a large bowl, combine the pumpkin, sugar, cinnamon, salt, ginger and nutmeg. Stir in walnuts. Fold in softened ice cream. Spoon into crust. Sprinkle remaining crumb mixture over top. Freeze until firm, about 3 hours.
1 piece: 351 cal., 18g fat (8g sat. fat), 39mg chol., 234mg sod., 46g carb. (33g sugars, 2g fiber), 5g pro.

❄ STRAWBERRY GELATO

You'll love this smooth and creamy gelato with bright strawberry flavor and just a hint of sea salt and honey.
—*Shelly Bevington, Hermiston, OR*

PREP: 10 min. + chilling
PROCESS: 25 min./batch + freezing
MAKES: 1½ qt.

- 2 cups whole milk
- 2 Tbsp. light corn syrup
- 1 Tbsp. honey
- ¾ cup sugar
- ½ tsp. sea salt
- 2½ cups fresh strawberries (about 12 oz.), halved
- ½ cup heavy whipping cream
- 1 tsp. lemon juice

1. Place first 6 ingredients in a blender; cover and blend. While blending, gradually add cream, blending just until combined. Remove to a bowl; stir in lemon juice. Refrigerate, covered, until cold, about 4 hours.

2. Fill cylinder of ice cream maker no more than two-thirds full; freeze according to manufacturer's directions. (Refrigerate any remaining mixture until ready to freeze.)

3. Transfer ice cream to freezer containers, allowing headspace for expansion. Freeze until firm, 3-4 hours.

½ cup: 160 cal., 6g fat (4g sat. fat), 18mg chol., 124mg sod., 26g carb. (25g sugars, 1g fiber), 2g pro.

COOL-KITCHEN TIP

Corn syrup and honey prevent ice crystals from forming in this smooth frozen treat. Try fresh raspberries or blackberries instead of strawberries, if you like. If your berries are tart, you may want to add more sugar or honey.

QUICK MANGO SORBET

Last summer, I decided to try my hand at making a passion fruit and mango sorbet. But fresh fruits require more prep and are difficult to find ripened at the same time. So I experimented using frozen fruit and juice, and *voila!* Both are readily available and inexpensive too.
—*Carol Klein, Franklin Square, NY*

TAKES: 5 min. • **MAKES:** 2½ cups

- 1 pkg. (16 oz.) frozen mango chunks, slightly thawed
- ½ cup passion fruit juice
- 2 Tbsp. sugar

Place all ingredients in a blender; cover and process until smooth. Serve immediately. If desired, for a firmer texture, cover and freeze at least 3 hours.
½ cup: 91 cal., 0 fat (0 sat. fat), 0 chol., 2mg sod., 24g carb. (21g sugars, 2g fiber), 1g pro.

CREAMY COFFEE PIE

It's easy to stir mini marshmallows, mini chocolate chips and crushed sandwich cookies into coffee ice cream to create this irresistible frozen dessert.
—*Cherron Nagel, Columbus, OH*

PREP: 25 min. + freezing
MAKES: 8 servings

- 15 Oreo cookies, finely crushed (about 1½ cups), divided
- ¼ cup butter, melted
- 2 pints coffee ice cream, softened
- 1 cup miniature marshmallows
- 1 cup miniature semisweet chocolate chips
- 2 cups whipped topping
- 2 Tbsp. caramel ice cream topping
- 2 Tbsp. hot fudge ice cream topping, warmed
- Additional Oreo cookies, optional

1. Combine 1¼ cups crushed cookies and butter. Press onto bottom and up the sides of a 9-in. pie plate. In a large bowl, combine ice cream, marshmallows, chocolate chips and the remaining crushed cookies. Spoon into crust. Freeze for 30 minutes.
2. Spread whipped topping over pie. Drizzle with caramel and hot fudge toppings. Freeze, covered, overnight. (May be frozen up to 2 months.) Remove from freezer 10-15 minutes before cutting. If desired, serve with additional cookies.
1 piece: 528 cal., 30g fat (17g sat. fat), 40mg chol., 265mg sod., 63g carb. (47g sugars, 3g fiber), 5g pro.

FROZEN VANILLA GREEK YOGURT

It's so simple and easy to make your own frozen Greek yogurt, you might even want to get the kids in on the fun.
—Taste of Home *Test Kitchen*

PREP: 15 min+ chilling
PROCESS: 15 min+ freezing
MAKES: 2½ cups

- 3 cups reduced-fat plain Greek yogurt
- ¾ cup sugar
- 1½ tsp. vanilla extract
- 1 Tbsp. cold water
- 1 Tbsp. lemon juice
- 1 tsp. unflavored gelatin

1. Line a strainer or colander with 4 layers of cheesecloth or 1 coffee filter; place over a bowl. Place yogurt in prepared strainer; cover yogurt with sides of cheesecloth. Refrigerate 2-4 hours.
2. Remove yogurt from cheesecloth to a bowl; discard strained liquid. Add sugar and vanilla to yogurt, stirring until sugar is dissolved.
3. In a small microwave-safe bowl, combine cold water and lemon juice; sprinkle with gelatin and let stand for 1 minute. Microwave on high for 30 seconds. Stir and let mixture stand 1 minute or until gelatin is completely dissolved; cool slightly. Stir the gelatin mixture into the yogurt. Cover and refrigerate until cold, about 40 minutes.
4. Pour yogurt mixture into cylinder of ice cream freezer; freeze according to the manufacturer's directions.
5. Transfer frozen yogurt to a freezer container. Freeze 2-4 hours or until firm enough to scoop.
½ cup: 225 cal., 3g fat (2g sat. fat), 8mg chol., 57mg sod., 36g carb. (36g sugars, 0 fiber), 14g pro.

❄ BELLINI ICE

This ice is fashioned after the Bellini, a peach and white Italian wine sparkler. The tart white grape juice paired with sweet ripe peaches creates a fantastic flavor combination. For a beautiful presentation, place some fresh peach slices in a large wine goblet, top with Bellini ice, and garnish with a kiwi slice.
—*Deirdre Cox, Kansas City, MO*

PREP: 10 min. + freezing
MAKES: 6 servings

- 2 medium peaches, peeled and quartered
- 2 cups white grape juice
- 1 cup lemon-lime carbonated water
- ¼ cup lime juice
  Optional: Fresh peach slices and kiwi slices

1. Place peaches in a food processor. Cover and process until pureed. Transfer to an 11x7-in. dish. Stir in the grape juice, carbonated water and lime juice. Freeze for 1 hour.
2. Stir with a fork; freeze 2-3 hours longer or until completely frozen, stirring every 30 minutes.
3. Stir with a fork just before serving; spoon into dessert dishes. Serve with peach and kiwi slices if desired.
1 serving: 65 cal., 0 fat (0 sat. fat), 0 chol., 5mg sod., 16g carb. (14g sugars, 1g fiber), 1g pro. **Diabetic exchanges:** 1 fruit.

READER RAVE
"This is a great treat on the hot summer days!"
—DVIOLA, TASTEOFHOME.COM

❄ WATERMELON BOMBE DESSERT

When cut, this sherbet dessert looks like watermelon slices—complete with seeds. It is fun to eat and refreshing, too.
—*Renae Moncur, Burley, ID*

PREP: 20 min. + freezing
MAKES: 8 servings

- About 1 pint lime sherbet
- About 1 pint pineapple sherbet
- About 1½ pints raspberry sherbet
- ¼ cup miniature semisweet chocolate chips

1. Line a 1½-qt. bowl with plastic wrap. Press a thin layer of lime sherbet against the inside of the bowl. Freeze, uncovered, until firm. Spread a thin layer of pineapple sherbet evenly over lime sherbet layer. Freeze, uncovered, until firm. Pack raspberry sherbet in the center of the sherbet-lined bowl. Smooth the top to resemble a cut watermelon.
2. Cover and freeze until firm, about 8 hours. Just before serving, uncover bowl of molded sherbet. Place a serving plate on the bowl and invert. Remove bowl and peel off plastic wrap.
3. Cut the bombe into wedges; press a few chocolate chips into the raspberry section of each wedge to resemble watermelon seeds.
1 piece: 205 cal., 4g fat (2g sat. fat), 8mg chol., 60mg sod., 43g carb. (35g sugars, 0 fiber), 2g pro.

COOL STRAWBERRY CREAM

This fruity, luscious dessert makes a wonderful ending to a special dinner. When fresh strawberries are not available, I substitute two packages of the frozen unsweetened kind, thawed and drained.
—Joyce Cooper, Mount Forest, ON

PREP: 30 min. + freezing
MAKES: 12 servings

- 2 pkg. (8 oz. each) cream cheese, softened
- ¾ cup sugar
- ½ cup sour cream
- 3 cups fresh strawberries, mashed
- 1 cup whipped topping

BLUEBERRY SAUCE
- 1 pkg. (12 oz.) frozen unsweetened blueberries
- ⅓ cup sugar
- ¼ cup water

1. Line a 9x5-in. loaf pan with a double thickness of foil; set aside. In a large bowl, beat the cream cheese, sugar and sour cream until smooth. Fold in strawberries and whipped topping. Pour into prepared pan. Cover and freeze for several hours or overnight.
2. In a small saucepan, bring the blueberries, sugar and water to a boil; cook and stir for 3 minutes. Cool slightly. Transfer to a blender; cover and process until pureed. Refrigerate until chilled.
3. Remove dessert from the freezer 15-20 minutes before serving. Use foil to lift out of pan; remove foil. Cut dessert into slices with a serrated knife. Serve with blueberry sauce.

1 piece with about 2 Tbsp. sauce: 198 cal., 10g fat (6g sat. fat), 27mg chol., 62mg sod., 26g carb. (23g sugars, 2g fiber), 2g pro.

FUDGE SUNDAE PIE

My son always asks for this frozen yogurt pie for his birthday. Complete with peanut butter, fudge topping and nuts, it tastes ice cream parlor–good ... but it's healthier.
—Margaret Riley, Tallahassee, FL

PREP: 20 min. + freezing
MAKES: 8 servings

- ¼ cup plus 3 Tbsp. light corn syrup, divided
- 3 Tbsp. reduced-fat butter
- 2 Tbsp. brown sugar
- 2½ cups crisp rice cereal
- ¼ cup reduced-fat creamy peanut butter
- ¼ cup fat-free hot fudge ice cream topping, warmed
- ¼ cup chopped unsalted peanuts
- 4 cups fat-free vanilla frozen yogurt, softened

1. In a large saucepan, combine ¼ cup corn syrup, the butter and brown sugar. Bring to a boil; cook and stir for 1 minute.
2. Remove from the heat; stir in cereal until blended. Press into a greased 9-in. pie plate.
3. In a small bowl, combine the peanut butter, hot fudge topping and remaining 3 Tbsp. corn syrup. Set aside ⅓ cup for topping. Spread remaining mixture over crust; sprinkle with half of the peanuts. Top with frozen yogurt. Freeze, covered, for 6 hours or until firm.
4. Warm reserved peanut butter mixture; drizzle over pie. Sprinkle with remaining peanuts. Let stand at room temperature for 5 minutes before cutting.

1 piece: 300 cal., 7g fat (2g sat. fat), 7mg chol., 253mg sod., 53g carb. (33g sugars, 1g fiber), 9g pro.

HOMEMADE VANILLA ICE CREAM

We think this is the best ice cream recipe ever. With only four ingredients, it just might be the easiest, too.
—Taste of Home *Test Kitchen*

PREP: 5 min.
PROCESS: 20 min. + freezing
MAKES: 1¼ qt.

- 2 cups heavy whipping cream
- 2 cups half-and-half cream
- 1 cup sugar
- 2 tsp. vanilla extract

Combine all ingredients, stirring to dissolve sugar completely. Fill cylinder of ice cream maker no more than two-thirds full; freeze according to manufacturer's directions. (Refrigerate any remaining mixture until ready to freeze.) Serve immediately or store in covered containers in freezer.

½ cup: 308 cal., 22g fat (14g sat. fat), 78mg chol., 37mg sod., 23g carb. (23g sugars, 0 fiber), 3g pro.

Raspberry or Strawberry Ice Cream: Substitute 2 cups fresh or frozen berries for 1 cup of half-and-half. Puree berries in a blender or food processor; stir into the other ingredients before freezing.

COOL-KITCHEN TIP

If you don't have an ice cream maker, pour the ice cream mixture into a shallow glass or metal container you've chilled in the freezer. Keep in the coldest part of the freezer until almost firm, but still soft enough to be stirred.

For the next 3 hours, check the ice cream every 30 minutes and stir or mix with a hand mixer to keep it aerated and creamy.

CHOCOLATE-COFFEE BEAN ICE CREAM CAKE

At our school, we celebrate faculty birthdays. I needed a quick recipe that would be appealing to everyone. This tall, impressive dessert certainly fit my needs and was a huge hit.
—Karen Beck, Alexandria, PA

PREP: 15 min. + freezing
MAKES: 12 servings

- 1¾ cups chocolate wafer crumbs (about 28 wafers)
- ¼ cup butter, melted
- 2 qt. coffee ice cream, softened
- ⅓ cup chocolate-covered coffee beans, finely chopped
- 2¼ cups heavy whipping cream
- 1 cup plus 2 Tbsp. confectioners' sugar
- ½ cup plus 1 Tbsp. baking cocoa
- ½ tsp. vanilla extract
   Chocolate curls and additional chocolate-covered coffee beans

1. In a small bowl, combine wafer crumbs and butter; press onto the bottom and up the sides of a greased 9-in. springform pan. Freeze for 10 minutes.
2. In a large bowl, combine ice cream and finely chopped chocolate-covered coffee beans; spoon over crust. Cover and freeze for 2 hours or until firm.
3. In a large bowl, beat cream until it begins to thicken. Add confectioners' sugar, cocoa and vanilla; beat until stiff peaks form. Spread over ice cream. (Pan will be full.)
4. Cover and freeze for 4 hours or overnight. Remove from the freezer 10 minutes before serving. Garnish with chocolate curls and coffee beans.

1 piece: 512 cal., 36g fat (20g sat. fat), 105mg chol., 185mg sod., 46g carb. (34g sugars, 1g fiber), 7g pro.

STICK WITH IT

Popsicles are the ultimate summer treat—
but why run after the ice cream truck when
you can make them at home in any flavor you like?

❄ BLUEBERRY CREAM POPS

Blueberry-and-cream pops are such a
fun afternoon snack. And they're simple
to make!
—*Cindy Reams, Philipsburg, PA*

PREP: 15 min. + freezing • **MAKES:** 8 pops

- ⅔ **cup sugar**
- ⅔ **cup water**
- 2 **cups fresh or frozen blueberries, thawed**
- ¼ **cup heavy whipping cream**
- 8 **freezer pop molds or 8 paper cups (3 oz. each) and wooden pop sticks**

1. For sugar syrup, in a small saucepan,
combine sugar and water; bring to a boil,
stirring to dissolve sugar. Cool completely.
2. Meanwhile, in a bowl, coarsely mash
blueberries; stir in cream and the sugar
syrup. Spoon into molds or paper cups.
Top molds with holders. If using cups,
top with foil and insert pop sticks through
foil. Freeze until firm. To serve, let pops
stand at room temperature 10 minutes
before unmolding.
1 pop: 112 cal., 3g fat (2g sat. fat), 10mg
chol., 3mg sod., 22g carb. (21g sugars,
1g fiber), 0 pro.

❄ ORANGE CREAM POPS

For a lower-fat alternative to ice cream-
filled pops, try this citrus novelty. The
tangy orange flavor will make your taste
buds tingle, while the silky smooth texture
offers cool comfort.
—*Taste of Home Test Kitchen*

PREP: 10 min. + freezing
MAKES: 10 pops

- 1 **pkg. (3 oz.) orange gelatin**
- 1 **cup boiling water**
- 1 **cup vanilla yogurt**
- ½ **cup 2% milk**
- ½ **tsp. vanilla extract**
- 10 **freezer pop molds or 10 paper cups (3 oz. each) and wooden pop sticks**

1. In a large bowl, dissolve gelatin in the
boiling water. Cool to room temperature.
2. Stir in the yogurt, milk and vanilla. Pour
¼ cup mixture into each mold or paper
cup. Top molds with holders. If using cups,
top with foil and insert pop sticks through
foil. Freeze until firm.
1 pop: 58 cal., 1g fat (0 sat. fat), 2mg chol.,
41mg sod., 11g carb. (11g sugars, 0 fiber),
2g pro. **Diabetic exchanges:** 1 starch.

✳ COCONUT MILK STRAWBERRY-BANANA POPS

These four-ingredient freezer pops are a delicious way to use up a pint of fresh strawberries. You'll love the hint of tropical flavor, thanks to the coconut milk.
—Taste of Home *Test Kitchen*

PREP: 10 min. + freezing
MAKES: 12 pops

- 1   can (13.66 oz.) coconut milk
- 1   pint fresh strawberries, chopped, divided
- 1   medium banana, sliced
- 2   Tbsp. maple syrup
- 12 freezer pop molds or 12 paper cups (3 oz. each) and wooden pop sticks

Place coconut milk, 1½ cups strawberries, banana and syrup in a blender; cover and process until smooth. Divide remaining strawberries among 12 molds or paper cups. Pour pureed mixture into molds or cups, filling ¾ full. Top molds with holders. If using cups, top with foil and insert pop sticks through foil. Freeze until firm, at least 4 hours.

1 pop: 51 cal., 3g fat (3g sat. fat), 0 chol., 5mg sod., 7g carb. (5g sugars, 1g fiber), 1g pro.

✳ STRAWBERRY-ROSEMARY YOGURT POPS

We planted strawberries a few years ago, and these tangy-sweet frozen yogurt pops are my very favorite treats to make with them! Try using other yogurt flavors like lemon, raspberry or blueberry. You may also substitute the rosemary with your favorite herb or simply omit it.
—*Carmell Childs, Orangeville, UT*

PREP: 20 min. + freezing • **MAKES:** 6 pops

- 1   cup chopped fresh strawberries
- 2   Tbsp. balsamic vinegar
- 2   Tbsp. strawberry preserves
- 2   fresh rosemary sprigs
- 1½ cups vanilla yogurt
- 6   freezer pop molds or paper cups (3 oz. each) and wooden pop or lollipop sticks

1. In a small bowl, mix strawberries, vinegar, preserves and rosemary. Let stand 30 minutes; discard rosemary.
2. Spoon 2 Tbsp. yogurt and 1 Tbsp. strawberry mixture into each mold or paper cup. Repeat layers. Top molds with holders. If using cups, top with foil and insert pop sticks through foil. Freeze until firm.

1 pop: 81 cal., 1g fat (0 sat. fat), 3mg chol., 42mg sod., 16g carb. (15g sugars, 1g fiber), 3g pro. **Diabetic exchanges:** 1 starch.

P. 262

NO-BAKE DESSERTS

Rethink summer desserts! Browse this collection of cakes, cheesecakes, pies, cookies, trifles and more—splendid meal-enders made without an oven.

SUMMER STRAWBERRY SHORTCAKE SOUP

When folks are longing for a sweet and refreshing treat, this soup is sure to hit the spot. To serve it with dinner or as an appetizer, simply omit the shortcake.
—*Joan Hallford,*
North Richland Hills, TX

PREP: 15 min. + chilling
MAKES: 4 cups

- 2 cups fresh or frozen strawberries, hulled
- 1½ cups unsweetened pineapple juice
- ½ cup white grape juice
- ⅓ cup confectioners' sugar
- ½ cup moscato wine or additional white grape juice
- ½ cup sour cream
- 6 individual round sponge cakes
  Whipped cream and additional strawberries

1. Place the strawberries in a blender; cover and process until pureed. Add the fruit juices and confectioners' sugar; cover and process until smooth. Transfer to a bowl; whisk in wine and sour cream. Refrigerate, covered, until chilled, 1-2 hours. Stir.
2. Serve with sponge cakes topped with whipped cream and sliced strawberries.
¾ cup: 227 cal., 6g fat (3g sat. fat), 32mg chol., 191mg sod., 37g carb. (27g sugars, 1g fiber), 3g pro.

OLD-FASHIONED BANANA CREAM PIE

This fluffy, no-bake pie is full of old-fashioned flavor, with only a fraction of the work. Because it uses instant pudding, it's ready in just minutes.
—*Perlene Hoekema, Lynden, WA*

TAKES: 10 min. • **MAKES:** 8 servings

- 1   cup cold 2% milk
- 1   pkg. (3.4 oz.) instant vanilla pudding mix
- ½   tsp. vanilla extract
- 1   carton (12 oz.) frozen whipped topping, thawed, divided
- 1   graham cracker crust (9 in.)
- 2   medium firm bananas, sliced
      Additional banana slices, optional

1. In a large bowl, whisk milk, pudding mix and vanilla 2 minutes (mixture will be thick). Fold in 3 cups whipped topping.
2. Pour 1⅓ cups pudding mixture into pie crust. Layer with banana slices and remaining pudding mixture. Top with remaining whipped topping. If desired, garnish with additional banana slices. Refrigerate until serving.
1 piece: 311 cal., 13g fat (9g sat. fat), 2mg chol., 213mg sod., 43g carb. (29g sugars, 1g fiber), 2g pro.

Chocolate & Peanut Butter Banana Cream Pie: Substitute 1 chocolate crumb crust (9 in.) for the graham cracker crust. Arrange the banana slices on crust. In a microwave-safe bowl, mix ¾ cup peanut butter and 2 oz. chopped chocolate; microwave on high 1-1½ minutes or until blended and smooth, stirring every 30 seconds. Spoon over bananas. Pour pudding mixture over top. Garnish with remaining whipped topping. Just before serving, garnish pie with 2 Tbsp. chopped salted peanuts.

PEANUT BUTTER PRETZEL BARS

My secret to these rich no-bake bites? Pretzels in the crust. They add a salty crunch to the classic peanut butter and chocolate pairing.
—*Jennifer Beckman, Falls Church, VA*

PREP: 15 min. + chilling • **MAKES:** 4 dozen

- 1   pkg. (16 oz.) miniature pretzels
- 1½   cups butter, melted
- 1½   cups peanut butter
- 3   cups confectioners' sugar
- 2   cups semisweet chocolate chips
- 1   Tbsp. shortening

1. Line a 13x9-in. baking pan with foil, letting ends extend up sides. Set aside 1½ cups pretzels for topping. In a food processor, pulse remaining pretzels until fine crumbs form. In a large bowl, mix butter, peanut butter, confectioners' sugar and pretzel crumbs.
2. Press mixture into prepared pan. In a microwave, melt chocolate chips and shortening; stir until smooth. Spread over the peanut butter layer. Break the reserved pretzels and sprinkle over top; press down gently. Refrigerate, covered, until set, about 1 hour. Lifting with foil, remove from pan. Cut into bars.
1 bar: 201 cal., 13g fat (6g sat. fat), 15mg chol., 233mg sod., 22g carb. (12g sugars, 1g fiber), 3g pro.

NO-BAKE CHOCOLATE HAZELNUT THUMBPRINTS

This recipe is so easy! A few years ago, a friend gave me a recipe for chocolate peanut treats that didn't require baking. I thought it was a quick and clever way to whip up a batch of sweets without heating up the kitchen, so I started making different variations of them. They're so yummy!
—*Lisa Speer, Palm Beach, FL*

PREP: 30 min. + chilling
MAKES: about 3½ dozen

- 1 carton (8 oz.) spreadable cream cheese
- 1 cup semisweet chocolate chips, melted
- ½ cup Nutella
- 2¼ cups graham cracker crumbs
- 1 cup finely chopped hazelnuts, toasted
- 1 cup whole hazelnuts, toasted

1. Beat cream cheese, melted chocolate chips and Nutella until blended. Stir in graham cracker crumbs. Refrigerate until firm enough to roll, about 30 minutes.
2. Shape mixture into 1-in. balls; roll in chopped hazelnuts. Make an indentation in the center of each with the end of a wooden spoon handle. Fill with a hazelnut. Store between layers of waxed paper in an airtight container in the refrigerator.
Note: To toast nuts, bake in a shallow pan in a 350° oven for 5-10 minutes or cook in a skillet over low heat until lightly browned, stirring occasionally.
1 cookie: 111 cal., 8g fat (2g sat. fat), 3mg chol., 46mg sod., 10g carb. (6g sugars, 1g fiber), 2g pro.

BANANA SPLIT ICEBOX CAKE

One day, a friend showed me how to make a traditional icebox cake with just some cream and graham crackers. I make it extra special with the fruit.
—*Shelly Flye, Albion, ME*

PREP: 30 min. + chilling
MAKES: 10 servings

- 1 carton (16 oz.) frozen whipped topping, thawed
- 1 cup sour cream
- 1 pkg. (3.4 oz.) instant vanilla pudding mix
- 1 can (8 oz.) crushed pineapple, drained
- 24 whole graham crackers
- 2 medium bananas, sliced
  Toppings: Chocolate syrup, halved fresh strawberries and additional banana slices

1. In a large bowl, mix the whipped topping, sour cream and pudding mix until blended; fold in pineapple. Cut a small hole in the tip of a pastry bag. Transfer pudding mixture to bag.
2. On a flat serving plate, arrange 4 graham crackers in a rectangle. Pipe about 1 cup pudding mixture over crackers; top with about ¼ cup banana slices. Repeat layers 5 times. Refrigerate, covered, overnight.
3. Just before serving, top with the chocolate syrup, strawberries and additional banana slices.
1 piece: 405 cal., 15g fat (11g sat. fat), 16mg chol., 372mg sod., 60g carb. (30g sugars, 2g fiber), 4g pro.

READER RAVE
"I've made this many times over the years, and it's always a hit."
—OWLTREE, TASTEOFHOME.COM

PINEAPPLE CHEESECAKE

A co-worker shared the recipe for this easy, elegant dessert years ago, and our family has enjoyed it many times since.
—*Phoebe Carre, Mullica Hill, NJ*

PREP: 15 min. + chilling
MAKES: 10 servings

- 2 pkg. (8 oz. each) cream cheese, softened
- ½ cup sugar
- 1 can (20 oz.) crushed pineapple, drained
- 1 carton (8 oz.) frozen whipped topping, thawed
- 2 pkg. (3 oz. each) ladyfingers (about 48)
- 1 pint fresh strawberries, sliced

1. In a large bowl, beat the cream cheese and sugar until smooth. Stir in pineapple. Fold in whipped topping.
2. Place ladyfingers around the sides and on the bottom of a greased 9-in. springform pan. Pour filling into pan. Cover and refrigerate for 8 hours or overnight. Carefully remove sides of pan. Top with strawberries.
1 piece: 366 cal., 20g fat (13g sat. fat), 82mg chol., 263mg sod., 41g carb. (33g sugars, 1g fiber), 5g pro.

COOL-KITCHEN TIP
You can also top this pineapple cheesecake with toasted coconut, sprigs of fresh mint, mango, raspberries or thin slices of lime.

NO-BAKE COOKIE BUTTER BLOSSOMS

Chewy and sweet, these easy treats mix Rice Krispies, cookie spread and chocolate in an unforgettable spin on an old favorite.
—*Jessie Sarrazin, Livingston, MT*

PREP: 25 min. + standing
MAKES: about 2½ dozen

- 1 cup Biscoff creamy cookie spread
- ½ cup corn syrup
- 3 cups Rice Krispies
- 32 milk chocolate kisses

In a large saucepan, combine the cookie spread and corn syrup. Cook and stir over low heat until blended. Remove from heat; stir in Rice Krispies until coated. Shape level tablespoonfuls of mixture into balls; place on waxed paper. Immediately press a kiss into the center of each cookie. Let stand until set.
1 cookie: 93 cal., 4g fat (1g sat. fat), 1mg chol., 22mg sod., 14g carb. (10g sugars, 0 fiber), 1g pro.

LAYERED LEMON PIE

This is a great ending for almost any meal. Kids and adults all enjoy it, and the creamy lemon filling is always a hit with my husband.
—*Elizabeth Yoder, Belcourt, ND*

PREP: 20 min. + chilling
MAKES: 8 servings

- 1 pkg. (8 oz.) cream cheese, softened
- ½ cup sugar
- 1 can (15¾ oz.) lemon pie filling, divided
- 1 carton (8 oz.) frozen whipped topping, thawed
- 1 graham cracker crust (9 in.)

In a small bowl, beat cream cheese and sugar until smooth. Beat in half the pie filling. Fold in the whipped topping. Spoon into crust. Spread the remaining pie filling over cream cheese layer. Refrigerate for at least 15 minutes before serving.
1 piece: 526 cal., 24g fat (13g sat. fat), 104mg chol., 251mg sod., 72g carb. (61g sugars, 1g fiber), 6g pro.

NO-BAKE APPLE PIE

We always have an abundance of apples in the fall, so I like to make this easy pie. My husband is diabetic, and this recipe fits into his diet ... but everyone enjoys it.
—*Shirley Vredenburg, Ossineke, MI*

PREP: 20 min. + chilling
MAKES: 8 servings

- 1 pkg. (0.3 oz.) sugar-free lemon gelatin
- ½ tsp. ground cinnamon
- ¼ tsp. ground nutmeg
- 1¾ cups water, divided
- 5 medium tart apples, peeled and sliced
- 1 pkg. (0.8 oz.) sugar-free cook-and-serve vanilla pudding mix
- ½ cup chopped nuts
- 1 reduced-fat graham cracker crust (9 in.)
  Whipped topping, optional

1. In a large saucepan, mix the gelatin, cinnamon, nutmeg and 1½ cups water. Add apples; bring to a boil. Reduce heat; simmer, covered, until apples are tender, about 5 minutes.
2. In a bowl, mix the pudding mix and remaining ¼ cup water; stir into apple mixture. Cook until thickened, about 1 minute, stirring occasionally. Remove from heat; stir in nuts. Transfer to crust.
3. Refrigerate at least 2 hours before serving. If desired, serve the pie with whipped topping.
1 piece: 202 cal., 8g fat (1g sat. fat), 0 chol., 152mg sod., 30g carb. (17g sugars, 2g fiber), 3g pro. **Diabetic exchanges:** 1½ fat, 1 starch, 1 fruit.

READER RAVE

"This pie is awesome. My mom even asked me for the recipe."
—CDSHELBY, TASTEOFHOME.COM

PEANUT BUTTER SILK PIE

My youngest son wanted to have homemade pies placed around his wedding cake, and this was one of his requests.
—*Lee Steinmetz, Lansing, MI*

PREP: 10 min. + chilling
MAKES: 8 servings

- ¾ cup peanut butter
- 4 oz. cream cheese, softened
- 1 cup confectioners' sugar
- 1 carton (8 oz.) frozen whipped topping, thawed
- 1 graham cracker crust (9 in.)
  Salted chopped peanuts
  Optional: Chocolate syrup, peanut butter ice cream topping and additional whipped topping

In a large bowl, beat the peanut butter, cream cheese and confectioners' sugar until smooth. Fold in whipped topping; pour into prepared crust. Refrigerate at least 2 hours. Before serving, sprinkle with peanuts. If desired, garnish with chocolate syrup, ice cream topping and additional whipped topping.
1 piece: 434 cal., 27g fat (11g sat. fat), 16mg chol., 276mg sod., 40g carb. (29g sugars, 2g fiber), 8g pro.

PINA COLADA ICEBOX CAKE

This icebox cake has all the flavors of a pina colada. It takes just one bite to escape to a tropical island!
—*Rachel Lewis, Danville, VA*

PREP: 25 min. + chilling
MAKES: 12 servings

- 1 pkg. (8 oz.) cream cheese, softened
- ½ cup confectioners' sugar
- ½ tsp. rum extract
- 1 can (13.66 oz.) coconut milk, divided
- 1 pkg. (3.4 oz.) instant vanilla pudding mix
- 1 container (8 oz.) frozen whipped topping, thawed
- 15 whole graham crackers
- 1 can (20 oz.) crushed pineapple, drained
- 1 cup sweetened shredded coconut, toasted

1. In a large bowl, beat cream cheese, confectioners' sugar and extract until smooth. Gradually beat in 1 cup coconut milk. Add pudding mix; beat on low speed until smooth. Fold in whipped topping.
2. Pour the remaining coconut milk into a shallow dish. Quickly dip half the graham crackers into the coconut milk; allow excess to drip off. Arrange crackers in a single layer in the bottom of a 13x9-in. baking dish, breaking to fit as needed. Layer with half each of the cream cheese mixture, pineapple and coconut. Repeat layers. Refrigerate, covered, for at least 4 hours before serving.
Note: To toast coconut, bake in a shallow pan in a 350° oven for 5-10 minutes or cook in a skillet over low heat until golden brown, stirring occasionally.
1 piece: 377 cal., 20g fat (15g sat. fat), 19mg chol., 259mg sod., 47g carb. (33g sugars, 1g fiber), 3g pro.

PEACH BAVARIAN

Fruit molds are my specialty. This one, with its refreshing peach taste, makes a colorful salad or dessert.
—*Adeline Piscitelli, Sayreville, NJ*

PREP: 15 min. + chilling
MAKES: 8 servings

- 1 can (15¼ oz.) sliced peaches
- 2 pkg. (3 oz. each) peach or apricot gelatin
- ½ cup sugar
- 2 cups boiling water
- 1 tsp. almond extract
- 1 carton (8 oz.) frozen whipped topping, thawed
   Additional sliced peaches, optional

1. Drain the peaches, reserving ⅔ cup juice. Chop peaches into small pieces.
2. In a large bowl, dissolve gelatin and sugar in the boiling water. Stir in reserved juice. Chill until slightly thickened. Stir extract into whipped topping; gently fold into gelatin mixture. Fold in peaches.
3. Pour into an oiled 6-cup mold. Chill overnight. Unmold onto a serving platter; garnish with additional peaches if desired.
1 serving: 249 cal., 5g fat (5g sat. fat), 0 chol., 53mg sod., 47g carb. (47g sugars, 0 fiber), 2g pro.

BERRIES WITH RICOTTA CREAM

Fresh, high-quality ingredients really make a difference in this dessert. If you don't have access to fresh-picked berries, use whatever fruit is in season near you.
—*Thomas Faglon, Somerset, NJ*

TAKES: 10 min. • **MAKES:** 6 servings

- 1 cup part-skim ricotta cheese
- ½ cup heavy whipping cream
- ¼ cup honey
- 2 cups fresh blueberries
- 2 cups fresh raspberries
- ½ cup chopped hazelnuts, toasted

In a large bowl, beat ricotta, cream and honey until combined. Divide the berries among 6 dessert dishes. Top with cream and hazelnuts. Refrigerate until serving.
1 serving: 277 cal., 17g fat (7g sat. fat), 35mg chol., 48mg sod., 28g carb. (19g sugars, 5g fiber), 8g pro.

CHERRY CREAM CHEESE TARTS

It's hard to believe that just five ingredients and few minutes of preparation can result in these delicate and scrumptious tarts!
—*Cindi Mitchell, Waring, TX*

TAKES: 10 min. • **MAKES:** 2 tarts

- 3 oz. cream cheese, softened
- ¼ cup confectioners' sugar
- ⅛ to ¼ tsp. almond or vanilla extract
- 2 individual graham cracker shells
- ¼ cup cherry pie filling

In a small bowl, beat the cream cheese, sugar and extract until smooth. Spoon into the shells. Top with pie filling. Refrigerate until serving.
1 tart: 362 cal., 20g fat (10g sat. fat), 43mg chol., 265mg sod., 42g carb. (29g sugars, 1g fiber), 4g pro.

NO-BAKE OREO CHEESECAKE

Oreo cookies and cheesecake— how can you go wrong? I made 20 of these crowd-pleasing desserts in all different sizes for my wedding, and they were a hit.
—*Leanne Stinson, Carnduff, SK*

PREP: 40 min. + chilling
MAKES: 8 servings

24 Oreo cookies, crushed
 6 Tbsp. butter, melted
FILLING
 1 envelope unflavored gelatin
 ¼ cup cold water
 1 pkg. (8 oz.) cream cheese, softened
 ½ cup sugar
 ¾ cup 2% milk
 1 cup whipped topping
10 Oreo cookies, coarsely chopped

1. In a small bowl, mix the crushed cookies and melted butter. Press onto bottom of a greased 9-in. springform pan. Refrigerate until ready to use.
2. In a small saucepan, sprinkle gelatin over the cold water; let stand 1 minute. Heat and stir over low heat until gelatin is completely dissolved. Let stand 5 minutes.
3. In a large bowl, beat cream cheese and sugar until smooth; gradually add milk. Beat in gelatin mixture. Fold in whipped topping and chopped cookies. Spoon over the crust.
4. Refrigerate, covered, overnight. Loosen sides of cheesecake with a knife; remove the rim from pan. If desired, garnish with additional chopped cookies.
1 piece: 499 cal., 30g fat (16g sat. fat), 53mg chol., 374mg sod., 53g carb. (37g sugars, 1g fiber), 7g pro.

COOL-KITCHEN TIP
After your cheesecake has set up properly in the fridge, you can freeze the whole thing, or just the leftovers. Place it in an airtight container and freeze for up to 3 months. Just thaw before serving.

COCONUT PISTACHIO PIE

This two-ingredient crust consisting of coconut and butter is a must try!
—Taste of Home *Test Kitchen*

PREP: 20 min. + chilling
MAKES: 8 servings

- 2½ cups sweetened shredded coconut, lightly toasted
- ⅓ cup butter, melted
- 2 cups cold 2% milk
- 2 pkg. (3.4 oz. each) instant pistachio pudding mix
- 1 cup whipped topping
  Chopped pistachios, optional

1. In a small bowl, combine coconut and butter. Press onto the bottom and up the sides of a greased 9-in. pie plate. Refrigerate for at least 30 minutes or until firm.

2. In a small bowl, whisk the milk and pudding mixes for 2 minutes. Let stand for 2 minutes or until soft-set. Spread 1½ cups over crust.

3. Fold whipped topping into remaining pudding; spread over the pie. If desired, sprinkle with chopped pistachios. Cover; refrigerate at least 2 hours before serving.

1 piece: 365 cal., 21g fat (16g sat. fat), 25mg chol., 513mg sod., 41g carb. (35g sugars, 1g fiber), 3g pro.

COOL-KITCHEN TIP
We recommend you use 2% milk in this pie. Fat-free or 1% milk won't give it a nice, firm texture.

BUTTERSCOTCH PUDDING TORTE

We really wanted a butterscotch-flavored pudding dessert. After searching many cookbooks, I came up with this version.
—Judith Kuehl, Merrill, WI

PREP: 15 min. + chilling
MAKES: 15 servings

- 1 pkg. (16 oz.) cream-filled vanilla sandwich cookies, crushed
- ½ cup butter, melted
- 1 pkg. (8 oz.) cream cheese, softened
- 1 cup confectioners' sugar
- 1 carton (12 oz.) frozen whipped topping, thawed, divided
- 2½ cups cold 2% milk
- 2 pkg. (3.4 oz. each) instant butterscotch pudding mix

1. Set aside 1 cup cookie crumbs for topping. In a small bowl, combine the remaining cookie crumbs and butter. Press into a greased 13x9-in. dish. In a large bowl, beat the cream cheese and confectioners' sugar until smooth. Fold in 1½ cups whipped topping. Spread over crust.

2. In a small bowl, whisk milk and pudding mix for 2 minutes; let stand for 2 minutes or until soft-set. Spoon over cream cheese layer. Top with the remaining whipped topping. Sprinkle with reserved crumbs. Cover and refrigerate for at least 2 hours.

1 piece: 413 cal., 22g fat (12g sat. fat), 36mg chol., 414mg sod., 49g carb. (33g sugars, 0 fiber), 4g pro.

CREAMY BISCOFF PIE

I tasted Biscoff cookie butter at a grocery store one day, and it was so delicious I decided to create a no-bake pie with it. You can make it your own by substituting peanut butter or another kind of spread and matching toppings.
—*Katrina Adams, Mount Olive, AL*

PREP: 20 min. + freezing
MAKES: 2 pies (8 servings each)

- 1 pkg. (8 oz.) cream cheese, softened
- 1 cup Biscoff creamy cookie spread
- ¾ cup confectioners' sugar
- 2 cartons (8 oz. each) frozen whipped topping, thawed (6 cups total), divided
- 2 graham cracker crusts (9 in.)
- ¼ cup caramel sundae syrup
- 4 Biscoff cookies, crushed

In a large bowl, beat the cream cheese, cookie spread and confectioners' sugar until combined. Fold in 1 carton whipped topping. Divide mixture between crusts. Top with remaining container whipped topping. Drizzle with the syrup; sprinkle with cookie crumbs. Freeze, covered, until firm, at least 4 hours.

1 piece: 367 cal., 21g fat (10g sat. fat), 14mg chol., 187mg sod., 40g carb. (31g sugars, 0 fiber), 3g pro.

REFRIGERATOR LIME CHEESECAKE

I made this for a Father's Day party, and it was a hit! I guarantee compliments when you serve this fantastic dessert.
—*Cher Anjema, Kleinburg, ON*

PREP: 30 min. + chilling
MAKES: 12 servings

- 32 soft ladyfingers, split
- 1 envelope unflavored gelatin
- ¼ cup lime juice, chilled
- 2 pkg. (8 oz. each) cream cheese, softened
- 1 cup sugar
- 6 oz. white baking chocolate, melted and cooled
- 2 tsp. grated lime zest
- 1 cup heavy whipping cream, whipped
  Optional: Fresh strawberry and lime slices

1. Arrange 20 ladyfingers around the edges and 12 ladyfingers on the bottom of an ungreased 8-in. springform pan. In a small saucepan, sprinkle gelatin over cold lime juice; let stand 1 minute. Heat over low heat, stirring until gelatin is completely dissolved; cool.

2. Meanwhile, beat cream cheese and sugar until smooth. Gradually beat in melted chocolate, lime zest and gelatin mixture. Fold in whipped cream. Pour into prepared pan. Cover and refrigerate until set, about 3 hours. Remove side of pan. If desired, garnish with strawberry and lime slices.

1 piece: 408 cal., 25g fat (16g sat. fat), 100mg chol., 267mg sod., 42g carb. (35g sugars, 0 fiber), 6g pro.

BLUEBERRY PIE WITH GRAHAM CRACKER CRUST

We live in blueberry country, and this pie is a perfect way to showcase the luscious berries. A neighbor made this pie for us when we had a death in the family several years ago. Our whole family enjoys it.
—R. Ricks, Kalamazoo, MI

PREP: 20 min. + chilling
MAKES: 8 servings

- ¾   cup sugar
- 3   Tbsp. cornstarch
- ⅛   tsp. salt
- ¼   cup water
- 4   cups fresh blueberries, divided
- 1   graham cracker crust (9 in.)
    Whipped cream

1. In a large saucepan, combine sugar, cornstarch and salt. Gradually add the water, stirring until smooth. Stir in 2 cups of blueberries. Bring to a boil; cook and stir until thickened, 1-2 minutes. Remove from heat; cool to room temperature.

2. Gently stir remaining blueberries into cooled blueberry mixture. Spoon into crust. Refrigerate, covered, until chilled, 1-2 hours. Serve with whipped cream.

Graham cracker crust (9 in.): Combine 1½ cups crushed graham cracker crumbs (24 squares), ¼ sugar and ⅓ cup melted butter. Press onto the bottom and up the sides of an ungreased 9-in. pie plate. Bake at 375° until lightly browned, 8-10 minutes. Cool on a wire rack before filling.

1 piece: 230 cal., 6g fat (1g sat. fat), 0 chol., 159mg sod., 46g carb. (35g sugars, 2g fiber), 1g pro.

READER RAVE

"Wow! What an easy pie to make. The taste was perfect ... not too sweet, but delicious!"

—JIMODY, TASTEOFHOME.COM

ROSE & RASPBERRY FOOL

I came up with this recipe when I was going through a floral phase, putting rose or lavender in everything. This dessert is easy to make, but it's also elegant to serve company.
—Carolyn Eskew, Dayton, OH

PREP: 15 min. + chilling
MAKES: 8 servings

- 2   cups fresh or frozen raspberries
- 6   Tbsp. sugar, divided
- 1½   cups heavy whipping cream
- 1   tsp. rose water
    Fresh mint leaves

1. In a small bowl, lightly crush the raspberries and 2 Tbsp. sugar. Cover and refrigerate 1-2 hours.

2. In a large bowl, beat cream until it begins to thicken. Add remaining 4 Tbsp. sugar and the rose water; beat until soft peaks form. Gently fold in raspberry mixture. Spoon into dessert dishes. Garnish with mint leaves and, if desired, additional berries. Serve immediately.

½ cup: 206 cal., 16g fat (10g sat. fat), 51mg chol., 13mg sod., 14g carb. (12g sugars, 2g fiber), 2g pro.

POSSUM PIE

This recipe was found in a box of recipes that were used in the cafe we own back in the early 1950s, when it was know as Mount Aire Camp. Since then, the pie has been on our menu.
—David Heilemann, Eureka Springs, AR

PREP: 20 min. + chilling
MAKES: 8 servings

- 6 oz. cream cheese, softened
- ¾ cup confectioners' sugar
- 1 graham cracker crust (9 in.)
- ¼ cup chopped pecans
- 1¾ cups cold milk
- ¾ tsp. vanilla extract
- ¼ cup instant vanilla pudding mix
- ⅓ cup instant chocolate pudding mix
- ½ cup heavy whipping cream, whipped
- 12 to 16 pecan halves

1. In a small bowl, beat the cream cheese and sugar until smooth. Spoon into crust. Sprinkle with chopped pecans.
2. In a bowl, whisk the milk, vanilla and pudding mixes for 2 minutes. Let stand for 2 minutes or until soft-set. Spoon over the pecans. Refrigerate for at least 4 hours. Top with whipped cream and pecan halves.

1 piece: 388 cal., 24g fat (10g sat. fat), 44mg chol., 276mg sod., 40g carb. (32g sugars, 1g fiber), 5g pro.

LEMON ICEBOX CAKE

This easy cake, with subtle lemon flavor and a pleasant crunch from the cookies, is a stunning centerpiece.
—Peggy Woodward, Shullsburg, WI

TAKES: 20 min. + chilling
MAKES: 8 servings

- 3 cups heavy whipping cream
- 3 Tbsp. sugar
- 3 Tbsp. grated lemon zest
- 63 Marie biscuits or Maria cookies
  Lemon slices, optional

1. In a large bowl, beat the cream, sugar and lemon zest on high until stiff peaks form. Cut a small hole in the corner of a pastry bag. Fill with whipped cream.
2. On a serving plate, arrange 7 cookies in a circle, placing 1 cookie in the center. Pipe ⅔ cup whipped cream over the cookies. Repeat the layers 8 times. Refrigerate overnight.
3. If desired, garnish with lemon slices.

1 piece: 530 cal., 37g fat (23g sat. fat), 102mg chol., 158mg sod., 44g carb. (17g sugars, 2g fiber), 6g pro.

COOL-KITCHEN TIP
If you don't have any Maria cookies on hand, no worries! You can also use graham crackers or vanilla wafers for this icebox dessert.

FRESAS CON CREMA

This refreshing dessert is wonderful when berries are in season. Media crema is a rich, unsweetened cream found in the baking aisle or ethnic food section of the grocery store.
—Taste of Home *Test Kitchen*

TAKES: 10 min. • **MAKES:** 4 servings

- 1 can (7.6 oz.) media crema table cream
- 3 Tbsp. sweetened condensed milk
- 1 tsp. vanilla extract
- 3 cups chopped fresh strawberries
  Fresh mint leaves, optional

In a small bowl, whisk crema, sweetened condensed milk and vanilla. Divide the strawberries among 4 serving dishes. Top with milk mixture. Garnish with mint if desired.

¾ cup: 241 cal., 17g fat (10g sat. fat), 43mg chol., 58mg sod., 21g carb. (14g sugars, 2g fiber), 2g pro.

COOL-KITCHEN TIP
Mexican crema is similar to creme fraiche. It's very thick, creamy and slightly tangy. Creme fraiche can be a great substitute if you can't find Mexican crema at the store.

CONTEST-WINNING RASPBERRY CREAM PIE

This recipe is delicious with either fresh-picked or frozen raspberries. That means you can make it year-round. One bite of raspberry pie will instantly turn winter to summer.
—Julie Price, Nashville, TN

PREP: 30 min. + chilling
MAKES: 8 servings

- 1½ cups crushed vanilla wafers (about 45 wafers)
- ⅓ cup chopped pecans
- ¼ cup butter, melted

FILLING
- 1 pkg. (8 oz.) cream cheese, softened
- ⅔ cup confectioners' sugar
- 2 Tbsp. orange liqueur
- 1 tsp. vanilla extract
- 1 cup heavy whipping cream, whipped

TOPPING
- 1 cup sugar
- 3 Tbsp. cornstarch
- 3 Tbsp. water
- 2½ cups fresh or frozen raspberries, divided

1. Combine the wafer crumbs, pecans and butter. Press onto the bottom and up the sides of a greased 9-in. pie plate.
2. In a large bowl, beat the cream cheese, confectioners' sugar, orange liqueur and vanilla until light and fluffy. Fold in the whipped cream. Spread into the crust. Chill until serving.
3. In a small saucepan, combine the sugar and cornstarch; stir in the water and 1½ cups raspberries. Bring to a boil; cook and stir for 2 minutes or until thickened. Transfer to a bowl; refrigerate until chilled.
4. Spread topping over filling. Garnish with remaining 1 cup berries.
Note: If using frozen raspberries, use without thawing to avoid discoloring the batter.
1 piece: 507 cal., 28g fat (14g sat. fat), 70mg chol., 196mg sod., 61g carb. (46g sugars, 4g fiber), 4g pro.

NO-BAKE CHOCOLATE CHIP CANNOLI CHEESECAKE

I make this cheesecake in the summer for a flavorful and refreshing treat. I love the added bonus of not having to turn on the oven in hot weather.
—Kristen Heigl, Staten Island, NY

PREP: 25 min. + chilling
MAKES: 8 servings

- 1 pkg. (4 oz.) cannoli shells
- ½ cup sugar
- ½ cup graham cracker crumbs
- ⅓ cup butter, melted

FILLING
- 2 pkg. (8 oz. each) cream cheese, softened
- 1 cup confectioners' sugar
- ½ tsp. grated orange zest
- ¼ tsp. ground cinnamon
- ¾ cup part-skim ricotta cheese
- 1 tsp. vanilla extract
- ½ tsp. rum extract
- ½ cup miniature semisweet chocolate chips
  Chopped pistachios, optional

1. Pulse cannoli shells in a food processor until coarse crumbs form. Add the sugar, cracker crumbs and melted butter; pulse just until combined. Press onto bottom and up sides of a greased 9-in. pie plate. Refrigerate until firm, about 1 hour.
2. Beat the first 4 filling ingredients until blended. Beat in the ricotta cheese and extracts. Stir in chocolate chips. Spread into crust.
3. Refrigerate, covered, until set, about 4 hours. If desired, top with pistachios.
1 piece: 548 cal., 36g fat (20g sat. fat), 88mg chol., 292mg sod., 51g carb. (38g sugars, 1g fiber), 8g pro.

MIXED BERRY TIRAMISU

Because I love tiramisu, I came up with this deliciously refreshing twist on the traditional coffee-flavored Italian dessert. Serve it from a glass bowl or in clear dishes to show off the layers.
—*Najmussahar Ahmed, Ypsilanti, MI*

PREP: 35 min. + chilling
MAKES: 12 servings

- 3 cups fresh raspberries
- 3 cups fresh blackberries
- 2 cups fresh blueberries
- 2 cups fresh strawberries, sliced
- 1⅓ cups sugar, divided
- 4 tsp. grated orange zest
- 1 cup orange juice
- 1 cup heavy whipping cream
- 2 cartons (8 oz. each) mascarpone cheese
- 1 tsp. vanilla extract
- 2 pkg. (7 oz. each) crisp ladyfinger cookies
  Additional fresh berries, optional

1. Place berries in a large bowl. Mix ⅓ cup sugar, orange zest and orange juice; toss gently with berries. Refrigerate, covered, 45 minutes.
2. Beat cream until soft peaks form. In another bowl, mix mascarpone cheese, vanilla and remaining 1 cup sugar. Fold in the whipped cream, a third at a time.
3. Drain the berries over a shallow bowl, reserving juices. Dip the ladyfingers in reserved juices, allowing excess to drip off; arrange ladyfingers in a single layer on bottom of a 13x9-in. dish. Layer with half the berries and half the mascarpone mixture; repeat the layers, starting with the ladyfingers.
4. Refrigerate, covered, overnight. Top with additional fresh berries before serving if desired.
Note: This recipe was prepared with Alessi brand ladyfinger cookies.
1 piece: 501 cal., 26g fat (14g sat. fat), 105mg chol., 77mg sod., 63g carb. (45g sugars, 5g fiber), 8g pro.

LAYERED STRAWBERRY POUND CAKE DESSERT

My mother's cousin shared this recipe more than 50 years ago. Our family has enjoyed it ever since, especially on a hot New Mexico day! It can be made the day before.
—*Vickie Britton, Hobbs, NM*

PREP: 20 min. + chilling
MAKES: 24 servings

- 1 loaf (10¾ oz.) frozen pound cake, thawed
- 1 pkg. (8 oz.) cream cheese, softened
- 1 can (14 oz.) sweetened condensed milk
- ⅓ cup lemon juice
- 1 carton (12 oz.) frozen whipped topping, thawed
- 1 container (16 oz.) frozen sweetened sliced strawberries, thawed

1. Cut pound cake into ½-in. slices; place in bottom of a 13x9-in. baking dish. In a large bowl, beat the cream cheese until smooth. Beat in milk and lemon juice until blended. Fold in 2⅔ cups whipped topping and 1½ cups strawberries with juice.
2. Spread mixture over pound cake. Top with the remaining whipped topping. Refrigerate, covered, at least 4 hours or overnight. Top with the remaining ½ cup strawberries in juice before serving.
1 piece: 195 cal., 10g fat (7g sat. fat), 34mg chol., 88mg sod., 24g carb. (20g sugars, 0 fiber), 3g pro.

QUICK & EASY TIRAMISU

No one can resist this classic cool and creamy dessert. It's quick to prepare but can be made ahead.
—Taste of Home *Test Kitchen*

PREP: 20 min. + chilling
MAKES: 6 servings

- 2   cups cold 2% milk
- 1   pkg. (3.4 oz.) instant vanilla pudding mix
- 1   cup heavy whipping cream
- 3   Tbsp. confectioners' sugar
- 28 soft ladyfingers, split
- 2½ tsp. instant coffee granules
- ½   cup boiling water
- 1   Tbsp. baking cocoa

1. In a large bowl, whisk the milk and pudding mix for 2 minutes. Let stand until soft-set, about 2 minutes. In a small bowl, beat cream until it begins to thicken. Add confectioners' sugar; beat until soft peaks form. Fold into pudding; cover and refrigerate.
2. Arrange half the ladyfingers, cut side up, in an 11x7-in. dish. Dissolve the coffee granules in the boiling water; drizzle half over the ladyfingers. Spread with half the pudding mixture. Repeat layers. Sprinkle with the cocoa. Refrigerate until serving.
1 piece: 384 cal., 19g fat (11g sat. fat), 123mg chol., 379mg sod., 47g carb. (33g sugars, 1g fiber), 7g pro.

COOL-KITCHEN TIP
Can't find ladyfingers at your store? You can substitute store-bought sponge cake or pound cake. Just cut into slices.

WATERMELON FRUIT PIZZA

Fruit pizza is an easy and refreshing way to end a summer meal. Top it with any fruit you may have on hand and add other toppings like fresh mint, toasted shredded coconut or chopped nuts.
—Taste of Home *Test Kitchen*

PREP/COOK TIME: 10 min.
MAKES: 8 servings

- 4   oz. cream cheese, softened
- 4   oz. frozen whipped topping, thawed
- ½   tsp. vanilla extract
- 3   Tbsp. confectioners' sugar
- 1   round slice of whole seedless watermelon, about 1 in. thick
     Assorted fresh fruit
     Fresh mint leaves, optional

1. In a small bowl, beat cream cheese until smooth. Gently fold in the whipped topping, then vanilla and confectioners' sugar until combined.
2. To serve, spread watermelon slice with cream cheese mixture. Cut into 8 wedges and top with your fruit of choice. If desired, garnish with fresh mint.
1 piece: 140 cal., 7g fat (5g sat. fat), 14mg chol., 45mg sod., 17g carb. (16g sugars, 0 fiber), 1g pro. **Diabetic exchanges:** 1½ fat, 1 fruit.

NO-BAKE MANGO STRAWBERRY CHEESECAKE

Cheesecake is my mom's favorite dessert. I made this especially for her on Mother's Day to thank her for being such an awesome mom. Decorate to your own taste!
—Elizabeth Ding, El Cerrito, CA

PREP: 45 min. + chilling
MAKES: 12 servings

1¼ cups graham cracker crumbs
⅓ cup butter, melted
¼ cup sugar
FILLING
1 envelope unflavored gelatin
3 Tbsp. cold water
2 pkg. (8 oz. each) cream cheese, softened
1⅓ cups sugar
1 cup heavy whipping cream
2 tsp. vanilla extract
½ large mango, peeled and cubed (about ¾ cup)
4 fresh strawberries, chopped
GLAZE
1 envelope unflavored gelatin
3 Tbsp. plus ½ cup cold water, divided
½ large mango, peeled and cubed (about ¾ cup)
Optional: Whipped cream, mango pieces and sliced strawberries

1. In a small bowl, mix crumbs, butter and sugar. Press into bottom of a greased 8-in. springform pan.
2. For filling, in a microwave-safe bowl, sprinkle the gelatin over cold water; let stand 1 minute. Microwave on high for 10-20 seconds or just until the water is warm but not hot. Stir and let stand until gelatin is completely dissolved, about 1 minute. Cool until partially set.
3. In a large bowl, beat cream cheese and sugar until smooth. Gradually beat in cream, vanilla and gelatin mixture until blended. Fold in the mango and strawberries. Pour over the crust. Refrigerate while preparing the glaze.

4. For glaze, in another microwave-safe bowl, sprinkle gelatin over 3 Tbsp. cold water; let stand 1 minute. Microwave on high just until water is warm but not hot, 10-20 seconds. Stir; let stand until gelatin is completely dissolved, about 1 minute. Cool until partially set. Meanwhile, place mango and remaining ½ cup water in a food processor; process until pureed. Stir in gelatin mixture; pour over filling. Refrigerate, loosely covered, overnight.
5. Loosen side from the pan with a knife. Remove rim from pan. If desired, garnish cheesecake with whipped cream, mango pieces and strawberry slices.

1 piece: 417 cal., 27g fat (16g sat. fat), 74mg chol., 215mg sod., 42g carb. (35g sugars, 1g fiber), 5g pro.

READER RAVE

"This is a great recipe! I made this for Mother's Day, and it was a huge hit. Excellent taste. I will make again!"
—RENEEH2010, TASTEOFHOME.COM

BLACKBERRY WHITE CHOCOLATE CHEESECAKE CUPS

I read that white chocolate intensifies the flavor of blackberries. It's true!
—*Arlene Erlbach, Morton Grove, IL*

PREP: 25 min. + chilling
MAKES: 6 servings

- 1½ cups miniature pretzels
- 2 Tbsp. plus ⅓ cup sugar, divided
- 3 Tbsp. butter, melted
- 1 cup heavy whipping cream
- 1 pkg. (8 oz.) cream cheese, softened
- ½ cup confectioners' sugar
- 1 tsp. vanilla extract
- ½ cup white baking chips
- 1½ cups fresh blackberries
  Additional blackberries

1. Pulse pretzels in a food processor until fine crumbs form. Add 2 Tbsp. granulated sugar and the melted butter; pulse just until combined. Divide the mixture among 6 half-pint canning jars or dessert dishes.
2. For cheesecake layer, beat cream until stiff peaks form. In another bowl, beat cream cheese, confectioners' sugar and vanilla until smooth. Fold in 1½ cups of the whipped cream, then baking chips. Spoon over pretzel mixture. Refrigerate, covered, until cold, about 3 hours.
3. In a clean food processor, puree 1½ cups blackberries with remaining ⅓ cup sugar; remove to a bowl. Cover and refrigerate berry mixture and remaining whipped cream until serving.
4. To serve, top with the blackberry mixture, reserved whipped cream and additional blackberries.
1 serving: 553 cal., 38g fat (23g sat. fat), 102mg chol., 359mg sod., 49g carb. (38g sugars, 2g fiber), 6g pro.

A LAYERED APPROACH

For a guaranteed crowd-pleaser, present a parfait or trifle as a gorgeous dessert!

BERRY, LEMON & DOUGHNUT HOLE TRIFLE

I whipped up this quick yet impressive dessert in only a few minutes, after my son called and said he was bringing home his college roommates. It's been a family favorite ever since.
—*Ellen Riley, Murfreesboro, TN*

TAKES: 25 min. • **MAKES:** 10 servings

- 2 cups cold 2% milk
- 1 pkg. (3.4 oz.) instant lemon pudding mix
- 1 carton (8 oz.) frozen whipped topping, thawed and divided
- 16 to 32 plain doughnut holes
- 3 cups fresh strawberries, halved
- 2 cups fresh blueberries

1. In a large bowl, whisk milk and pudding mix for 2 minutes. Let stand for 2 minutes or until soft-set. Fold in 2½ cups whipped topping; set aside.
2. Place half of the doughnut holes in a 3-qt. trifle bowl; spread half the pudding mixture over the top. Top pudding with half the strawberries and blueberries. Repeat layers. Top with the remaining whipped topping. Chill until serving.
1 cup: 250 cal., 11g fat (7g sat. fat), 6mg chol., 250mg sod., 33g carb. (24g sugars, 2g fiber), 3g pro.

CAPPUCCINO MOUSSE TRIFLE

This is the easiest trifle I've ever made, yet it looks like I spent time on it. I like to pipe whipped topping around the edge of the bowl, grate chocolate in the center and sprinkle with cinnamon. It gets rave reviews.
—*Tracy Bergland, Prior Lake, MN*

PREP: 35 min. • **MAKES:** 20 servings

- 2½ cups cold milk
- ⅓ cup instant coffee granules
- 2 pkg. (3.4 oz. each) instant vanilla pudding mix
- 1 carton (16 oz.) frozen whipped topping, thawed, divided
- 2 loaves (10¾ oz. each) frozen pound cake, thawed and cubed
- 1 oz. semisweet chocolate, grated
- ¼ tsp. ground cinnamon

1. In a large bowl, stir the milk and coffee granules until dissolved; remove 1 cup and set aside. Add the pudding mix to the remaining milk mixture; beat on low speed for 2 minutes (mixture will be thick). Fold in half the whipped topping.
2. Place a third of the cake cubes in a 4-qt. serving or trifle bowl. Layer with a third of the reserved milk mixture, a third of the pudding mixture and a fourth of the chocolate. Repeat the layers twice. Garnish with remaining whipped topping and chocolate. Sprinkle with cinnamon. Cover and refrigerate until serving.
1 serving: 166 cal., 8g fat (6g sat. fat), 26mg chol., 139mg sod., 20g carb. (13g sugars, 0 fiber), 2g pro.

BANANA PUDDING PARFAIT

I blend cream cheese, sweetened condensed milk and whipped topping into instant pudding then layer this creamy concoction with vanilla wafers and sliced bananas. Served in a pretty glass bowl, the results make for a fancy yet fuss-free dessert.
—Edna Perry, Rice, TX

PREP: 15 min. + chilling
MAKES: 12 servings

- 1 pkg. (8 oz.) cream cheese, softened
- 1 can (14 oz.) sweetened condensed milk
- 1 cup cold 2% milk
- 1 pkg. (3.4 oz.) instant vanilla pudding mix
- 1 carton (8 oz.) frozen whipped topping, thawed
- 52 vanilla wafers
- 4 medium firm bananas, sliced

In a large bowl, beat cream cheese until smooth. Beat in condensed milk; set aside. In another bowl, whisk milk and pudding mix; add to cream cheese mixture. Fold in whipped topping. Place a third of the vanilla wafers in a 2½-qt. glass bowl. Top with a third of the bananas and pudding mixture. Repeat layers twice. Cover and refrigerate at least 4 hours or overnight. If desired, garnish with additional whipped topping, bananas and wafers.

¾ cup: 376 cal., 16g fat (10g sat. fat), 35mg chol., 225mg sod., 52g carb. (41g sugars, 1g fiber), 5g pro.

COOL-KITCHEN TIP
For best results, make this parfait with firm, unblemished bananas. If they're too ripe, they're more likely to bruise and turn brown. You can toss the sliced bananas with a teaspoon of lemon juice to prevent oxidizing.

PEACH MELBA TRIFLE

This dream of a dessert tastes extra good on a busy day, because you can make it ahead of time. If you don't have fresh peaches handy, use the canned ones.
—Christina Moore, Casar, NC

PREP: 20 min. + chilling
MAKES: 12 servings

- 2 pkg. (12 oz. each) frozen unsweetened raspberries, thawed
- 1 Tbsp. cornstarch
- 1½ cups fat-free peach yogurt
- ⅛ tsp. almond extract
- 1 carton (8 oz.) frozen reduced-fat whipped topping, thawed
- 2 prepared angel food cakes (8 to 10 oz. each), cut into 1-in. cubes (about 8 cups)
- 4 small peaches, peeled and sliced (about 2 cups)

1. In a large saucepan, mix raspberries and cornstarch until blended. Bring to a boil; cook and stir for 1-2 minutes or until thickened. Strain the seeds; cover and refrigerate.

2. In a large bowl, mix the yogurt and extract; fold in whipped topping. In a 4-qt. bowl, layer half each of the cake cubes, yogurt mixture and peaches. Repeat layers. Refrigerate, covered, at least 3 hours before serving. Serve with raspberry sauce.

⅔ cup: 201 cal., 3g fat (2g sat. fat), 1mg chol., 298mg sod., 41g carb. (10g sugars, 3g fiber), 4g pro.

P. 290

BONUS: BACKYARD GRILLING

Of course, one way to keep your house cool while you cook is to cook outside! Summer is the time for grilling, and these recipes will see you through the season in style.

ELOTE (MEXICAN STREET CORN)

Elote, otherwise known as Mexican street corn, is grilled, covered in mayo, and then sprinkled with chili powder, Cotija and cilantro. A squeeze of lime juice is the perfect finishing touch.
—*James Schend, Pleasant Prairie, WI*

PREP: 15 min. + soaking
GRILL: 25 min. • **MAKES:** 6 servings

- 6 medium ears sweet corn
- 2 Tbsp. olive oil
- ½ cup mayonnaise
- 2 to 3 tsp. chili powder
- 6 Tbsp. Cotija cheese
- ½ cup fresh cilantro leaves
  Lime wedges

1. Carefully peel back corn husks to within 1 in. of bottoms; remove silk. Brush corn with oil. Rewrap corn in husks; secure with kitchen string. Place in a Dutch oven; cover with cold water. Soak 20 minutes; drain.
2. Grill corn, covered, over medium heat until tender, 25-30 minutes, turning often.
3. Peel back husks. Spread mayonnaise over each ear; sprinkle with chili powder, cojita cheese and cilantro. Squeeze lime wedges over corn before serving.

1 ear: 278 cal., 22g fat (4g sat. fat), 14mg chol., 245mg sod., 20g carb. (6g sugars, 2g fiber), 5g pro.

GRILLED VEGETABLE PLATTER

These pretty summer veggies are perfect for entertaining. Grilling brings out their natural sweetness, and the easy marinade really perks up the flavor.
—*Heidi Hall, North St. Paul, MN*

PREP: 20 min. + marinating
GRILL: 10 min. • **MAKES:** 6 servings

- ¼ cup olive oil
- 2 Tbsp. honey
- 4 tsp. balsamic vinegar
- 1 tsp. dried oregano
- ½ tsp. garlic powder
- ⅛ tsp. pepper
  Dash salt
- 1 lb. fresh asparagus, trimmed
- 3 small carrots, cut in half lengthwise
- 1 large sweet red pepper, cut into 1-in. strips
- 1 medium yellow summer squash, cut into ½-in. slices
- 1 medium red onion, cut into wedges

1. Whisk the first 7 ingredients. Place 3 Tbsp. marinade in a large bowl; set remaining marinade aside. Add vegetables to bowl; turn to coat. Cover; marinate 1½ hours at room temperature.
2. Transfer vegetables to a grilling grid; place grid on grill rack. Grill vegetables, covered, over medium heat until crisp-tender, 8-12 minutes, turning occasionally.
3. Place vegetables on a large serving plate. Drizzle with reserved marinade.
1 serving: 144 cal., 9g fat (1g sat. fat), 0 chol., 50mg sod., 15g carb. (11g sugars, 3g fiber), 2g pro. **Diabetic exchanges:** 2 vegetable, 2 fat.

CHICKEN WITH PEACH-AVOCADO SALSA

This super fresh dinner is pure summer—juicy peaches, creamy avocado, grilled chicken and a kick of hot sauce and lime. To get it on the table even quicker, make the salsa ahead.
—*Shannon Norris, Cudahy, WI*

TAKES: 30 min. • **MAKES:** 4 servings

- 1 medium peach, peeled and chopped
- 1 medium ripe avocado, peeled and cubed
- ½ cup chopped sweet red pepper
- 3 Tbsp. finely chopped red onion
- 1 Tbsp. minced fresh basil
- 1 Tbsp. lime juice
- 1 tsp. hot pepper sauce
- ½ tsp. grated lime zest
- ¾ tsp. salt, divided
- ½ tsp. pepper, divided
- 4 boneless skinless chicken breast halves (6 oz. each)

1. For salsa, in a small bowl, combine peach, avocado, red pepper, onion, basil, lime juice, hot pepper sauce, lime zest, ¼ tsp. salt and ¼ tsp. pepper.
2. Sprinkle chicken with remaining ½ tsp. salt and ¼ tsp. pepper. On a lightly greased grill rack, grill chicken, covered, over medium heat 5 minutes. Turn; grill until a thermometer reads 165°, 7-9 minutes longer. Serve with salsa.
1 chicken breast half with ½ cup salsa: 265 cal., 9g fat (2g sat. fat), 94mg chol., 536mg sod., 9g carb. (4g sugars, 3g fiber), 36g pro. **Diabetic exchanges:** 5 lean meat, 1 fat, ½ starch.

COOL-KITCHEN TIP

If you do not have a grilling grid, use a disposable foil pan. Poke holes in the bottom of the pan with a meat fork to allow liquid to drain.

GREEN CHILE CHEESEBURGERS

A diner outside of Albuquerque, New Mexico, served the most amazing burgers topped with freshly roasted green chiles. They have a smoky flavor and a bit of a bite—perfect after a long day of driving.
—*James Schend, Pleasant Prairie, WI*

PREP: 20 min. • **GRILL:** 15 min.
MAKES: 6 servings

- 3 whole green chiles, such as Anaheim or Hatch
- 2 lbs. ground beef
- 1 tsp. salt
- ½ tsp. pepper
- 6 slices slices sharp cheddar cheese
- 6 hamburger buns, split and toasted
  Optional: Lettuce leaves, sliced tomato, sliced onion, bacon and mayonnaise

1. Grill peppers, covered, over high heat until all sides are blistered and blackened, 8-10 minutes, turning as needed. Immediately place peppers in a small bowl; let stand, covered, 20 minutes. Reduce grill temperature to medium heat.
2. Meanwhile, in a large bowl, combine beef, salt and pepper; mix lightly but thoroughly. Shape beef mixture into six ¾-in.-thick patties.
3. Peel off and discard charred skin from peppers. Cut peppers lengthwise in half; carefully remove stems and seeds. Cut into slices or coarsely chop.
4. Grill burgers, covered, over medium heat until a thermometer reads 160°, 5-7 minutes on each side. Top with cheese and chiles; grill, covered, until cheese is melted, 1-2 minutes longer. Top bun bottoms with burgers. If desired, serve with lettuce, tomato, onion, bacon and mayonnaise.

1 burger: 482 cal., 26g fat (11g sat. fat), 116mg chol., 552mg sod., 23g carb. (4g sugars, 1g fiber), 36g pro.

SKEWERED LAMB WITH BLACKBERRY-BALSAMIC GLAZE

This dish proves it takes only a few quality ingredients to make a classy main dish.
—*Elynor Townsend, Summerfield, WI*

PREP: 10 min. + marinating
GRILL: 10 min. • **MAKES:** 6 servings

- ½ cup seedless blackberry spreadable fruit
- ⅓ cup balsamic vinegar
- 1 Tbsp. minced fresh rosemary or 1 tsp. dried rosemary, crushed
- 1 Tbsp. Dijon mustard
- 1½ lbs. lean boneless lamb, cut into 1-in. cubes
- ¼ tsp. salt

1. In a small bowl, combine spreadable fruit, vinegar, rosemary and mustard. Pour ⅔ cup marinade into a shallow dish; add lamb. Turn to coat; cover and refrigerate for at least 1 hour. Cover and refrigerate the remaining marinade for basting.
2. Drain lamb, discarding marinade in dish. Thread lamb onto 6 metal or soaked wooden skewers. Place kabobs on a greased grill rack. Grill, covered, over medium heat (or broil 4 in. from the heat) until lamb reaches desired doneness (for medium-rare, a thermometer should read 135°; medium, 140°; medium-well, 145°), 10-12 minutes, turning once and basting frequently with reserved marinade. Sprinkle with salt before serving.

1 kabob: 255 cal., 9g fat (4g sat. fat), 103mg chol., 264mg sod., 9g carb. (7g sugars, 0 fiber), 32g pro. **Diabetic exchanges:** 5 lean meat, ½ starch.

KEY WEST FLANK STEAK

My husband, Jason, is the cook in our family. This is his recipe, inspired by his Colombian roots and our visits to Key West, Florida. Serve with sides of rice and fried plantains.
—*Gretchen Ospina, Columbia Heights, MN*

PREP: 20 min. + marinating
GRILL: 15 min. + standing
MAKES: 4 servings

1	large red onion, sliced
1	cup minced fresh cilantro
¼	cup white wine vinegar
¼	cup Key lime juice
3	Tbsp. extra virgin olive oil, divided
6	Key limes, halved
1	beef flank steak (1 lb.)
1	tsp. kosher salt
⅛	tsp. pepper

1. In a small bowl, combine onion, cilantro, vinegar, lime juice and 2 Tbsp. oil until blended. Pour 1 cup marinade into a large bowl or shallow dish. Add lime halves. Rub steak with remaining 1 Tbsp. oil; sprinkle with salt and pepper. Add to bowl; turn to coat. Refrigerate 8 hours or overnight. Cover and refrigerate the remaining marinade.

2. Drain steak, discarding marinade and limes in bowl. Place reserved marinade in a food processor; process until chopped.

3. Grill steak, covered, over medium heat or broil 4 in. from heat until meat reaches desired doneness (for medium-rare, a thermometer should read 135°; medium, 140°; medium-well, 145°), 6-8 minutes per side. Baste occasionally with reserved marinade. Let stand 10 minutes before thinly slicing steak across the grain.

3 oz. cooked steak: 271 cal., 16g fat (5g sat. fat), 54mg chol., 431mg sod., 12g carb. (3g sugars, 3g fiber), 23g pro.
Diabetic exchanges: 3 lean meat, 1½ fat.

GRILLED ELOTE FLATBREAD

Here's a fun twist on a classic Mexican dish! Keep your kitchen cooled down during the summer by grilling this fresh flatbread outdoors.
—*Amanda Phillips, Portland, OR*

PREP: 20 min. • **GRILL:** 15 min.
MAKES: 12 servings

- 2 medium ears sweet corn, husked
- 3 Tbsp. olive oil, divided
- 1 lb. fresh or frozen pizza dough, thawed
- ½ cup mayonnaise
- ⅓ cup crumbled Cotija cheese, divided
- ⅓ cup chopped fresh cilantro, divided
- 1 Tbsp. lime juice
- ½ tsp. chili powder
- ⅛ tsp. pepper

1. Brush corn with 1 Tbsp. oil. Grill corn, covered, over medium heat until lightly browned and tender, 10-12 minutes, turning occasionally. Cool slightly. Cut corn from cobs; transfer to a large bowl.
2. On a lightly floured surface, roll or press dough into a 15x10-in. oval (about ¼ in. thick); place on a greased sheet of foil. Brush top with 1 Tbsp. oil.
3. Carefully invert crust onto grill rack, removing foil. Brush top with remaining 1 Tbsp. oil. Grill, covered, over medium heat until golden brown, 2-3 minutes on each side. Remove from grill; cool slightly.
4. Add mayonnaise, 3 Tbsp. cheese, 3 Tbsp. cilantro, lime juice, chili powder and pepper to corn; stir to combine. Spread over warm crust. Sprinkle with remaining cheese and cilantro.
1 piece: 211 cal., 13g fat (2g sat. fat), 4mg chol., 195mg sod., 20g carb. (2g sugars, 1g fiber), 5g pro.

CHICKEN YAKITORI

I grew up in Tokyo, and some of my favorite memories include eating street food like this dish with my friends. Although we now live thousands of miles apart, my friends and I still reminisce about our nights sharing secrets and bonding over delicious meals. This one is easy to re-create at home, which makes it perfect for when I'm feeling homesick. I like to serve it with rice.
—*Lindsay Howerton-Hastings, Greenville, SC*

TAKES: 30 min. • **MAKES:** 6 servings

- ½ cup mirin (sweet rice wine)
- ½ cup sake
- ½ cup soy sauce
- 1 Tbsp. sugar
- 2 large sweet red peppers, cut into 2-in. pieces
- 2 lbs. boneless skinless chicken thighs, cut into 1½-in. pieces
- 1 bunch green onions

1. In a small saucepan, combine first 4 ingredients. Bring to a boil over medium-high heat. Remove from heat; set aside half the mixture for serving.
2. Thread peppers onto 2 metal or soaked wooden skewers. Thread chicken onto 6 metal or soaked wooden skewers. Grill chicken, covered, over medium heat until meat is cooked through, 10-12 minutes, turning occasionally and basting frequently with soy sauce mixture during the last 3 minutes. Grill peppers, covered, until tender, 4-5 minutes, turning occasionally. Grill onions, covered, until lightly charred, 1-2 minutes, turning occasionally. Serve chicken and vegetables with reserved sauce for dipping.
1 serving: 332 cal., 11g fat (3g sat. fat), 101mg chol., 1316mg sod., 14g carb. (11g sugars, 1g fiber), 32g pro.

BACON-WRAPPED STUFFED JALAPENOS

Sunday is grill-out day for my husband, Cliff, and these zesty peppers are one of his specialties. We usually feature them at our annual Daytona 500 party. They disappear from the appetizer tray in no time.
—*Therese Pollard, Hurst, TX*

PREP: 1 hour • **GRILL:** 40 min.
MAKES: 2 dozen

- 24   medium jalapeno peppers
- 1   lb. uncooked chorizo or bulk spicy pork sausage
- 2   cups shredded cheddar cheese
- 12   bacon strips, cut in half

1. Make a lengthwise cut in each jalapeno, about ⅛ in. deep; remove seeds. Combine sausage and cheese; stuff into jalapenos. Wrap each with a piece of bacon; secure with toothpicks.
2. Grill, covered, over indirect medium heat for 35-40 minutes or until a thermometer reads 160°, turning once. Move to direct heat and grill, covered, until bacon is crisp, 1-2 minutes longer.
Note: Wear disposable gloves when cutting hot peppers; the oils can burn skin. Avoid touching your face.
1 stuffed jalapeno: 132 cal., 10g fat (4g sat. fat), 30mg chol., 365mg sod., 1g carb. (1g sugars, 0 fiber), 8g pro.

CEDAR PLANK SALMON WITH BLACKBERRY SAUCE

Here's my favorite entree for a warm-weather cookout. The salmon has a rich grilled taste that's enhanced by the savory blackberry sauce. It's a nice balance of sweet, smoky and spicy.
—*Stephanie Matthews, Tempe, AZ*

PREP: 20 min. + soaking • **GRILL:** 15 min.
MAKES: 6 servings (¾ cup sauce)

- 2   cedar grilling planks
- 2   cups fresh blackberries
- 2   Tbsp. white wine
- 1   Tbsp. brown sugar
- 1½   tsp. honey
- 1½   tsp. chipotle hot pepper sauce
- ¼   tsp. salt, divided
- ¼   tsp. pepper, divided
- ¼   cup finely chopped shallots
- 1   garlic clove, minced
- 6   salmon fillets (5 oz. each)

1. Soak grilling planks in water for at least 1 hour.
2. In a food processor, combine the blackberries, wine, brown sugar, honey, hot pepper sauce, ⅛ tsp. salt and ⅛ tsp. pepper; cover and process until blended. Strain mixture and discard the seeds. Stir shallots and garlic into the sauce; set aside.
3. Place planks on grill over medium-high heat. Cover and heat until planks create a light to medium smoke and begin to crackle, about 3 minutes. Turn planks over.
4. Sprinkle salmon with remaining ⅛ tsp. salt and ⅛ tsp. pepper. Place on planks. Grill, covered, over medium heat for 12-15 minutes or until fish flakes easily with a fork. Serve with sauce.
1 fillet with 2 Tbsp. sauce: 304 cal., 16g fat (3g sat. fat), 84mg chol., 186mg sod., 10g carb. (6g sugars, 3g fiber), 29g pro. **Diabetic exchanges:** 4 lean meat, ½ starch.

THE BEST GRILLED SIRLOIN TIP ROAST

If you're looking for a flavorful cut of meat that's still pretty lean, give this sirloin tip roast recipe a try. I like to cook it slowly over indirect heat, mopping it frequently with red wine sauce.
—*James Schend, Pleasant Prairie, WI*

PREP: 40 min. + chilling
GRILL: 1½ hours + standing
MAKES: 6 servings

- 1   beef sirloin tip roast or beef tri-tip roast (2 to 3 lbs.)
- 1   Tbsp. kosher salt
- 2   tsp. dried thyme
- 2   tsp. garlic powder
- 1   tsp. coarsely ground pepper
- 1   small onion, chopped
- 2   Tbsp. olive oil, divided
- 1   bottle (750 ml) dry red wine
- 6   fresh thyme sprigs
- 1   garlic cloves, crushed
- ½   tsp. whole peppercorns
- 3   whole cloves

HORSERADISH-THYME BUTTER (OPTIONAL)

- 6   Tbsp. softened butter
- 2   Tbsp. prepared horseradish
- 3   Tbsp. fresh thyme leaves

1. Sprinkle roast with salt, thyme, garlic powder and ground pepper. Cover and refrigerate for at least 8 hours or up to 24 hours. Meanwhile, in a saucepan, saute onion in 1 Tbsp. oil until tender, about 5 minutes. Add wine, thyme, garlic, peppercorns and cloves. Simmer until reduced to ¾ cup. Cool; strain, discarding solids, and refrigerate.

2. Remove roast from the refrigerator 1 hour before grilling. Prepare grill for indirect heat, using a drip pan. Add wood chips according to manufacturer's directions.

3. Pat roast dry with paper towels. Brush with remaining 1 Tbsp. oil; place over drip pan. Grill, covered, over medium-low indirect heat, brushing with mop sauce every 20 minutes, until meat reaches desired doneness (for medium-rare, a thermometer should read 135°; medium, 140°; medium-well, 145°), 1½-2 hours. Let stand 15 minutes before slicing.

4. If desired, in a small bowl, stir together butter, horseradish and thyme. Serve on top of roast.

4 oz. cooked beef: 262 cal., 13g fat (4g sat. fat), 91mg chol., 1027mg sod., 3g carb. (1g sugars, 1g fiber), 32g pro.

SUGAR COOKIE S'MORES

Change up traditional s'mores by using sugar cookies and candy bars in place of the traditional ingredients. This fun twist on the campfire classic will delight everyone!
—Taste of Home *Test Kitchen*

TAKES: 15 min. • **MAKES:** 4 servings

- 8   fun-size Milky Way candy bars
- 8   sugar cookies (3 in.)
- 4   large marshmallows

1. Place 2 candy bars on each of 4 cookies; place on grill rack. Grill, uncovered, over medium-hot heat for 1-1½ minutes or until bottoms of cookies are browned.

2. Meanwhile, using a long-handled fork, toast marshmallows 6 in. from the heat until golden brown, turning occasionally. Remove marshmallows from fork and place over candy bars; top with remaining cookies. Serve immediately.

1 sandwich cookie: 271 cal., 10g fat (5g sat. fat), 13mg chol., 123mg sod., 43g carb. (31g sugars, 1g fiber), 3g pro.

GRILLED MAHI MAHI

Instead of grilling the usual hamburgers or chicken breasts, prepare this grilled mahi mahi and reel in raves!
—Taste of Home *Test Kitchen*

PREP: 20 min. + marinating
GRILL: 10 min. • **MAKES:** 8 servings

- ¾ cup reduced-sodium teriyaki sauce
- 2 Tbsp. sherry or pineapple juice
- 2 garlic cloves
- 8 mahi mahi fillets (6 oz. each)

TROPICAL FRUIT SALSA

- 1 medium mango, peeled and diced
- 1 cup chopped seeded peeled papaya
- ¾ cup chopped green pepper
- ½ cup cubed fresh pineapple
- ½ medium red onion, chopped
- ¼ cup minced fresh cilantro
- ¼ cup minced fresh mint
- 1 Tbsp. chopped seeded jalapeno pepper
- 1 Tbsp. lime juice
- 1 Tbsp. lemon juice
- ½ tsp. crushed red pepper flakes

1. In a shallow dish, combine the teriyaki sauce, sherry and garlic; add mahi mahi. Turn to coat; refrigerate for 30 minutes.
2. Meanwhile, in a large bowl, combine the salsa ingredients. Cover and refrigerate until serving.
3. Drain mahi mahi and discard marinade. Place mahi mahi on an oiled grill rack. Grill, covered, over medium heat or broil 4 in. from the heat until fish flakes easily with a fork, 4-5 minutes on each side. Serve with fruit salsa.
Note: Wear disposable gloves when cutting hot peppers; the oils can burn skin. Avoid touching your face.
1 fillet with ¼ cup fruit salsa: 195 cal., 2g fat (0 sat. fat), 124mg chol., 204mg sod., 12g carb. (9g sugars, 2g fiber), 32g pro.
Diabetic exchanges: 5 lean meat, 1 fruit.

BRATWURST & CHICKEN KABOBS

I made these lively chicken kabobs as a thank-you gift while visiting my relatives in Norway. They loved eating them almost as much as I loved cooking for them! If you prefer less heat in the chutney, you can use honey in place of pepper jelly. Also, any variety of vegetables will work with these.
—Anna Davis, Springfield, MO

PREP: 40 min. • **GRILL:** 10 min.
MAKES: 12 kabobs

- ¼ cup balsamic vinegar
- ¼ cup cider vinegar
- 2 Tbsp. pepper jelly
- 2 Tbsp. stone-ground mustard
- 1 tsp. salt
- ½ tsp. pepper
- ½ cup olive oil, divided
- 1 can (15 oz.) peach halves in light syrup, drained and cut into ½-in. cubes
- ⅔ cup minced onion
- 1 jar (12 oz.) mango chutney
- 6 boneless skinless chicken breasts (6 oz. each)
- 1 pkg. (14 oz.) fully cooked bratwurst links

- 2 each medium green pepper, sweet red pepper and yellow pepper
- 1 large onion
- 3 Tbsp. brown sugar bourbon seasoning

1. Whisk together vinegars, pepper jelly, mustard, salt and pepper. Gradually whisk in ⅓ cup olive oil until blended. Add peaches, minced onion and chutney.
2. Cut chicken into 1-in. cubes and bratwursts into 1-in. slices. Cut peppers into large squares and onion into cubes. Toss with brown sugar bourbon seasoning and the remaining oil.
3. On 12 metal or soaked wooden skewers, alternately thread meat and vegetables. Grill skewers, covered, on a greased grill rack over medium-high direct heat, turning occasionally, until chicken is no longer pink and vegetables are tender, 10-12 minutes. If desired, sprinkle with additional brown sugar bourbon seasoning during grilling. Serve with chutney sauce.
Note: We used McCormick brown sugar bourbon seasoning for this recipe.
1 kabob: 433 cal., 21g fat (5g sat. fat), 71mg chol., 1249mg sod., 37g carb. (24g sugars, 2g fiber), 23g pro.

THE BEST BABY BACK RIBS

I like to marinate racks of ribs before adding my zesty spice rub. Then I grill them to perfection. They always turn out juicy and loaded with flavor.
—*Iola Egle, Bella Vista, AR*

PREP: 10 min. + marinating
GRILL: 1 hour 20 min. • **MAKES:** 6 servings

- 2 racks baby back ribs (about 4½ lbs.)
- ¾ cup chicken broth
- ¾ cup soy sauce
- 1 cup sugar, divided
- 6 Tbsp. cider vinegar
- 6 Tbsp. olive oil
- 3 garlic cloves, minced
- 2 tsp. salt
- 1 Tbsp. paprika
- ½ tsp. chili powder
- ½ tsp. pepper
- ¼ tsp. garlic powder
   Dash cayenne pepper
   Barbecue sauce, optional

1. If necessary, remove thin membrane from ribs and discard. Combine broth, soy sauce, ½ cup sugar, the vinegar, olive oil and garlic. Place ribs in a shallow baking dish; pour two-thirds of the marinade over ribs. Turn to coat; refrigerate overnight, turning occasionally. Cover and refrigerate remaining marinade.
2. Drain ribs, discarding marinade in dish. Combine remaining ½ cup sugar, salt and seasonings; rub over both sides of ribs.
3. Grill ribs, covered, on an oiled rack over indirect medium heat for 30 minutes on each side.
4. Baste with reserved marinade, or, if desired, barbecue sauce. Move ribs to direct medium heat and cook until pork is tender, turning and basting occasionally, 20-40 minutes longer.
1 serving: 647 cal., 41g fat (13g sat. fat), 123mg chol., 2345mg sod., 30g carb. (29g sugars, 1g fiber), 37g pro.

BACON-BLUE CHEESE STUFFED BURGERS

These loaded burgers are a hearty meal in a bun. They're sure to satisfy the biggest appetites.
—*Christine Keating, Norwalk, CA*

PREP: 30 min. • **GRILL:** 10 min.
MAKES: 4 burgers

- 1½ lbs. lean ground beef (90% lean)
- 3 oz. cream cheese, softened
- ⅓ cup crumbled blue cheese
- ⅓ cup bacon bits
- ½ tsp. salt
- ½ tsp. garlic powder
- ¼ tsp. pepper
- 1 lb. sliced fresh mushrooms
- 1 Tbsp. olive oil
- 1 Tbsp. water
- 1 Tbsp. Dijon mustard
- 4 whole wheat hamburger buns, split
- ¼ cup mayonnaise
- 4 romaine leaves
- 1 medium tomato, sliced

1. Shape beef into 8 thin patties. Combine the cream cheese, blue cheese and bacon bits; spoon onto the center of 4 patties. Top with remaining patties and press edges firmly to seal. Combine the salt, garlic powder and pepper; sprinkle over patties.
2. Grill burgers, covered, over medium heat or broil 4 in. from the heat on each side until a thermometer reads 160° and juices run clear, 5-7 minutes.
3. Meanwhile, in a large skillet, saute the mushrooms in oil until tender. Stir in the water and mustard.
4. Serve the burgers on buns with mayonnaise, romaine, tomato and mushroom mixture.
1 burger: 701 cal., 43g fat (15g sat. fat), 149mg chol., 1280mg sod., 31g carb. (7g sugars, 5g fiber), 48g pro.
Herb & Cheese Stuffed Burgers: Omit blue cheese and bacon bits. Mix cream cheese with ¼ cup shredded cheddar cheese, 2 Tbsp. minced fresh parsley and 1 tsp. Dijon mustard. Season meat with ¾ tsp. crushed dried rosemary and ¼ dried sage. Proceed as recipe directs.

CHORIZO BURGERS

A chorizo burger? You bet! Pickled veggie toppers complement the spicy patties especially well.
—*Robert Johnson, Chino Valley, AZ*

PREP: 20 min. + standing • **GRILL:** 15 min.
MAKES: 2 servings

- ⅓ cup sugar
- ⅓ cup water
- ⅓ cup cider vinegar
- ½ large red onion, halved and thinly sliced
- 1 jalapeno pepper, seeded and sliced
- 6 oz. ground beef or bison
- ¼ lb. fresh chorizo or bulk spicy pork sausage
- ¼ tsp. salt
- ¼ tsp. pepper
- 2 sesame seed hamburger buns, split
- ½ cup fresh baby spinach
- 2 Tbsp. peeled and grated horseradish

1. In a large bowl, whisk sugar, water and vinegar together until sugar is dissolved. Add red onion and jalapeno; let stand at least 1 hour.

2. Combine beef and chorizo; shape into two ¾-in.-thick patties. Sprinkle with salt and pepper. Grill burgers, covered, over medium heat until a thermometer reads 160°, 6-8 minutes on each side. Grill buns over medium heat, cut side down, until toasted, 30-60 seconds. Drain the pickled vegetables. Serve burgers on buns with baby spinach, pickled vegetables and grated horseradish.

Note: Wear disposable gloves when cutting hot peppers; the oils can burn skin. Avoid touching your face.

1 burger: 555 cal., 30g fat (11g sat. fat), 103mg chol., 1264mg sod., 36g carb. (10g sugars, 5g fiber), 34g pro.

GRILLED LOBSTER TAILS

I had never made lobster at home until I tried this convenient and deliciously different grilled recipe. It turned out amazing, and has left me with little reason to ever order lobster at a restaurant again.
—*Katie Rush, Kansas City, MO*

PREP: 15 min. + marinating
GRILL: 10 min. • **MAKES:** 6 servings

- 6 frozen lobster tails (8 to 10 oz. each), thawed
- ¾ cup olive oil
- 3 Tbsp. minced fresh chives
- 3 garlic cloves, minced
- ½ tsp. salt
- ½ tsp. pepper

1. Using scissors, cut 3-4 lengthwise slits in underside of tail to loosen shell slightly. Cut top of lobster shell lengthwise down the center with scissors, leaving tail fin intact. Cut shell at an angle away from the center of the tail at base of tail fin. Loosen meat from shell, keeping the fin end attached; lift meat and lay over shell.

2. In a small bowl, combine the remaining ingredients; spoon over lobster meat. Cover and refrigerate for 20 minutes.

3. Place lobster tails, meat side up, on grill rack. Grill, covered, over medium heat until meat is opaque, 10-12 minutes.

1 lobster tail: 446 cal., 29g fat (4g sat. fat), 215mg chol., 869mg sod., 2g carb. (0 sugars, 0 fiber), 43g pro.

COOL-KITCHEN TIP

To remove the vein from a lobster tail, hold the fleshy end of the tail (where the tail originally connected to the body), locate the vein and gently pull with your fingers until it detaches from the tail. You can also use a small, sharp paring knife to get the vein started before completely loosening it with your fingers.

SPICY GRILLED EGGPLANT

This grilled side dish goes well with pasta or meats also made on the grill. Thanks to the Cajun seasoning, it gets more attention than an ordinary veggie.
—*Greg Fontenot, The Woodlands, TX*

TAKES: 20 min. • **MAKES:** 8 servings

- 2 small eggplants, cut into ½-in. slices
- ¼ cup olive oil
- 2 Tbsp. lime juice
- 3 tsp. Cajun seasoning

1. Brush eggplant slices with oil. Drizzle with lime juice; sprinkle with Cajun seasoning. Let stand 5 minutes.

2. Grill eggplant, covered, over medium heat or broil 4 in. from heat until tender, 4-5 minutes per side.

1 serving: 88 cal., 7g fat (1g sat. fat), 0 chol., 152mg sod., 7g carb. (3g sugars, 4g fiber), 1g pro. **Diabetic exchanges:** 1½ fat, 1 vegetable.

GRILLED MEDITERRANEAN ZUCCHINI SALAD

This grilled zucchini salad with Mediterranean dressing is the perfect side dish. I also like to add summer squash for a variation, or crumbled goat cheese when I want creaminess.
—Rashanda Cobbins, Milwaukee, WI

TAKES: 20 min. • **MAKES:** 4 servings

- 3 medium zucchini, thinly sliced
- ¼ cup olive oil, divided
- ¼ tsp. salt
- ¼ tsp. pepper
- ¼ cup chopped red onion
- 3 Tbsp. minced fresh mint
- 2 Tbsp. minced fresh parsley
- 1 medium lemon, juiced and zested
- ⅓ cup crumbled feta cheese
- 3 Tbsp. pine nuts, toasted

1. In a large bowl, combine zucchini and 2 Tbsp. olive oil. Add salt and pepper; toss to coat. Transfer to a grill wok or open grill basket; place on grill rack. Grill, covered, over medium-high heat until crisp-tender, 5-10 minutes, turning occasionally.
2. Transfer zucchini to a serving bowl; sprinkle with remaining 2 Tbsp. olive oil and red onion. When cooled slightly, sprinkle with mint, parsley, lemon juice and zest, and feta cheese. Stir gently. Sprinkle with pine nuts before serving.
1 cup: 220 cal., 20g fat (3g sat. fat), 5mg chol., 252mg sod., 8g carb. (4g sugars, 3g fiber), 5g pro.

SOUVLAKI PITA POCKETS

This is a favorite at our house, especially in summer. A quick trip to the market for a very few ingredients results in gourmet-style Greek sandwiches we often enjoy outdoors by the grill. Of course, a simple Greek salad on the side is a nice addition.
—Becky Drees, Pittsfield, MA

PREP: 20 min. + marinating
GRILL: 10 min. • **MAKES:** 6 servings

- 4 medium lemons, divided
- 4 Tbsp. olive oil
- 4 garlic cloves, minced
- 2 tsp. dried oregano
- ½ tsp. salt
- ¼ tsp. pepper
- 2 lbs. boneless skinless chicken breasts, cut into 1-in. pieces
- 6 whole pita breads
- 1 carton (8 oz.) refrigerated tzatziki sauce
  Optional toppings: Chopped tomatoes, chopped cucumber, sliced red onion and fresh dill sprigs

1. Cut 3 lemons crosswise in half; squeeze juice from lemons. Transfer juice to a large bowl or shallow dish. Whisk in oil, garlic, oregano, salt and pepper. Add chicken; turn to coat. Refrigerate 1 hour.
2. Drain chicken, discarding marinade. Thinly slice remaining lemon. On 6 metal or soaked wooden skewers, alternately thread chicken and lemon slices. Grill kabobs, covered, over medium heat (or broil 4 in. from heat) until chicken is no longer pink, about 10 minutes, turning occasionally.
3. Remove chicken from kabobs; discard lemon slices. Serve chicken with pita bread, tzatziki sauce and toppings as desired. Drizzle with additional olive oil if desired.
2 filled pita halves: 369 cal., 8g fat (2g sat. fat), 90mg chol., 462mg sod., 34g carb. (2g sugars, 1g fiber), 37g pro. **Diabetic exchanges:** 5 lean meat, 2 starch, 1 fat.

GARDEN-FRESH GRILLED VEGGIE PIZZA

I have four gardens, so I always have a great spread of produce. I created this appetizer using my top garden goodies.
—*Dianna Wara, Washington, IL*

PREP: 30 min. • **GRILL:** 15 min.
MAKES: 6 servings

- 3 Tbsp. olive oil
- 3 garlic cloves, minced
- 3 medium tomatoes, cut into ½-in. slices
- 1 large sweet red pepper, halved, stemmed and seeded
- 1 small zucchini, cut lengthwise into ¼-in.-thick slices
- 1 small onion, cut crosswise into ½-in. slices
- 1 tsp. coarsely ground pepper
- 1 prebaked 12-in. pizza crust
- ⅓ cup spreadable garden vegetable cream cheese
- 8 slices smoked provolone cheese, divided
- ½ cup minced fresh basil, divided
- ¼ cup shredded carrots
- 1 Tbsp. minced fresh oregano
- 1 tsp. minced fresh thyme

1. Mix oil and garlic; brush onto both sides of vegetables. Sprinkle with pepper. Grill, covered, over medium heat until tender, 4-5 minutes per side for pepper and onion, 3-4 minutes per side for zucchini and 2-3 minutes per side for tomatoes.
2. Coarsely chop pepper, onion and zucchini. Spread pizza crust with cream cheese; layer with 4 slices provolone and tomato slices. Sprinkle with ¼ cup basil, carrots, oregano and thyme. Top with grilled vegetables, then remaining cheese.
3. Grill pizza, covered, over medium heat until bottom is golden brown and cheese is melted, 5-7 minutes. Top with remaining ¼ cup basil.
1 serving: 395 cal., 22g fat (8g sat. fat), 23mg chol., 618mg sod., 36g carb. (6g sugars, 3g fiber), 16g pro.

COOL-KITCHEN TIP
Half the provolone is layered under the tomatoes to prevent the crust from becoming soggy. Shredded carrot may seem out of the ordinary for pizza, but it adds a subtle, pleasant sweetness.

GRILLED NECTARINES WITH BURRATA & HONEY

The classic Caprese gets a sweet makeover with this inspired summer starter. Burrata, mint and honey are served over nectarine halves—or any stone fruit you like—in this creamy, dreamy dish.
—Anthony Gans, Hawthorne, CA

TAKES: 15 min. • **MAKES:** 6 servings

- 3 medium ripe nectarines, halved and pitted
   Cooking spray
- 8 oz. burrata cheese
- 2 Tbsp. honey
- 12 fresh mint leaves
   Flaky sea salt, such as Maldon

1. Heat a grill pan over medium-high heat. Spritz cut sides of nectarines with cooking spray. Place cut sides down on pan. Grill until just tender, 4-5 minutes. Meanwhile, drain burrata; cut into 6 slices.
2. Arrange nectarine halves, cut side up, on a serving platter. Top with burrata, honey and mint; sprinkle with salt.
1 serving: 160 cal., 8g fat (5g sat. fat), 27mg chol., 60mg sod., 15g carb. (13g sugars, 1g fiber), 7g pro.

GRILLED CABBAGE

I don't really like cabbage, but I fixed this recipe and couldn't believe how good it was! We threw some burgers on the grill and our dinner was complete. I never thought I'd skip dessert because I was full from eating too much cabbage!
—Elizabeth Wheeler, Thornville, OH

TAKES: 30 min. • **MAKES:** 8 servings

- 1 medium head cabbage (about 1½ lbs.)
- ⅓ cup butter, softened
- ¼ cup chopped onion
- ½ tsp. garlic salt
- ¼ tsp. pepper

1. Cut cabbage into 8 wedges; place on a double thickness of heavy-duty foil (about 24x12 in.). Spread cut sides of cabbage with butter. Sprinkle with onion, garlic salt and pepper.
2. Fold foil around cabbage and seal tightly. Grill, covered, over medium heat until tender, about 20 minutes. Open foil carefully to allow steam to escape.
1 wedge: 98 cal., 8g fat (5g sat. fat), 20mg chol., 188mg sod., 7g carb. (4g sugars, 3g fiber), 2g pro. **Diabetic exchanges:** 1½ fat, 1 vegetable.

LEBANESE STREET SANDWICHES

Arayes are grilled Lebanese-style pitas stuffed with a seasoned meat mixture. They're commonly found throughout the food stalls that line the streets of Beirut. If you'd rather not use a grill, they can be baked in the oven or made in a panini press too.
—Nikki Haddad, Germantown, MD

PREP: 30 min. • **GRILL:** 10 min.
MAKES: 6 servings

- 2 large onions, coarsely chopped
- 1½ cups packed fresh parsley sprigs
- 1½ lbs. ground beef
- 1 large egg, lightly beaten
- 1 tsp. salt
- 6 whole pita breads
- 2 Tbsp. olive oil

TAHINI SAUCE
- ⅓ cup tahini
- 2 garlic cloves, minced
- ¼ cup lemon juice
- 2 Tbsp. water
- ⅛ tsp. salt

1. Place onions in a food processor; pulse until finely chopped. Remove and pat dry; transfer to a large bowl. Add parsley to processor; pulse until minced. Stir into onions. Add beef, egg and salt; mix lightly but thoroughly.
2. Slice pitas horizontally in half. Spread bottoms with meat mixture to edge. Replace pita tops; press lightly to adhere. Brush outsides of sandwiches with oil. Grill sandwiches, uncovered, over medium heat until a thermometer inserted into meat mixture reads 160°, 10-12 minutes, turning every 2 minutes. Cool slightly before cutting into quarters.
3. Combine sauce ingredients; serve with sandwiches.
1 sandwich: 545 cal., 28g fat (7g sat. fat), 101mg chol., 852mg sod., 42g carb. (3g sugars, 4g fiber), 30g pro.

SOURDOUGH BREAD BOWL SANDWICH

I created this recipe for when my husband and I go to the lake. I don't like to spend a lot of time hovering over a stove or grill, especially in the hot Oklahoma summer months, and this filling sandwich is ready in minutes. For extra flavor, brush melted garlic-and-herb butter over the top prior to cooking.

—*Shawna Welsh-Garrison, Owasso, OK*

PREP: 15 min. • **COOK:** 25 min. + standing
MAKES: 8 servings

- 1   round loaf sourdough bread (1½ lbs.)
- ½   cup honey mustard salad dressing
- 4   slices sharp cheddar cheese
- ⅓   lb. thinly sliced deli ham
- 4   slices smoked provolone cheese
- ⅓   lb. thinly sliced deli smoked turkey
- 1   Tbsp. butter, melted

1. Prepare campfire or grill for low heat. Cut a thin slice off top of bread loaf. Hollow out bottom of loaf, leaving a ½-in.-thick shell (save removed bread for another use). Spread dressing on inside of hollowed loaf and under the bread top. Layer inside with cheddar, ham, provolone and turkey. Replace top. Place on a piece of heavy-duty foil (about 24x18 in.). Brush loaf with butter. Fold foil edges over top, crimping to seal.

2. Cook over campfire or grill until heated through, 25-30 minutes. Let stand for 15 minutes before removing foil. Cut into wedges.

1 wedge: 346 cal., 17g fat (6g sat. fat), 46mg chol., 865mg sod., 30g carb. (5g sugars, 1g fiber), 19g pro.

COOL-KITCHEN TIP

This giant sandwich can be tricky to slice. Cut it with a serrated knife. Consider using skewers to hold layers together while you cut.

GRILLED BRUSCHETTA

This is my go-to appetizer in the summer when tomatoes and basil are fresh from the garden. A balsamic glaze takes this bruschetta recipe over the top. I like to use a Tuscan herb or basil-infused olive oil for this. But it works well with plain olive oil too.

—*Brittany Allyn, Mesa, AZ*

PREP: 30 min. • **GRILL:** 5 min.
MAKES: 16 servings

- ½   cup balsamic vinegar
- 1½   cups chopped and seeded plum tomatoes
- 2   Tbsp. finely chopped shallot
- 1   Tbsp. minced fresh basil
- 2   tsp. plus 3 Tbsp. olive oil, divided
- 1   garlic clove, minced
- 16   slices French bread baguette (½ in. thick)
     Sea salt
     Grated Parmesan cheese

1. In a small saucepan, bring vinegar to a boil; cook until liquid is reduced to 3 Tbsp., 8-10 minutes. Remove from heat.

2. Meanwhile, combine tomatoes, shallot, basil, 2 tsp. olive oil and garlic. Cover and refrigerate until serving.

3. Brush remaining 3 Tbsp. oil over both sides of baguette slices. Grill, uncovered, over medium heat until golden brown on both sides.

4. Top toasts with tomato mixture. Drizzle with balsamic syrup; sprinkle with sea salt and Parmesan. Serve immediately.

1 piece: 58 cal., 3g fat (0 sat. fat), 0 chol., 49mg sod., 7g carb. (3g sugars, 0 fiber), 1g pro. **Diabetic exchanges:** ½ starch, ½ fat.

FAVORITE GRILLED PORK CHOPS

I start preparing this entree the night before I plan to grill it. The fabulous marinade officially convinced my family to eat pork chops.
—*Erica Svejda, Janesville, WI*

PREP: 5 min. + marinating
GRILL: 20 min. • **MAKES:** 4 servings

- ½ cup Worcestershire sauce
- ¼ cup minced fresh parsley
- ¼ cup balsamic vinegar
- ¼ cup soy sauce
- 2 Tbsp. olive oil
- 1 tsp. minced garlic
- ½ tsp. pepper
- ¼ tsp. cayenne pepper
- 4 boneless pork loin chops (8 oz. each and 1 in. thick)

1. In a large bowl, combine the first 8 ingredients. Add pork chops; turn to coat. Refrigerate for 8 hours or overnight.
2. Drain and discard marinade. Grill pork chops, covered, over medium heat for 10-15 minutes on each side or until a thermometer reads 145°. Let meat stand for 5 minutes before serving.
1 pork chop: 328 cal., 14g fat (5g sat. fat), 109mg chol., 358mg sod., 3g carb. (2g sugars, 0 fiber), 44g pro.

GRILLED GARDEN VEGGIE PIZZA

Pile on the veggies—this crisp, grilled crust can take it! This colorful, healthy pizza looks as fresh as it tastes.
—*Diane Halferty, Corpus Christi, TX*

TAKES: 30 min. • **MAKES:** 6 servings

- 1 medium red onion, cut crosswise into ½-in. slices
- 1 large sweet red pepper, halved, stemmed and seeded
- 1 small zucchini, cut lengthwise into ½-in.-thick slices
- 1 yellow summer squash, cut lengthwise into ½-in.-thick slices
- 2 Tbsp. olive oil
- ½ tsp. salt
- ¼ tsp. pepper
- 1 prebaked 12-in. thin whole wheat pizza crust
- 3 Tbsp. jarred roasted minced garlic
- 2 cups shredded part-skim mozzarella cheese, divided
- ⅓ cup torn fresh basil

1. Brush vegetables with oil; sprinkle with salt and pepper. Grill, covered, over medium heat until tender, 4-5 minutes per side for onion and pepper, 3-4 minutes per side for zucchini and squash.
2. Separate onion into rings; cut pepper into strips. Spread pizza crust with garlic; sprinkle with 1 cup cheese. Top with grilled vegetables, then remaining cheese.
3. Grill pizza, covered, over medium heat until bottom is golden brown and cheese is melted, 5-7 minutes. Top with basil.
1 serving: 324 cal., 15g fat (6g sat. fat), 24mg chol., 704mg sod., 30g carb. (5g sugars, 5g fiber), 16g pro. **Diabetic exchanges:** 2 starch, 2 medium-fat meat, 1 fat.

SKILLET-GRILLED CATFISH

You can use this recipe with any thick fish fillet, but I suggest catfish or haddock. The Cajun flavor is great.
—*Traci Wynne, Denver, PA*

TAKES: 25 min. • **MAKES:** 4 servings

- ¼ cup all-purpose flour
- ¼ cup cornmeal
- 1 tsp. onion powder
- 1 tsp. dried basil
- ½ tsp. garlic salt
- ½ tsp. dried thyme
- ¼ to ½ tsp. white pepper
- ¼ to ½ tsp. cayenne pepper
- ¼ to ½ tsp. pepper
- 4 catfish fillets (6 to 8 oz. each)
- ¼ cup butter
  Optional: Lemon wedges and minced fresh parsley

1. In a large shallow dish, combine the first 9 ingredients. Add catfish, 1 fillet at a time, and turn to coat.
2. Place a large cast-iron skillet on a grill rack over medium-high heat. Melt butter in the skillet; add catfish in batches, if necessary. Grill, covered, until fish just begins to flake easily with a fork, 5-10 minutes on each side. If desired, serve with lemon wedges and fresh parsley.
1 fillet: 222 cal., 15g fat (8g sat. fat), 51mg chol., 366mg sod., 14g carb. (0 sugars, 1g fiber), 8g pro.

STUFFED SMOKY PORK BURGERS

These stuffed burgers are far from ordinary. The ground pork makes them juicy and extra flavorful. Stuffing them takes a bit of extra time, but it's well worth it!
—*Francine Lizotte, Langley, BC*

PREP: 30 min. + chilling
GRILL: 15 min. • **MAKES:** 12 servings

- 2 lbs. ground beef
- 2 lbs. ground pork
- ½ cup panko bread crumbs
- ½ cup finely chopped red onion
- 3 Tbsp. minced fresh basil
- 2 tsp. smoked paprika
- ½ tsp. salt
- ½ tsp. pepper
- ¾ cup finely chopped fresh pineapple
- ¾ cup barbecue sauce
- 12 bacon strips, cooked and crumbled
  Sliced Jarlsberg cheese, optional
- 12 hamburger buns, split
  Optional: Additional barbecue sauce, chopped red onion and fresh basil

1. In a large bowl, combine the first 8 ingredients, mixing lightly but thoroughly. Shape into 24 thin patties. Divide pineapple, barbecue sauce and bacon over center of 12 patties; top with remaining patties, pressing edges firmly to seal. Refrigerate, covered, for 1 hour.
2. Grill burgers, covered, over medium heat or broil 4 in. from heat until a thermometer reads 160°, 7-8 minutes on each side. If desired, top with cheese; grill, covered, until cheese is melted, 1-2 minutes longer. Serve on buns and, if desired, top with additional barbecue sauce, red onion and fresh basil.
1 burger: 508 cal., 25g fat (9g sat. fat), 105mg chol., 724mg sod., 33g carb. (10g sugars, 1g fiber), 35g pro.

SPICED GRILLED CHICKEN WITH CILANTRO LIME BUTTER

This grilled chicken gets a lovely pop of color and flavor from the lime butter—don't skip it!
—Diane Halferty, Corpus Christi, TX

PREP: 20 min. • **GRILL:** 35 min.
MAKES: 6 servings

- 1   Tbsp. chili powder
- 1   Tbsp. brown sugar
- 2   tsp. ground cinnamon
- 1   tsp. baking cocoa
- ½   tsp. salt
- ½   tsp. pepper
- 3   Tbsp. olive oil
- 1   Tbsp. balsamic vinegar
- 6   bone-in chicken breast halves (8 oz. each)

CILANTRO LIME BUTTER
- ⅓   cup butter, melted
- ¼   cup minced fresh cilantro
- 2   Tbsp. finely chopped red onion
- 1   Tbsp. lime juice
- 1   serrano pepper, finely chopped
- ⅛   tsp. pepper

1. In a small bowl, combine the first 8 ingredients. Brush over chicken.
2. Place chicken skin side down on grill rack. Grill, covered, over indirect medium heat for 15 minutes. Turn; grill 20-25 minutes longer or until a thermometer reads 165°.
3. Meanwhile, in a small bowl, combine the cilantro lime butter ingredients. Drizzle over chicken before serving.
Note: Wear disposable gloves when cutting hot peppers; the oils can burn skin. Avoid touching your face.

1 chicken breast half with 1 Tbsp. lime butter: 430 cal., 27g fat (10g sat. fat), 138mg chol., 411mg sod., 5g carb. (3g sugars, 1g fiber), 40g pro.

GRILLED PORK TENDERLOIN WITH CHERRY SALSA MOLE

The combination of pork and cherries has long been a favorite of mine. The hint of spice and chocolate in the salsa makes the combination even more special.
—Roxanne Chan, Albany, CA

PREP: 25 min. • **GRILL:** 15 min. + standing
MAKES: 6 servings

- 2   pork tenderloins (¾ lb. each)
- 1   Tbsp. canola oil
- ½   tsp. salt
- ¼   tsp. ground cumin
- ¼   tsp. chili powder
- 1   cup pitted fresh or frozen dark sweet cherries, thawed, chopped
- 1   jalapeno pepper, seeded and minced
- ½   cup finely chopped peeled jicama
- 1   oz. semisweet chocolate, grated
- 2   Tbsp. minced fresh cilantro
- 1   green onion, thinly sliced
- 1   Tbsp. lime juice
- 1   tsp. honey
      Salted pumpkin seeds or pepitas

1. Brush tenderloins with oil; sprinkle with salt, cumin and chili powder. Grill, covered, over medium heat until a thermometer reads 145°, 15-20 minutes, turning occasionally. Let stand 10-15 minutes.
2. Meanwhile, combine cherries, jalapeno, jicama, chocolate, cilantro, green onion, lime juice and honey. Slice pork; serve with cherry salsa and pumpkin seeds.

3 oz. cooked pork with ¼ cup salsa: 218 cal., 8g fat (3g sat. fat), 64mg chol., 248mg sod., 11g carb. (9g sugars, 2g fiber), 23g pro. **Diabetic exchanges:** 3 lean meat, ½ starch, ½ fat.

FOILED AGAIN!

Convenient to prep ahead of time, easy to cook and serve, and a snap to clean up—what's not to love about grilled foil-packet meals?

SALMON GRILLED IN FOIL

This tender salmon steams up in foil packets, meaning easy cleanup later.
—*Merideth Berkovich, The Dalles, OR*

TAKES: 20 min. • **MAKES:** 4 servings

- 4 salmon fillets (4 oz. each)
- 1 tsp. garlic powder
- 1 tsp. lemon-pepper seasoning
- 1 tsp. curry powder
- ½ tsp. salt
- 1 small onion, cut into rings
- 2 medium tomatoes, seeded and chopped

1. Place salmon, skin side down, on a double thickness of heavy-duty foil (about 18x12 in.). Combine the garlic powder, lemon pepper, curry powder and salt; sprinkle over salmon. Top with onion and tomatoes. Fold foil over fish and seal tightly.
2. Grill, covered, over medium heat for 10-15 minutes or until fish flakes easily with a fork. Open foil carefully to allow steam to escape.
1 packet: 232 cal., 13g fat (3g sat. fat), 67mg chol., 482mg sod., 5g carb. (3g sugars, 1g fiber), 24g pro. **Diabetic exchanges:** 3 lean meat.

CHICKEN OLE FOIL SUPPER

These Tex Mex–style chicken packets can be assembled ahead and frozen if you like. Just thaw them overnight in the fridge, then grill as directed. I like to serve them with warm tortillas and fresh fruit on the side.
—*Mary Peck, Salina, KS*

TAKES: 30 min. • **MAKES:** 4 servings

- 1 can (15 oz.) black beans, rinsed and drained
- 2 cups fresh or frozen corn (about 10 oz.), thawed
- 1 cup salsa
- 4 boneless skinless chicken breast halves (4 oz. each)
- ¼ tsp. garlic powder
- ¼ tsp. pepper
- ⅛ tsp. salt
- 1 cup shredded cheddar cheese
- 2 green onions, chopped

1. Mix beans, corn and salsa; divide among four 18x12-in. pieces of heavy-duty foil. Top with chicken. Mix seasonings; sprinkle over chicken. Fold foil over chicken, sealing tightly.
2. Grill packets, covered, over medium heat until a thermometer inserted in chicken reads 165°, 15-20 minutes. Open foil carefully to allow steam to escape. Sprinkle with cheese and green onions.
1 packet: 405 cal., 13g fat (6g sat. fat), 91mg chol., 766mg sod., 34g carb. (8g sugars, 6g fiber), 37g pro. **Diabetic exchanges:** 4 lean meat, 2 starch, 1 fat.

FOIL-PACKET POTATOES & SAUSAGE

My family enjoys camping and cooking over a fire. These hearty foil-packet meals turn out beautifully over a campfire, on the grill or even in the oven at home.
—*Julie Koets, Elkhart, IN*

PREP: 20 min. • **COOK:** 30 min.
MAKES: 8 servings

- 3 lbs. red potatoes, cut into ½-in. cubes
- 2 pkg. (12 oz. each) smoked sausage links, cut into ½-in. slices
- 4 bacon strips, cooked and crumbled
- 1 medium onion, chopped
- 2 Tbsp. chopped fresh parsley
- ¼ tsp. salt
- ¼ tsp. garlic salt
- ¼ tsp. pepper
  Additional chopped fresh parsley, optional

1. Prepare campfire or grill for medium heat. In a large bowl, toss potatoes with sausage, bacon, onion, parsley, salts and pepper.
2. Divide mixture among eight 18x12-in. pieces of heavy-duty nonstick foil, placing food on dull side of foil. Fold foil around potato mixture, sealing tightly.
3. Place packets over campfire or grill; cook 15 minutes on each side or until potatoes are tender. Open packets carefully to allow steam to escape. If desired, sprinkle with additional parsley.
1 packet: 414 cal., 25g fat (10g sat. fat), 61mg chol., 1181mg sod., 31g carb. (4g sugars, 3g fiber), 17g pro.

COOL-KITCHEN TIP
If you don't have heavy-duty foil on hand, use a double thickness of regular foil.

STEAK & POTATO FOIL PACKS

As a park ranger, I often assemble foil packs, toss them into my backpack with some ice, and cook them over a campfire when I set up camp. At home I use my grill.
—*Ralph Jones, San Diego, CA*

PREP: 20 min. • **GRILL:** 20 min.
MAKES: 8 servings

- 2 beef top sirloin steaks (1½ lbs. each)
- 3 lbs. red potatoes, cut into ½-in. cubes
- 1 medium onion, chopped
- 4 tsp. minced fresh rosemary
- 1 Tbsp. minced garlic
- 2 tsp. salt
- 1 tsp. pepper
  Additional minced rosemary, optional

1. Prepare grill for medium heat or preheat oven to 450°. Cut each steak into 4 pieces, for a total of 8 pieces. In a large bowl, combine steak, potatoes, onion, rosemary, garlic, salt and pepper.
2. Divide mixture among eight 18x12-in. pieces of heavy-duty foil, placing food on dull side of foil. Fold foil around the potato mixture, sealing tightly.
3. Place packets on grill or in oven; cook until potatoes are tender, 8-10 minutes on each side. Open packets carefully to allow steam to escape. If desired, sprinkle with additional rosemary.
1 packet: 348 cal., 7g fat (3g sat. fat), 69mg chol., 677mg sod., 29g carb. (2g sugars, 3g fiber), 40g pro. **Diabetic exchanges:** 5 lean meat, 2 starch.

INDEX